DO I NEED TO SEE A THERAPIST?

Hero, an imprint of
Legend Times Group Ltd, 51 Gower Street, London, WC1E 6HJ
hero@hero-press.com | www.hero-press.com

Print ISBN: 9781800316843
Ebook ISBN: 9781800316850
Set in Times. Printing managed by Jellyfish Solutions Ltd

DO I NEED TO SEE A THERAPIST?

HOW TO UNDERSTAND YOUR EMOTIONS AND MAKE THERAPY WORK FOR YOU

DONNA MARIA BOTTOMLEY

CONTENTS

To my husband Mike and daughter Tilly. Thank you for being so patient over the past year as I stressed about this book! You are my world and I love you very much.

I would also like to acknowledge the clients I have had the honour of sitting with over the years. You may think I have forgotten you but I have not. I often think of you and wonder how you are.

DISCLAIMER

There are many therapies, directories and organizations listed in this book which I hope will help to show that you do have choice when it comes to therapy. I have tested each link as of September 2020 and have provided as much information as possible, but neither I as the author nor the publisher of this book can guarantee the complete accuracy, efficacy or appropriateness of any of these suggestions for you personally.

Without knowing your personal situation, it is impossible to give a guarantee that any of the suggestions described in this book will work for you. If you find that any of the material is triggering for you and makes you feel worse, please leave that part of the book, look at the appendix for the helpline numbers or seek the personal support of your doctor, therapist or someone you trust and who can support you.

For some people the fear of emotions and the fear of bodily sensations can go hand in hand. I want to help you with this, but as with any fear it is important to take a graded approach and not flood yourself with feelings. So only do what feels right for you. Please seek support if you are struggling.

ACKNOWLEDGEMENTS

Thank you so very much to Christian Müller, my editor at Hero. If I had to write a wish list of everything I wanted in an editor, it would be you I would use as my model.

To my clinical supervisors, Colin Howard, of Howard Psychology Ltd, and Elizabeth Doggart, of Elizabeth Doggart Associates Ltd, for introducing me to several exciting neurobiological developments in psychotherapy that have given my practice a new dimension. It is an exciting time for therapy as we are increasingly seeing the science behind what we do in practice.

Also, thank you Clare Mackintosh for your words of encouragement about this book when we met at Monty Lit Fest in 2019. Your words reached me at a time when they were most needed.

I also acknowledge – with a mixture of emotions – lockdown, home-schooling, and Zoom, because, despite the struggles, I am heartened to see that the pandemic experience has placed mental health (or emotional health as I prefer to call it) front and centre. It doesn't seem unusual to speak about emotions on TV or social media at the moment and this is a huge step forward from where things have been in the past.

PREFACE

I started writing this book in 2017 as a CBT therapist of seventeen years who had recently qualified as an EMDR (Eye Movement Desensitization and Reprocessing) therapist and was incorporating this new method into my practice. In EMDR the instruction to notice that an emotion has been activated and to place it somewhere in your body, was the start of a significant change for me in my psychotherapy practice. EMDR threw a light on how unprocessed emotions and negative beliefs about the self could be released and processed through the body, and not just processed cognitively by the thinking brain.

Much has changed since 2017 for me personally, and of course much has changed in the world too. In my therapy work I have now travelled deeper into the science of emotions and the connection between the nervous system and midbrain and its role in emotional health. Polyvagal theory has shown me the key role that the vagal nerve plays in our feeling-states. 'Heartache' and 'gut feelings' are real, and we now have a way to describe how they happen and what they are. When we notice our 'gut feelings' we are in touch with the interoceptive network that travels from body to brain and back again.

I am now a 'brainspotting' therapist as well as an EMDR therapist. Brainspotting is a slightly gimmicky name for an extraordinarily powerful therapy. It was developed by David Grand and grew out of his EMDR practice. It involves not only noticing what is happening in our body when we feel emotionally activated, but also noticing where our gaze falls. The place where our eyes look when we are experiencing a strong emotion is part of that feeling-state and is connected to activity in our midbrain. By combining eye gaze with interoceptive awareness we can gain insight into what is happening in our brain and nervous system and learn how to tolerate and process our feelings. Notice where your eyes look when you are thinking about a memory.

As I used these processes more and more with my clients, I began to see that the reluctance to start therapy and the issues that people described, often coincided with a wariness about emotions themselves and either losing control or being overwhelmed and worrying about not being able to cope. I realized that, in writing this book, there was an opportunity to offer what I had learned to more people than I could see one-to-one in practice. It felt too important to keep to myself. So, in this book I have set out to combine the fear of therapy with the fear of emotion and offer my methods as to how you can understand and master your feeling-states by developing your interoceptive awareness.

Now, my journey along the way has also given me my own parallel process to deal with. Through researching sensations and the processing of information by the brain I started to realize my own sensory processing differences. My 'spiky profile' shows that I am 'neurodivergent', and many things make sense about my life now that I have discovered this. I have also come to realize the key role that interoceptive awareness plays in my own emotional health, and I am so much better at identifying what I am feeling as a result.

I have learned that my body will give me the pure truth of a feeling if I listen to it, whereas my thinking brain is so busy trying to predict what is happening that it often gets it wrong. By understanding that this thought activity is a prediction, not the truth, and by noticing what my body is doing, I can work out how to soothe and level things out.

This is a blend of meta-cognitive awareness (noticing) and appraising interoceptive/body information in a non-threatening way. It is not the only solution to everything, but it is an important tool for emotional health. I deliberately use the term *emotional health* rather than *mental health*, because I believe it more accurately represents the vital two-way connection between brain and body. Mental health as a term still seems to split body and brain. It no longer makes sense to do this.

FOREWORD

I wanted to include the thoughts of my clients as well as those of my clinical supervisors in the foreword of this book. My practice has been and continues to be influenced and informed by them and their perceptions matter to me a great deal.

Two of my clients very kindly agreed to comment and I asked them the following questions. To protect their confidentiality their names have not been published.

* * * *

1. Did you feel anxious about coming to therapy in case it made you feel emotions you didn't want to feel?

Client 1: My understanding before therapy was that my thoughts and feelings needed to be kept under control, shut away. That I could train my brain to think and feel the negative stuff less and that therapy might bring all the 'bad' memories back to the surface. I also thought therapy might help me control my brain. I didn't trust or understand my emotions a lot of the time because they didn't make sense to me and I felt they often worked against me. I felt like therapy would be like letting someone into your mind and I was scared to do that: it didn't feel safe to be vulnerable. At the same time as these worries, I believed therapy could help me with the right therapist.

Client 2: I wasn't so much anxious, rather I felt I'd failed, and that accepting I needed to see someone for support was a sign of that failure and the fact I couldn't cope. I also felt embarrassed that maybe people would judge me for needing to see a 'head doctor'.

2. Did you have a sense of what you thought would happen if you let certain emotions come out?

Client 1: I felt so full of anger and sadness that I didn't know how to release it, but worried if I did that it would pour out of me uncontrollably and I thought I might not be able to stop. I guess it was unknown to me what might come out and how it would look; it was unknown territory for my mind, and I don't like to feel out of control.

Client 2: Again, it was worry that I was failing or conceding defeat by needing that support. If I broke my leg or had the flu I would have no issue seeking medical help. Yet the fact it was a mental issue made me feel I was weak and had failed in some way. I was worried I would be judged, not so much by a therapist, but by colleagues and friends. That it might change their perception of me and make them trust me less.

3. Did any of these fears/worries come true?

Client 1: My worries and fears didn't come true. I smile at myself for the imaginative extremes I went to and how different that was from my experience. I asked a lot of questions and started understanding thoughts and emotions until I felt safe and able to let things start to come out. I never felt pushed and trusted that nothing bad would happen to go to certain places in my mind, remember and feel what I had been carrying round for so long and was finally, bit by bit, able to let it go.

Client 2: Once I overcame my own hesitations I quickly realized that asking for help was actually a sign of strength and courage, not weakness. From our first session I felt comfortable, yet I perhaps was guarded at first, as I had barriers up to protect myself mentally from further anguish and didn't want to fully accept how poorly I was. I wanted you to give me a quick solution and then I could get back on the treadmill, whereas what I needed was a sustained period of mental support and rest to truly reflect on where I'd got to and how I wanted to move forward. Far from being unsupportive or judgemental, my colleagues and friends rallied round me and made me feel loved and cared for. I even achieved a top performer rating for 2020 despite being poorly during it. People actually admired my acceptance of needing help and it inspired them.

4. What would you say to someone who is struggling, but worries that seeing a therapist will make them feel overwhelmed by their emotions?

Client 1: To someone who is fearful of being overwhelmed I would say: ask questions, talk through what your fears are and what will happen. I learnt to trust in my emotions.

Client 2: I would say that things likely won't get better until you get help and give yourself some kindness. That the brain is a critical part of your body that needs just as much looking after as your heart, your kidneys or any other organs. Mental health is something we all have and nobody is able to be mentally healthy all the time. Therapists are not there to judge or scold you, they are there to work with you and teach you different coping strategies that make you a stronger, more capable person. People will actually admire you for getting help and it may in turn give others the courage to seek help themselves so you are not only having a positive impact on you, but others too.

* * * *

I also wanted to ask the views of my two clinical supervisors whose practices both sit in the cutting edge of psychotherapy and neuroscience and whom I have learned so much from. This book feels very much like the culmination of their teachings, and it felt very important to me to include their thoughts in this book.

Colin Howard, Howard Psychology Ltd

This book is a refreshing review of the latest therapeutic modalities, and neurobiological research, and Donna has provided the information in a way that makes it accessible to the layperson. This is incredibly helpful and allows the reader to make a truly informed decision about starting their own therapeutic journey. Donna has combined information that is relevant to those who are interested in understanding how the mind and body combine to store, and process information, as well as the interruptions to that process. Donna has also addressed the core fears and misconceptions that people can have about starting therapy. This book will be an incredibly helpful resource for those who are considering entering into therapy, and will provide the reader with a clear and informed awareness of the latest approaches.

Elizabeth Doggart, Elizabeth Doggart Associates Ltd

Working in the helping professions it has been my pleasure to know Donna through our professional relationship, for many years. In that time, I have watched her grow and develop an extensive knowledge and experience in the world of counselling and psychotherapy.

The world of counselling and psychotherapy has undergone considerable growth since the pioneering work of Freud in the 1890s, and that process of development has in turn brought with it increased knowledge, understanding, but also a high degree of complexity. Indeed, there has been such an emergence of paradigms each purporting to help the troubled individual address their adversities by different methods, that there are now over 400 psychotherapeutic 'routes to Rome' (Prochaska and Norcross, 1994). The dilemma then, for the client, is that in finding themselves in a time of crisis or distress, a time when it can itself be very hard to make decisions, is that they need to choose from the many treatments on offer, exactly which will be the right one for them. Of course, there are many approaches that have made more of an impact through the media than others and have slipped into common language. For example, there is cognitive behavioural therapy (CBT), psychodynamic therapy, Gestalt therapy, integrative psychotherapy, and client-centred therapy, to name but a few. Such popularized 'talking therapies have focused very much on the role of our thoughts, or our feelings, or our behaviours, as almost discrete entities. But if we look to simply talking through our thoughts to try and cope with our distress, are we perhaps being guilty of committing Descartes's error (Damasio, 1995)? Perhaps it is not sufficient to declare 'I think therefore I am', believing that simply talking through our problems and changing our thoughts will find the solution we need. Science tells us we are physical beings, our mind, which is housed in a highly complex neural network of cells (our brain) and is an extension of our central nervous system, is part of our entire body. Thoughts, feelings and behaviours are in fact interrelated and interdependent of each other (Ellis, 1994). Recently, newer approaches have emerged that focus on the whole person, approaches such as eye movement desensitization and reprocessing (EMDR), somatic experiencing and also the lesser known but very effective brainspotting (BSP). Such approaches have been guided by developments in neurosciences, increasing our understanding of our cellular biochemical-electrical being.

So far I have only touched on a few of the developments in the field of counselling and psychotherapy and choices on offer, and it's clear that there is a wealth of choice, and we can run the risk of succumbing to 'information overload' when we ask questions such as: what kind of counselling should I have? What is out there? How will I benefit? Who do I turn to? How will I know that this is the right therapy for me?

'Do I need to see a therapist?' It's a question people may ask themselves in times of stress and confusion and then may not be sure or may even be fearful about what might be the next steps to take. This book will help the reader find the answers to these questions. Donna has set out in a clear and precise way an informative and valuable guide on how to navigate through the maze of services and approaches, bringing a much-needed torch that will illuminate the way forward for clients and may also be of benefit to therapists. Donna has achieved this with a critical but compassionate eye, her focus always being to help the client, and with refreshing clarity. Counselling and therapy is about making choices and this book will help to determine your choice from a much more informed position.

LIST OF FIGURES
AND TABLES

INTRODUCTION

Imagine placing a lemon onto a chopping board and slicing your knife through the bulging yellow belly of the fruit. You cut the lemon in half, and then half again. Then you pick up one of the quarters and bring it to your lips, biting into the sharp flesh and sucking the juice. Pause there. What do you notice in your body right now? Is there a little bit more saliva in your mouth? Did you move your lips slightly, or pucker them? Did your upper body pull back at the thought of biting into the lemon? Notice these small events that are happening in your body right now.

Where is the lemon? It doesn't exist: you imagined it; you visualized it. Yet your body reacted as if it were real.

Your brain just made a 'simulation'. It represented what you deliberately imagined and what you know about lemons to simulate the experience of biting into that slice of lemon. You may have had other thoughts or memories pop up. For example, I've just had a memory of throwing out some bad lemons that were green and powdery. But when I wrote the first draft of this paragraph a tasty memory of the smell and feeling in my mouth of warm lemon drizzle cake came up for me. Today though, a newer memory of the bad lemons was triggered first instead of that lovely lemon drizzle cake.

Now, bring up a memory of a time when you felt proud. Did you manage to get through a whole day at work despite having very little sleep the night before? Did you have an interview for a job and manage to get through it, even though you felt so on edge just before that you thought about cancelling and not going through with it? Or have you finally finished that degree after several long years? If you got through it, whatever your 'it' is, say to yourself now, 'I did it!' Repeat, 'I, did it.' Say it again: 'I *did* it!' What happened in your body as you said this? Did you smile? Did you look upwards, or to the side? Did you lean back, or straighten up your posture? Notice that shift in your body, and where your gaze went to. Each of these micro-expressions (Ekman & Friesen, 1974) are connected to the feeling of pride that is connected to that memory. When you feel proud in other situations, notice if you have the same sensations and shifts in your body.

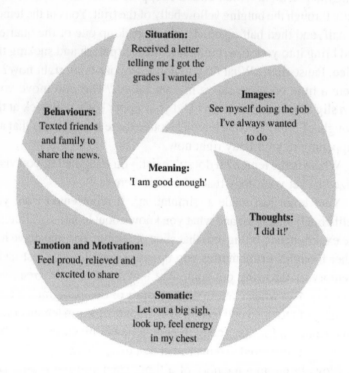

Fig. 1. – Formulation of an instance of pride

Let's try this again with a different memory. Bring up a time when you made a small mistake. Maybe you accidentally said 'luv you, bye' to the guy from EE on the phone (me), or tripped over, recovered then slipped again and face-planted in the mud in front of the other parents at school pickup (also me). OK, that's not really a mild embarrassment! But what memory comes up for you? Let your mind flick through, and when you settle on one, notice the moment in the memory when you felt the most embarrassed. See the image of that moment. Now, notice what your body is doing right now. Are you frowning? Looking down or clenching your teeth? Do you notice any gripping or tension anywhere?

These are some of the bodily expressions that are connected to the feeling of embarrassment for you. Notice how your body is reacting to what you are visualizing.

Now do a quick scan of your body. Check that your shoulders are not hunched forwards. Notice if you're clenching your toes or holding tension anywhere else. Take a slow, deep breath in, then let this breath 'flop' out. Take another big, deep breath in, and let this breath 'flop' out like a big sigh.

When we think about something or recall a memory, this can trigger a set of physiological responses in our bodies (Smith et al., 2017; Levenson, 1994). We have just witnessed what happens for us when we visualize biting into a lemon, and then we noticed what happened when we recalled a memory with an emotion attached to it (in this case, mild embarrassment). These were quick exercises recalling relatively minor events, yet they provoked physical reactions which we then mindfully noticed. We deliberately attended to what was happening in our bodies. Usually in the course of a day we do not pay this much attention to the bodily sensations that accompany our thoughts. But all of these events are still occurring even though we may not be deliberately attending to them. So imagine the journey that your brain and body go through in just one hour of a day, as you think about, experience and respond to the many things that are happening within and around you.

Each event can also trigger other thoughts, memories and bodily actions. For example, when we thought about the lemon, we may have had other thoughts, images and memories come into our awareness. If you have had a bad experience with lemons this exercise could have activated an unpleasant memory too, and with this you would have had some activation in your body. Now just in case that has happened for you, I would like to invite you to notice that what has been triggered is a *memory* of something. It is a memory. The event is not happening right now. Your body can relax.

Given all of this activity that is taking place outside our awareness, it's not surprising that we can end up experiencing aches or pains or find ourselves in twisted or slumped postures. It is normal not to notice any of this, of course, until we have cause to check our posture, or pain intrudes, for example with headaches or backaches towards the end of a long day.

Now bring up a memory of a time when you felt relaxed and free. Maybe at the start of your holiday, feeling warm and hopeful as you step through the automatic doors of the airport arrivals lounge into the sun-baked air. The freedom of no expectations or demands on your time; just the anticipation of sunshine. Take a deep breath in and breathe out slowly as you imagine your scene. Notice how this feels in your body. In your holiday scene, what are the sounds and the smells around you? Notice these and how you feel as you imagine this place. What word or phrase would you use to describe how it makes you feel? Pause there and let's do a quick body scan. Notice that feeling and where your gaze goes to as you imagine this place and this feeling. Are you looking up, to the left or right, or straight ahead? Are you sitting back in your seat, smiling or tilting your head? Is there anything else that your body is doing? All these small movements are part of a network of activities taking place within and between your brain and body. You have evoked this feeling and these sensations deliberately and mindfully. You can choose to evoke this feeling for yourself anytime you choose.

What we think about has a direct link to what happens physically in our bodies. Just thinking about a slip or trip is enough to make us frown, feel a little more tense or look down. It does not have to be something big and traumatic to make us feel contracted, tense or slumped. Our nervous system registers this and our brain interprets what it thinks is happening as a result of the tension and the slump in our bodies. We then have thoughts that are congruent with this feeling of tension.

24

Conversely, thinking about a place where we feel relaxed and content can result in a different experience. It can be something small that makes us smile and feel proud. This smile causes a physical shift in our face via our facial muscles, and we might also shift our posture and feel the sense of pride in our chest. All of these physical changes are transmitted via the vagal nerve to our brain, which predicts what it thinks is happening as a result.

It is normal not to be aware of these events, but this two-way relationship between what the brain predicts and how the body responds, and how the brain responds to what the body is preparing for, is a main part of this book. I want to show you how you can learn more about emotions and how to manage them by noticing what happens physically in your body, and not being afraid of these sensations. My belief is that if we can understand more about what happens physically between our brain and body, then we will be less wary of emotions, and will find it easier to process them rather than suppress them.

Managing emotions is not just about looking at what happens with our thoughts and what we then do behaviourally. It is also about noticing the intelligent two-way relationship between our sensorimotor systems and our brain, in particular the role of our interoceptive network which I will say more about as we move through this book.

I believe that seeing a therapist is difficult for some of us because of a fear of becoming overwhelmed by emotion. The way the mental health system has treated us traditionally has not helped, and has perhaps unintentionally shown us that emotions are to be feared. We have seen or heard of people being rendered crazy and losing control of the agency over their own lives. As a result, we have a default position of trying to suppress and control what we feel. But this suppression and distraction can take its toll and lead to more problems.

If we can become curious, rather than wary, of what we are experiencing, then we can make way for change and construct new ways of being that can become new stories for ourselves. This is the aim of therapy. But therapy isn't always an easy process. We do not always stop to notice what our bodies are doing, like we did just now, and even if we do, the way this can feel can be overwhelming or confusing or frightening. Sometimes we can become scared or frustrated at our own sensations and thoughts. Have you ever felt yourself getting a lump in your throat or felt tears coming and then immediately tried to hide or suppress this? We have adapted to be able to delay certain expressions if we predict it isn't safe or appropriate to display them at that moment. It is quite amazing that we can do this. But pushing away and trying to avoid feelings can become a habit. Over time this can lead to us becoming wary of letting our feelings be expressed in case they overwhelm us. We worry that if we do let them out, we won't be able to cope.

The judgements of others can influence us too. Maybe we've learned to feel ashamed of getting upset because of what we are told this would mean if we do. But this avoidance of getting upset can also mean that we then avoid therapy until things get really bad. This can be a killer.

In this book I want to offer you an alternative to the fear of getting upset. I will explore the fears we can have which prevent us from seeking help: the fear of our own emotions, the fear of therapy and our fears of other people judging us. I also want to unpack how fear and avoidance work and offer strategies for how we can manage them differently.

I also want to help make the process of therapy easier by discussing how to unpack what is upsetting you, how to choose a therapist and how to enter the process in a way that will help you get the most out of it. I have also included a chapter on alternatives to traditional 'talking' therapies and how to help yourself if you would prefer not to see a therapist. I hope that this book will be a useful handbook to keep with you as you navigate the world of therapy, and I do hope that it will help to make emotions and therapy a bit less daunting.

Before we go on to the first chapter, I'd like you to ask yourself these three questions, and score each one between 0 (not at all) and 10 (completely agree):

EMOTIONS

1. I often don't understand my emotions or where they come from. ☐

2. I wish I didn't feel emotions. ☐

3. I hate the sensations of some emotions. ☐

Add these three to get your total score for your current discomfort with emotions.

Total score ☐

Now do the same for therapy:

THERAPY

1. I feel uncomfortable about seeing a therapist ☐

2. I don't know how or where to look to find help for myself ☐

3. I don't want to try therapy ☐

Add these three to get your total score for your current thoughts about therapy.

Total score ☐

If you'd like to try an established and more scientific questionnaire, have a look at this link:

www.researchgate.net/publication/340660428_Emotion_Beliefs_Questionnaire_EBQ_Copy_of_questionnaire_and_scoring_instructions

27

CHAPTER ONE

The Fear of Therapy

Sometimes 'Last Resort' is the
first prudent step taken by you.
Nitin Yadav

I am often a last resort for my clients. Someone they'd rather not see, in a place they don't really wish to be. Sometimes they mention it, sometimes not, but it's in the words they use and the way they position themselves: the assumption that they should know how to sort things out on their own rather than be here with me. 'Why can't I stop it?' 'Why does it upset me so much?' 'Why can't I just forget about it?'

They tell me how they've been distracting themselves from their 'it' by running, dieting, drinking, smoking or generally keeping so busy that the 'it' cannot take over. The 'it' has become their shadow ghoul, and the fear of it is very real. They may have tried self-help books, or mindfulness apps, which may or may not have helped (when you're trying to avoid your 'it' you don't really want to give it space by doing mindfulness!). But I am usually one of the options at the end of the list. The reason I am a last resort is sometimes thrown into the air in frustration during our initial meeting – 'I feel stupid: why can't I sort this out myself?' – or is whispered as a question – 'Does this mean I'm going mad?'

In this chapter I want to explore this fear of therapy and of getting upset. Why do we delay getting help, and why are we so afraid of getting upset? What do we think it means about us if we see a therapist? I use the word 'we' because from my practice I know that therapists and doctors, along with other people in responsible positions, are not immune to this difficulty in seeing a therapist. We can often feel that we should be able to sort things out for ourselves without needing help, and we worry about being considered unfit to practise if we do seek help.

WHY DO WE DELAY GETTING HELP?

PROCRASTINATION

We all put things off sometimes, especially when there is uncertainty. But we can often procrastinate without realizing that we are doing so. I will book an appointment with my GP when it becomes apparent that I need to. But if I need to call the local garage to book my car in, I will rarely do it straight away. I don't want to be without my car, and I feel hesitant and awkward when I'm with mechanics, like I'm out of my depth, and could be judged as foolish or silly. So I delay. This delaying behaviour is procrastination. Whenever we are unsure, uncertain or uneasy about something, we will usually distract ourselves, either knowingly or unknowingly (Lauderdale, 2017). We can then get stuck in a cycle of avoidance where the need to procrastinate will be reinforced (Gautam et al., 2019). There has been some research showing that the brain gets a hit of dopamine (the reward chemical) when we put something off. This would indicate that trying to stop procrastinating is like trying to stop a bad habit and can be just as difficult.

FEAR OF JUDGEMENT

I know that underneath my reticence to speak to a mechanic is a fear of looking stupid or being laughed at. When I'm at the garage I hide this by deliberately making silly jokes at my own expense, in an effort to try to control the outcome and the laughs. It's a situation in which I know I'm more vigilant for signs that tell me I might be sounding silly. This is the self-fulfilling prophecy of anxiety. We become hypervigilant for what might go wrong, but this means we are more likely to see signs of our worst-case scenarios. When we are in this mode our brains are predicting what might happen and as a result we are more likely to see these things. If you look out for what might go wrong, you will likely find it.

When we put off or try to suppress our struggles with our own body and mind then there can be consequences. Yousaf et al.'s 2015 systematic review found that men were more likely to delay seeking help until their symptoms became serious. One of the reasons that came out in the study was the fear of talking to health professionals. The participants reported that this made them feel out of control. This fear ties in with research that sadly shows higher statistics for male suicide (Office for National Statistics, 2015) and how things can become very bad before help is sought, if it is sought at all. The gender difference is quite pronounced in the research literature and is often spoken about as a difference in terms of whether a person prefers to talk about emotions or instead focuses on solving a problem (Liddon, Kingerlee & Barry, 2018). Although this finding does seem to be well documented, it is important to consider there may be many reasons for this difference. For example, there could be a bias in the way that participants are categorized in such studies. Also, society's expectations of gender can be a reason why we might make certain judgements. The expectations on men to be stoic and not show emotions are still widespread, although several recent campaigns have tried to chip away at this mindset. See for example the recent efforts within rugby union, Prince William's mental health initiatives and the ongoing work of CALM (the Campaign Against Living Miserably).

Another systematic review (Clement et al., 2015) found that there wasn't a clear male-female split, and that other groups were affected disproportionally as well. It demonstrated how the fear of judgement when it comes to mental health affected people from ethnic minorities, as well as certain professions such as the military and health workers. There is also a growing awareness from the neurodivergent community of how mental health systems have incorrectly judged and misdiagnosed them for many years.

Difficulty talking to professionals showed up as one of the barriers to people seeking help in Clement et al.'s study. But other fears were also present. The fears that were found to be most associated with delays in seeking help were thoughts about oneself being in some way 'weak' or 'crazy' (judgements about the self), and social judgements about seeking help for mental health (judgements from others). Fears about disclosure and confidentiality and the impact on employment were also present in this study. This is another key area of importance, because people have reported in previous studies that they have lost their jobs due to mental health (Nelson & Kim, 2011). The judgements of others matter to us as much as the judgements we place upon ourselves. In a biopsychosocial sense the two are closely linked and one informs the other. Our brains rush to judge because the brain needs to quickly categorize. It does this based on our shared social norms and our personal past experience. If you want to see this in action, aim to 'notice' the quick thoughts that you have in response to items in the news or on social media.

It is clear that fear – either of the judgements people are making of themselves or of what they fear others are making about them – is a barrier to people seeking help, and in my practice I see that this fear can affect a great many of us. I see mothers with young babies who are terrified of being judged if they admit to feeling anxious or low. I see police officers, GPs and teachers, both male and female, who are in positions of responsibility. They keep their feelings to themselves out of fear of being judged not fit to practise, or of being considered 'weak', by themselves just as much as by others.

There have been damning statistics showing that black men are judged much more harshly by the psychiatric system, and as a result are logically going to find it very difficult to seek help. Sadly, this can mean that their difficulties will be much more severe by the time they do get help.

The fear of judgement keeps people silent and struggling, until they find a way out of their difficulties one way or the other. The high rates of addictive behaviours and suicide amongst doctors is a particularly shocking commentary on this unseen struggle to cope (Gerada, 2018a).

There are some other factors to take into account here, such as cost, availability and not being aware that therapy could be helpful. All of these play a role. The cost of private therapy can be outside many people's budgets, and as a result there are many who are on agonizingly long NHS waiting lists. However, there does still remain a great deal of fear when it comes to seeking help, particularly a fear of judgement (Topkaya, 2015), and what this judgement could ultimately lead to.

Some of my clients only decided to come to me once they started thinking of taking their own lives. There is no clearer indication of just how hard it can be for people to seek help.

POWERLESSNESS

In many of the studies on delays seeking help, there is mention of feeling out of control when talking to health professionals as well as the fear of being judged. In my practice I hear this too. I'd like to show you an example:

Therapist (T): How do you feel about being here and seeing me?
Client (C): Like I must be really crazy or something.
T: If you were crazy, what would that mean about you?
C: That I've lost it, got no control, can't be trusted any more.
T: And if you can't be trusted and have lost control, what would that mean?
C: I wouldn't be able to do anything, I'd have no choices, other people would tell me what to do.
T: And if that happened, what would that mean?
C: I'd be powerless.

In this example I have used a technique called the 'downward arrow' to get to the belief that was underneath this client's worry about seeing me. This form of questioning was developed by the founder of cognitive therapy, Dr Aaron Beck, as a way of getting to a 'core belief' of what something means to that person (Beck et al., 1979).

For the client above, we followed a chain of meaning that led us to her core belief that seeing a therapist could mean she would be made powerless. As a result, it was incredibly difficult for her to come and see me, and she had put it off many times. It is important to note that she would not necessarily have been aware that this was the reason why she was delaying seeking help. We are not always conscious of how our core beliefs filter our perceptions and interpretations.

Being rendered powerless is something that is potentially dangerous from a survival point of view, so it makes sense that we would be motivated to avoid anything that could trigger this feeling. However, not all of us will have this fear triggered to the same degree when it comes to seeing a therapist. Our past experiences shape the strength of our beliefs as well as what we believe, and some of us may have been surrounded by positive messages about what it means to see a therapist. Nevertheless, anxieties about having our power and control taken from us are a core human fear (Millings & Carnelley, 2015), and different things can trigger this in us.

HELPLESSNESS

Here's another example from my practice, and sadly quite a common one:

T: What does it mean to you to be seeing a therapist?
C: It means I need help.
T: What does it mean to you if you need help?
C: If I need help it means I'm weak.
T: Needing help means you are weak?
C: Yes.
T: What does it mean about you if you are weak?
C: That I'm helpless.

In this example the client believed that needing help was something that made him feel he was weak. When we looked at what being 'weak' meant, we got to the fear that this could leave him helpless and at the mercy of others. This is a potentially dangerous state for us humans: to be rendered helpless. Our instinct will be to avoid anything that might make us feel powerless or helpless.

If we have had experiences where we have been rendered powerless or helpless and have feared for our lives and sense of agency, then this feeling will be remembered and laid down as a fear memory. We learn through our experiences in the world and with those around us. This teaches us what could be dangerous or problematic. Cognitive behavioural researchers, led by Aaron Beck, state that we develop core beliefs as a result of our early and significant experiences (Osmo et al., 2018). These core beliefs help us to categorize and filter the way we see the world. Barrett (2017) calls them our 'concepts' and states they are the brain's way of making sense of the large amount of input and activity within and around us. Beck and fellow researchers have found that these beliefs (or 'Schemas' as Jeffrey Young calls them) can be the filter through which we then come to view certain situations. Sometimes this can cause us problems if we hold a particular negative, rigid belief about something we fear is happening but that isn't actually happening.

For example, imagine growing up in an environment where high achievement is the norm and is expected. You are praised when you achieve and are expected to win. You strive for the top position or grade and feel ignored or punished if you don't achieve. If this is what is expected of you, you will want to achieve and not 'fail'. You might also feel unloved if not achieving. In this sense you could develop a belief that to be 'good enough' you have to be the best, be perfect, pass every exam, get an A grade. Anything other than achieving success can trigger feelings of failure and not being good enough, or feelings of worthlessness. I have painted an extreme example here, but this belief about needing to achieve to feel good enough can be something that isn't verbalized, or maybe even noticed, until something happens to trigger it. A failure on an exam can be a time when a belief like this can be seen. Instead of seeing the many different reasons why they didn't pass that exam, a person might go straight to the negative label of 'I'm a failure'. This is where the beliefs can become unhelpful, because the person's sense of self is tied up with needing to be 'good enough'. If they don't meet their standards or expectations, then they judge themselves and feel even worse. Sadly, the way that the brain then retrieves memories where we have had the same feeling, means that we are likely to have other thoughts and images and feelings which we may label as 'failure' and then this can colour the way we see the present. We can then become stuck in low mood and feeling like everything we do is a failure.

If you are feeling upset about a particular event or situation, sometimes this can be because you hold a particular belief about what that event means to you. In Appendix One I have put a list of the most common beliefs that I have come across in my practice, along with some ideas of how we can work on developing more constructive and helpful ones. It takes time to develop the newer beliefs though so go easy on yourself if you are going to try this. This is a good example of where therapy can help you to release the power of these core beliefs or schemas.

We can develop beliefs in many different ways, but for things that are potentially dangerous for us, it is clear that we very quickly learn to fear those things. Our brain has a survival circuit that is able to come online swiftly to alert us to anything that might be dangerous for us. Anything that could potentially render us vulnerable to attack, powerless or helpless will not be overlooked by the brain.

Unfortunately, psychiatry and our approach to mental health have historically not helped with these fears, and it could be argued they are the origin of some of them. As a result, the way that we perceive mental health and therapy can be through a particularly negative lens, unless we have had experiences that have enabled us to develop more accepting beliefs. The history of how people have been treated in asylums and psychiatric institutions has understandably helped to reinforce a fear of being rendered powerless. We not only have our individual beliefs here but also shared social norms for psychiatry, therapy and mental health.

SHARED BELIEFS AND ATTITUDES

> "We are what we imagine. Our very existence consists in our imagination of ourselves."
> N. Scott Momaday (quoted in Connor, 2011, p. 232)

Our past experiences help us to create our future predictions of the world. Our perceptions of therapy come, like most perceptions do, from the way we have been shaped and what has been modelled to us from others. As a result, we can all have very different perceptions of the same situation. Look at what happened in 2015 with the 'dress on the Internet' (en.wikipedia.org/wiki/The_dress) and how people could not agree on one definitive answer. This shows that even colour perception is not the same for all of us. We perceive, think about and react to an event in our own unique way, albeit within the confines of particular structures. For example there were commonalities in the colours people saw and the range was small. There were two main categories that people seemed to be in with regards to the dress; black and blue, or white and gold. People didn't end up saying colours such as pink and green, red and blue, black and turquoise for example.

Our brains are geared towards efficiency, and one way that this can be seen is through the manner in which we share concepts with others in our sociocultural groups. The way that we see and understand situations is shaped by the wider societal and familial attitudes that we experience. For example, if I said, 'Thank goodness it's Friday tomorrow,' it's likely that you would know that I'm referring to the end of the working week, and a chance to be free of work demands until Monday. Your individual circumstances may mean that you don't personally have the 'Friday feeling', but you might still understand the concept.

We are influenced not just by our own thoughts and behaviours, but by what we share and experience from significant others and from the world around us (Van der Kolk, 2010). Research suggests that our brains do this in order to categorize and work more efficiently. We streamline our understanding into shared concepts to construct a 'social reality' (Barrett, 2018).

These shared concepts have a role to play when it comes to mental health and therapy. Psychiatry, psychology and mental health have long been associated with the exertion of control and being locked up against one's will and subjected to inhumane chemical and physical treatments (Hari, 2018). The psychiatrist Thomas Szasz wrote in 1961 about how people were having their personal responsibility taken away from them and were being diagnosed as 'deviant' and 'ill', when they should instead have been taught how to understand and manage their experiences (Szasz, 2010). That this was written over fifty years ago shows just how long change takes to happen, because psychiatry is still being criticized for its treatment of mental illness today. Diagnoses and drugs are sadly still the first line of treatment in psychiatry (Filer, 2019; Hari, 2018), and the term 'mental illness' is still being used, even though Szasz argued over half a century ago that this was not a helpful label for people and their suffering.

I recall watching the film *One Flew over the Cuckoo's Nest* when I was younger. It became my model for what mental illness was, until my experiences brought the full reality into view. The film is a snapshot in time of how little understanding psychiatry had for what was happening in the human brain, and why people might be distressed. The back story of the main narrator – a mixed-race man who became known as 'Chief Bromden' – tells of him witnessing the loss of his family's livelihood: salmon fishing. As a result, his father lost his work and with it his sense of pride and being able to provide for his family. He descended into alcoholism and died. Bromden then fought as a soldier in the Second World War and later suffered a breakdown whilst on a military base. Looking at this through today's eyes, it's apparent that he suffered key impactful events in his life prior to experiencing the stress of combat. He was suffering. Unfortunately, his behaviour was viewed with fear and suspicion instead. Bromden's Native American cultural heritage meant that he viewed situations through a different lens to those in the military base, and the ways he used language to discuss his fears and sadness became viewed as madness. He was diagnosed as a paranoid schizophrenic and held against his will at the asylum (Connor, 2011).

In the film we also see the treatment of Jack Nicholson's character Randle P. McMurphy. In several scenes we witness him enraged at being restrained and told he cannot leave, with his fury taken as evidence of his madness instead of a normal reaction in the context of being held down and rendered powerless. The behaviour of the staff is almost a lesson in how not to understand someone else's distress.

We also see the institution's regular drug routine and how people were heavily tranquillized in order to control their unpredictable, difficult-to-understand 'conditions'. The drugs used at that time were anti-psychotic medications such as chlorpromazine, which had serious side effects. Some of the outward signs of these effects were repetitive behaviours such as rocking, drooling and involuntary movements of the tongue. These became stereotyped as being due to 'madness', but they were actually due to the side effects of the crude medications that targeted wide areas of the brain. One of the complications that they caused was called 'drug-induced' Parkinson's symptoms. Psychiatry later came to add another type of medication to the mix to counteract these effects, with drugs such as procyclidine. But this meant that the person's brain and body had two sets of side effects to cope with, on top of the distress that brought them into contact with the psychiatric system in the first place.

Cuckoo's Nest was a work of fiction, but it resembled real life for my parents' generation. A search of the literature throws up many stories of people who have been treated in similar ways in real psychiatric institutions. Not enough was known about the brain to offer information about what emotions were, or what psychological health was. The brain seemed a mysterious 'black box', and even psychologists referred to it as such. One of the most well-known and influential figures in psychology at the time was B.F. Skinner. It was Skinner's practices that *Cuckoo's Nest* was said to be a commentary on (Connor, 2011). He developed the theory of learned behaviour and the important role of reward and punishment in shaping this learning. But he placed importance on only observable actions being worthy of scientific study, not functions taking place inside the brain such as memories, thoughts and perceptions (Goleman, 1987).

Skinner's focus on the observable had been a reaction to the dominance of Sigmund Freud and his concept of the unconscious and unseen aspects of the brain. Freud explored what people 'said' and saw this as being indicative of unconscious processes taking place inside their brains. He developed a 'talking therapy', which he called psychoanalysis, based on this theory of what was happening beneath the surface. His main view was that people were driven by instincts that they were not conscious of, and that talking therapy could bring these unconscious patterns into the person's conscious awareness. The problem that Skinner and the behaviourists had with this approach was that you could not 'see' or measure these unconscious processes.

In their own ways each was trying to understand the mysteries of the brain, but the two approaches went about this in very different ways. Both though seemed to take a disorder-focused approach, looking at how to correct what they thought was *wrong* with a person if that person was struggling or not behaving as expected.

Freud pathologized certain conditions; for example, the term 'hysteria' was originally used by him to label females who were anxious, particularly if they displayed any physical symptoms that doctors were unable to explain. But physical illnesses, and what it meant to be 'healthy', were just as much of a mystery as the brain was at the time. It seems hard to believe now, but in the 1930s and 40s smoking was considered healthy. Doctors were still being used in advertisements showing the supposed benefits of smoking up until the 1950s (Gardner & Brandt, 2006; Lawrence, 2009).

As a result of how little was known about the brain, psychiatric treatments were crude and at times downright inhumane, as was seen in the *Cuckoo's Nest* film. Even the way that people were spoken about when they 'became' a patient implied that they were 'less than' human. The lack of knowledge and understanding is the cause of this, not the people themselves. We can see the language of the psychiatric system here in the UK in documents from the not-too-distant past. Take a look at this website devoted to the history of High Royds Hospital: www.highroydshospital.com. High Royds was West Yorkshire's best-known Victorian asylum.

Residents were labelled with words such as 'pauper', 'lunatic' and 'degenerate stock'. These were official terms used to discuss people who were deemed to be defective and 'less than'. As if their suffering was their fault, rather than because not enough was known about how to help them. These labels of ignorance are a sorry and sad sight. It is little wonder we have grown to fear psychiatry, given its history.

Local author and historian Mark Davis has worked to document the history of High Royds and its former patients and staff in his book *Voices from the Asylum*. I visited High Royds and met Mr Davis and some of the hospital's former residents and staff. I will not forget the stories I heard of pain, separation and misunderstanding. Even the building itself left its mark on me, with many sleepless nights for months after my visit. If a building can capture the energies of what occurs within its walls, then High Royds is still holding on to the screams of those it imprisoned.

For my parents' generation I see clear reasons why they would have learned to fear mental illness, the psychiatric system, the brain and emotions. Showing too much emotion could get you locked up and labelled as disordered – and so they 'kept calm and carried on'. These fears are still present today though, whether passed down from our parents or generated by our own experiences. They show that there is still work to do with regards to our understanding of distress. People are still held against their will in psychiatric hospitals; people are still being misdiagnosed and given major tranquillizers; and people are still being restrained. It can feel like change will never happen sometimes, as it can be so painfully slow.

I recall being a service user/carer member of a group setup by NICE to draw up guidelines for the use of restraint and tranquillizers in acute psychiatric settings. This was in 2003 and the death of Rocky Bennett in a psychiatric unit in 1998 (Carvel, 2004) was a strong driving force in making sure that the guidance clearly set out what was not appropriate. Our guidelines stated that physical restraint and force were to be the last resort and should be avoided if possible (Royal College of Nursing, 2005). It is deeply saddening to know that this guidance did not prevent further tragedies. The death of Seni Lewis in 2010 is evidence of this: Seni died from being physically restrained for more than thirty minutes by eleven police officers. In 2015 there was an update to the NICE guidelines for physical restraint; however, this still did not stop the practice. In 2018 the *Guardian* newspaper reported an 'alarming rise' in injuries due to restraint

Seni's family have worked hard to push for change since his death, and in 2018 'Seni's Law' was passed (Mind, 2018). This law now means that mental health units have to reduce their use of force and physical restraint. Change can take time, because beliefs and attitudes take time to shift. But we must keep going.

In the arena of psychiatric diagnoses change is happening. Take a look at these quotes:

> the biomedical diagnostic approach in psychiatry is not fit for purpose. Diagnoses frequently and uncritically reported as 'real illnesses' are in fact made on the basis of internally inconsistent, confused and contradictory patterns of largely arbitrary criteria. The diagnostic system wrongly assumes that all distress results from disorder and relies heavily on subjective judgements about what is normal.

> Professor Peter Kinderman, University of Liverpool

> Perhaps it is time we stopped pretending that medical-sounding labels contribute anything to our understanding of the complex causes of human distress or of what kind of help we need when distressed.

> Professor John Read, University of East London

These conclusions came as the result of a study by Allsopp and colleagues at the University of Liverpool in 2019. They are a good example of how research can back up what is already apparent anecdotally, but sadly not respected or given credibility. Service users and campaign groups such as 'Drop the Disorder' have been reporting for many years about their experiences with diagnoses that do not represent what they have experienced. Thankfully they are now being vindicated by science. This is significant, because it directly challenges psychiatry's reliance on the language of disorder and diagnosis. Without these, the field of mental health has to look more holistically at why a person is struggling, opening the door to us being able to access help sooner, without having to fit a particular diagnosis. If we do not have to be judged by a diagnosis, then we do not have to judge ourselves as having a particular disorder or diagnosis. Perhaps instead we will be able to use different words to talk about what we are experiencing; words which are not quite so judgemental.

Psychotherapies have also been shifting and changing, especially over the past decade. Through a cross-fertilization between neuroscientists and psychotherapists, we are beginning to see new insights into what takes place inside the brain and body, and how trauma and our early attachment relationships shape us. Daniel Siegel, Bessel van der Kolk, Peter Levine, Stephen Porges, Frank Corrigan, David Grand and Francine Shapiro, to name but a few, have all produced exciting work in this area, and I have included some of their work in the references section of this book. The work that resulted in the Adverse Childhood Experiences scale has also led to a pronounced shift in our understanding of the impact of our early experiences. We now have a way of being able to discuss and help those who have experienced developmental or attachment-based trauma. By this I mean the effects on a person of living with abusive and/ or neglectful and traumatic early experiences, particularly with those who are meant to keep us safe.

What this means in practice is that underneath our relationship struggles and battles with how we feel are body-brain systems that are operating in a particular way for a reason. The things we experience are not necessarily due to us being disordered.

Our body's internal systems are continually sending messages up to our brain and vice versa. Psychological health is no longer only about what happens in the brain, and physical health is no longer only about what happens from the neck down.

With the new science of brain-body interaction we are beginning to get our hands on a new vocabulary and way of understanding psychological health. We need this so that we can reassess what is normal and stop judging ourselves and others when it comes to what we are experiencing. We also need more emotional 'granularity' (Barrett, 2017): more words for describing how we feel, so we can choose from a wider range. At the moment we have a limited vocabulary to use to describe our struggles. This traps us into describing how we feel with limited categories that pathologize. 'I'm stressed' or 'I'm anxious' can mean such a wide variety of sensations and thoughts and behaviours. It's a good thing that we are using those words more openly, but we can now aim to notice earlier how we feel and detect more subtle shifts. The science of interoception and CBT's 'automatic thoughts' are two examples of how we can aim to notice what is happening within us.

In this chapter, we have looked at some of the reasons we can feel wary of seeking help for our mental health. The way that people have been mistreated in mental health services throughout history, and still are in some parts of psychiatry today, is responsible for some of this fear. As a result, we have learned as a society to fear showing emotions or behaviours that may be considered 'mad', lest we be locked up. This has resulted in a way of coping that emphasizes the importance of suppressing emotions and not showing how we feel.

In the next chapter I'd like to delve deeper into what actually happens when we feel an emotion, and the ways that we try to keep control of our emotions for fear of being overwhelmed. Through our struggles to suppress we can get into unhelpful patterns that can cause us even more distress. I will also be highlighting the emotion of fear and how it can keep us caught in a vicious cycle and will take a look at the fear of fear itself.

CHAPTER TWO

The Trouble with Emotions

Feeling scared is a core emotional state. But what is an emotion and why do we have them? In this chapter I'm going to give you an overview of emotions, especially the emotion of fear: what it is, why we have it and how we can manage it. In my practice I see the difference it can make when we know how to manage our emotions, especially the emotional state of anxiety. I've heard from my clients that they have felt more in control and more confident, and felt better both physically and psychologically. But I also know from my own experiences that understanding more about emotions generally and how to manage them can make situations easier to untangle, and life more straightforward as a result.

THE MONSTER IN THE BEDROOM

Imagine your five-year-old daughter wakes you up during the night to tell you she had a bad dream and is feeling scared that there are monsters in her bedroom. What would you do?

The way you respond will give her information about what happens when she is afraid. She will likely be experiencing the activation of fear in her body, with the many sensations of sympathetic arousal in preparation for danger. Some of these include a fast, racing heartbeat, quick shallow breaths, wobbly legs, a fluttery feeling in the stomach area, a dry mouth and possibly a need to go to the toilet. She will also likely have scary worst-case-scenario thoughts and images running through her mind as well.

All of these sensations, thoughts, images and behaviours are normal responses to the perception of something frightening, such as bad dreams or shadows in the bedroom. But your daughter won't necessarily be thinking about why her body is reacting this way, and will instead be focused on the monsters and how scared she feels. Her instinctive response will be to get away from the danger and look for safety.

In our efforts to comfort and reassure our children we may say things like 'there's no monster', or 'don't be scared' or 'don't worry'. But when we say this it can be confusing, because it is effectively telling them that all the things they are experiencing shouldn't be happening and they should just 'stop' feeling.

We want to take their distress away and solve the problem. But we don't need to do as much as we might think. Helping them to feel safe to feel their feelings is key.

Researchers have found that an effective strategy can be simply to label what is happening, rather than try to stop or suppress it. For example, explaining to your daughter that this is the feeling of fear. It is there because something frightened her. The wobbly, fluttery sensation in their body is normal; it will come, but it will also go away soon. This strategy is called 'affect labelling', and it has been found to be a surprisingly simple but effective strategy for understanding and regulating. Of course we need to adapt what we say to our child's age, but the combination of labelling the feeling that they are having, whilst acknowledging the way this feeling physically feels can be a helpful way to process emotions. A review by researchers Jared Torre and Matthew Lieberman at the University of California detailed how putting into words (either by speaking or writing) the way that you feel can lead to reductions in negative feelings that can have lasting effects.

When we label what we are feeling, we are doing a few things: we are turning our attention towards something and bringing that into our conscious awareness; we are noticing our body's response and assessing this response in light of what is actually happening in our environment. We are pausing; and hopefully we are also accepting rather than dismissing or judging. Finally, we are attaching a conceptual label which – depending on what it is – can change the way that our brain reacts in the future. The labelling of our bodily sensations is important here, because it can be these which we learn to fear. If we label our bodily sensations as something to be wary of then we will feel worried or scared the next time we notice them.

Try it the next time you feel worried, annoyed or sad. Notice what your body is doing, and label what you notice. For example, if you find yourself keyed up and having angry thoughts, pause. Notice what is happening in your chest, stomach, hands, arms and head, or any other ways your body is expressing this and label what you notice, e.g., 'I'm feeling really annoyed right now, can feel my heart beating hard, and my face is flushed.' But here's the tricky part: notice without putting an immediate judgement in place. This activation in your body will calm down again if you let it. The judgements that our thoughts are usually making at this time are the things that can disrupt the emotion from coming and going. For example with anger, the thoughts 'You never…', 'I can't bear this' or 'You should…' will all maintain the angry feeling. If you switch from these thoughts into what is happening in your body, you can help yourself to get to the other side of this emotional wave – not by trying to get rid of the feeling, just by noticing and gently unclenching and breathing. Don't try to rush it and you will find it goes away quicker.

If someone close to you is upset, comfort them with your presence and gently try to help them to label what they are noticing in their body, instead of trying to solve their problem straight away. You could, for example, prompt them to put what they feel into words by saying something open-ended like 'I can see that you are upset – do you feel sad?' You don't have to use the word 'sad'; you can keep it more open if you like: 'What does it feel like?' Let them have the feeling, let them know it is OK to notice it. Be curious rather than trying to judge or rush to problem-solve. 'I can understand it must feel…' or 'It's not a nice feeling but it makes sense you'd be feeling like that. Let it come. It's a wave. It will soon pass'. By doing this you will be validating what they are experiencing and showing that they don't have to 'get rid' of it. They (and you) can tolerate this. It is just our body's way of sending messages back and forth. There might be a lot of activity, but it is normal. It's a wave. Let it come and it will go.

This can be hard at night when our children are woken by nightmares and seem to have persistent scary thoughts that can't be calmed. We can feel pressured to take away their distress – quickly, so that we can all get back to sleep. But this teaches them that they must do something to take away that feeling if they get it again. Show them instead that the feeling is normal, but importantly that they are safe right now. This is what we try to do when we tell them not to worry and that there isn't a monster. Rather than tell them not to feel what they feel, we could instead let them know what the feeling is and why it is there. Then we can show them how to check if they are safe and comfort them with our presence to help them to know what this sense of safety feels like. Feeling safe and being comforted by a trusted person is vital for our development. It's our model for learning how to soothe ourselves. Comfort your little one with your presence and let them know that they are safe. Don't be alarmed if they pop back up with more scary thoughts; just comfort them again and let them know they are safe and notice where they feel safe in their body. It's difficult to be patient late at night, so don't judge yourself. If you do get snappy, that's OK. Be honest and own how you feel – label it. You could show them how you let a feeling come and go. A study by Sara Waters and colleagues (Waters et al., 2020) has found that this style of emotional regulation is more helpful for parent-child relationships than suppressing emotions.

I know that when I was younger, I wasn't told about emotions or what they were. I grew up not paying much attention at all to feelings, especially bodily sensations. I learned not to interrupt or disturb my parents at night, because their response taught me either to feel ashamed – 'Don't be so stupid: there aren't monsters in your room!' – or to be more afraid of their anger if I woke them up. I learned it wasn't OK to share what I was feeling, so I kept silent.

I mention this because just knowing what a feeling is, and that it is normal, can be something many of us do not have a real physical experience of. We might know it rationally, but knowing something rationally is very different from having an internal physical experience of it. It's common to be wary of emotions, lest they overwhelm us and cloud our capacity to cope. So we avoid letting ourselves get upset. This can become an aversion, and the more we reinforce an aversion the stronger our belief becomes that we need to avoid that thing.

From the clients I have spoken to over the years, I know I was not alone in not understanding what emotions were. My teachers did not speak about emotions and thoughts and how to manage them. To be fair to my parents, they weren't shown how to manage emotions when they were growing up either. There was very little understanding of what to do when others around us were upset. As a result, the discomfort we felt would be quickly turned into a judgement; of ourselves or others with labels such as 'sissy', 'weakling' or 'weirdo'. We ridiculed, ignored or avoided.

It is my hope that this is perhaps changing. We know so much more about what happens in our brains now, and we are learning all the time about what does or doesn't help. We can pass on a different attitude to our young people, and we can learn different ways to regulate our own emotions too. This is important because trouble regulating our emotions leads us into coping strategies that involve distraction and avoidance, for example anxiety disorders, depression, addiction, self-harm and eating disorders.

WHAT ACTUALLY ARE EMOTIONS?

Would it surprise you to know that there doesn't appear to be one agreed-upon definition of what emotions actually are? Daniel Siegel, in his book *The Neurobiology of 'We'* (2011), likens emotions to messages and explains how they signal something to us about ourselves, others or our environment. Peter Levine (2010), the founder of the trademarked 'somatic experiencing' approach, separates 'emotion' and 'feeling' by explaining that a 'feeling' is our awareness of our internal bodily sensations and bodily postures, and an 'emotion' is the expression and action that can result from that feeling-state. For example, if we are called back by our boss just as we are leaving the office and spoken to in a way we don't like, we might feel a clenching in our stomach, or a heat in our face, or feel our hearts beginning to beat fast. Our thoughts might start coming thick and fast: 'What? How dare you!' Or we may find in that moment we are blank and simply staring at our boss. Our nervous system is in a state of high arousal at this point, and the feeling is not a pleasant one because of the thoughts going through our mind and how we perceive this state of high arousal. But as it is our boss, we are likely to restrain ourselves from saying anything in that moment. We might go home, see our house in a mess, and have the thought 'why can't you clean up the mess, for God's sake!', then blow up at our spouse. This would be the expression of the emotion of anger. We 'felt' a certain way, and we expressed the 'emotion' of anger.

Alternatively, we may not say anything when we get home. We might withdraw and disconnect from those around us and silently ruminate instead. With the same 'feelings' we then repress instead of express that feeling-state. This can lead us to start to replay past experiences and feel even worse as we start to blame ourselves or feel resentful towards others. The activation in our nervous system is not needed, so it reduces. But this reduction may not feel pleasant: it might instead feel like a flattening of our energy. This, along with the fact we are alone and have withdrawn from others can give us a feeling of disconnection. This is a feeling of depression instead of anger.

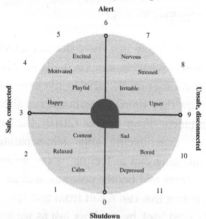

Fig. 2 – Dial of arousal, safety and connection

In the diagram above, the dial represents our activation or arousal level, from calm to high alert to shutdown. This arousal is activation in our central nervous system, which determines how mobilized we are for action. This, in combination with what our brain predicts is happening, is what leads to a feeling-state. For example, with high arousal we could have a feeling-state of either excitement or nervousness, or a blend of the two. Performers can move through both states from nervous to excited to elated as they prepare for, then proceed with and complete a performance. If the performance goes well, they can move from nervousness to elation and then to contented tiredness as their arousal level drops. But if they perceive the performance hasn't gone well, they could progress from nervousness to rumination and low mood instead, as their bodily arousal level drops.

Feeling safe and connected is an important part of our feeling-state. If we perceive that we are safe and we feel connected, then this can help us to tolerate both increases and decreases in our arousal level. If we feel threatened or helpless in association with feeling unsafe and disconnected from others, then this sets us up for anxiousness, aggression and/or depression.

A performance that goes well and makes us feel elated afterwards is a case in point here. Notice how nervous and worried you feel just before you go on. As the performance ends and you feel you have done well and you feel the connection from the audience, this makes you feel elated and excited. Your arousal level is the same as it was before you went on, but the emotional experience is very different. By contrast, a performance that you think hasn't gone well can make you have negative thoughts that turn this arousal into an unpleasant feeling that you will want to get away from. You might then withdraw and disconnect from people. This will make you more likely to ruminate on what went wrong. The dip in arousal, coupled with post-event rumination can make you feel upset and low.

In day-to-day life we may not have these extreme arousal experiences, but our nervous systems are still acting and reacting to everything that is going on around and within us. Moments of safety or threat, connection or rupture are normal. But they can become sticky when we think they mean something more significant.

Exercise: Where would you put yourself on your own dial right now?

Do a quick scan of your body. Are there any aches, pains or feelings of tension anywhere? Stretch out and adjust if you need too. With your next breath out, try and extend it a little, then make your next in-breath a deep, slow breath, and as you exhale pucker your lips so that the hole your breath escapes through is small, like the diameter of a string of spaghetti. Breathe out a long string of spaghetti. Now take a big breath in and let it flop out, like a big sigh. Once again, big breath in and let it flop out like a big sigh. Check your body for any tension, then release it.

Where would you put yourself on the dial now?

In Lisa Feldman Barrett's book *How Emotions Are Made* (2017), she describes how our brain and body work together to predict and balance out what is needed for a particular situation. She uses the term 'body budget' to describe this internal activity that can give rise to feeling-states that we don't always notice.

For example, in a given moment, how much energy do our muscles need? Do we need to run away from something? Or just support our bodies in a chair? Do we need an increased amount of oxygen to power our movements? Do we need more glucose pumped into our system in preparation for a task? All of this is going on in the background. It's a sensory world that we can be oblivious to. It's part of our 'interoceptive network'.

Interoception is the perception of our internal bodily sensations, such as our heart rate, muscle tension, breathing rate. Our nervous system (which includes our gut and heart) is continuously assessing and sending messages to the brain using this network. It is now being considered a vital part of our emotional feeling-states (Critchley & Garfinkel, 2017; Barrett, 2017; Levine, 2010). Have you ever noticed what happens in your body when you are annoyed or excited? There can be many events taking place; for example, fast heartbeat, flushed face, tense hands, wide eyes, shallow breathing, and a feeling of jitteriness. These events are perceived by our brain, and our brain responds and makes predictions about what it thinks is happening based on these events.

When we are activated, with a fast heartbeat and quick shallow breathing, we are mobilized for action and we are alert. What is it that we need to be alert for? Is it something interesting and exciting, or is it something we don't like? Are we safe or unsafe? Do we feel connected or disconnected? Our past experience and our core beliefs and expectations will shape what decisions our brain makes and inform what emotion we then express. So, although our bodily sensations are part of the picture, it is what our brain predicts is happening as a result of getting this feedback from our environment and body that leads to the expression of a particular emotion.

Here's an example of a situation that can lead to a different emotion depending on how the brain perceives the signals it is being fed:

Situation: You arrive home and hear loud noises, voices and music coming from inside your house			
Somatic	Thoughts	Emotion	Action
Heart racing, shallow breathing, tension in head	Why is it always so chaotic in my house?!	Irritated, annoyed	Stomp into the house and tell them to be quiet.
Heart racing, shallow breathing, dry mouth, muscles feel rigid	Who the hell is in my house?	Scared, nervous	Freeze outside the door and listen for clues to what is happening. Take phone out of pocket to call 999.
Heart racing, shallow breathing, warm feeling in chest	Wow it's the surprise party – I knew they were planning this!	Excited and nervous	Smile, take a quick look in your mirror, and open the door.

Table 1. – Same situation, different interpretations

The expression of an emotion is not universal, however, even though we used to think it was. Two people may both be having angry thoughts, feeling tense and activated at the same situation, but they might express this feeling very differently. One person could be shouting, gesturing wildly or even hitting out, whereas another might be rigid and restrained and stare quietly at the object of their anger instead.

Peter Levine's research would say that prior to this expression of anger there would have been a particular feeling-state in the person's body, made up of various sensations and muscle movements, that then became either a free expression of aggressive rage or an inhibitory (restrained) expression of seething anger.

In Hilary Jacobs Hendel's book *It's Not Always Depression*, she discusses how we can inhibit the expression of our emotions when it doesn't feel safe to express a core feeling-state: e.g., feeling unable to express frustration or anger, either because it doesn't feel safe to (in which case an anxious arousal will occur) or because it feels wrong to (in which case a feeling of withdrawing and guilty thoughts may take place). This can be a common experience for new mothers, or in those of us who have lost someone to suicide. We can sometimes find it easier to blame ourselves for what we believe we have done, than to be annoyed at the person we care for. The feeling we then construct is one of guilt, which can lead to us feeling even more upset and isolated. Blaming ourselves also helps us to continue believing that we could have done something to change things; that we had some control over things. That we were not powerless.

When feelings of guilt ('I have done something bad') are accompanied by critical judgements and self-attacking behaviours, they can become shame ('I am bad'). This is an emotion that can severely inhibit us and keep us locked in a wordless and cold place. From this place of silence, it can be very hard to heal. Shame loves silence. It feels safe within silence. Shame keeps us shut down and disconnected. If we look back at the dial from Figure 2, shame can be reduced the more that we accept and feel safe with ourselves and with others. Experiences of safety, connection and compassion can loosen the padlocks of shame. Speaking it out loud (with those whom we feel safe with), whilst connecting to what our bodies are really feeling, can free us from the prison of shame.

Emotions are our brain's way of signalling to us when something important is happening, is about to happen or has happened. They are fast and often occur outside our awareness (Gilbert, 2010). It is important for our survival that we have a system that can detect and report from body to brain and back again, without being slowed down to wait for us to become aware of it and decide what to do. So we do need these events to be happening outside of our awareness, but when they intrude into our awareness it is for a reason. It is at this point that we can cause ourselves more difficulties with the way that we then manage what we become aware of. My argument here is that many of us have either learned or been taught that we should either fear what we become aware of or should try to suppress and avoid it. This can set us up for a struggle and a fight.

WHAT IS FEAR?

The rapid assessment of danger is key to our survival. If we did not have this, we would do things that would likely lead to us getting into serious harm, such as walking out in front of traffic, or driving our cars too fast for the conditions on the road. We need quick warnings of potential danger – much quicker than we can assess using conscious thought alone. Neuroscience researchers believe that we have a survival circuit in our brain which coordinates all the information that is sensed or picked up from the environment. This circuit helps us assess and respond to threat swiftly and efficiently, but our body is an intelligent part of this activity too. It isn't only the brain that is playing a role here. Stephen Porges has coined the term 'neuroception' to describe the way our nervous system picks up on information from our environment and transmits danger or safety signals via the vagus nerve to the brain.

The perception of threat is something that takes place outside of our conscious awareness. This is important because it is essential to our survival that our system is able to predict and assess danger as swiftly as possible. Our bodies are continuously picking up information from our environment, and our brains use this, in association with our prior experiences, to make a prediction about what is happening right now. If a danger signal is perceived, then our protective fight/ flight mechanism is set in action. A surge of adrenaline and cortisol is released, glucose rushes to the brain, blood pressure increases and our heart pumps more blood around the body to the muscles. Breathing quickens to get oxygen to the large muscles, readying them for action (they can twitch or feel wobbly at this point). Digestion slows down, because digesting food has to take a back seat whilst the body deals with danger. This can give us the sensation we often call 'butterflies', and the reduction of saliva gives us a dry mouth. The effects of adrenaline can be felt in our heads too, where we can notice disturbances in our vision and perception, such as seeing things more brightly or in a daze or from far away. We have an impulse to 'do' something. Usually this is to get away from the threat or remove it somehow. This is fight or flight. But if we are trapped and cannot get away from the danger, we feel helpless fear and can enter 'freeze' or immobilization mode, where an extra process in our nervous system makes us shut down. This is the extreme end of the survival response and can lead to feeling cut off and dissociated from what's going on around us. This 'freeze' response is often overlooked when people talk about fear and the 'fight or flight' response. But it is important, because when we are in life-threatening danger we become immobile and we cannot run or fight. Only when our threat system detects an escape or potential safety will we be able to move out of freeze mode.

Many victims of assault have given themselves a hard time because they believe they should have fought, or said no, or run away. But the way they behaved was not within their control. When the freeze response has been activated you cannot do anything until your system feels it is safe to move. A deeper part of the brain is in charge. So if you have ever been paralysed by this 'rabbit in the headlights' freeze response, please do not blame yourself for it. It is your threat system responding to what it perceives is a serious danger, and it is forcing you to keep safe in the only way it knows how.

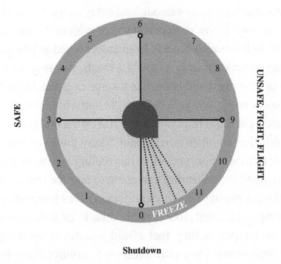

Fig. 3 – The dial of fight/flight/freeze showing the shift from safe to unsafe/threat/life-threat

In the diagram above we can see that the dial of our rising arousal level takes us into fight or flight. But if a danger becomes life-threatening, our freeze response comes online to shut us down and render us immobile.

On this dial I have also plotted an engagement-disengagement dimension to show that when we feel safe, we are able to connect to others comfortably, however when we move into fight/flight and then freeze, we disengage from our safe connections with others and can dissociate/shutdown. When we are feeling really stressed, nervous or annoyed, our connections with others can suffer. If we have experienced events in our lives where others have treated us badly and we have not been able to trust, then we will be set up to feel unsafe and shut off from other people. This can complicate things for us because we will be conflicted between wanting to feel safe and comforted by others, but having a corresponding wariness or instinct to withdraw from others instead.

Hopefully, the majority of the time we will be at the low-middle part of the dial, or engaged and comfortably aroused at a mid-way point.

It is normal to have spikes throughout a day as we deal with whatever comes our way. If you've ever had a near miss in the car, for example the traffic lights turning quickly from amber to red as you slip through, or having to brake sharply to avoid a crash, you may have noticed a feeling in your chest and belly, like a surge or a shakiness. Your heart might be thumping, and your head might hurt a little. This is the activation of the fight/flight response as you rise on the dial from low-middle up to high alert and then down again. Many things can set this off in our modern world. For some of us this feeling is so unpleasant and set off so unpredictably that they can come to fear the feeling itself.

Some people will have experienced these sensations during something unpleasant, like a panic attack, or a distressing event. What can happen is they feel afraid whenever anything triggers similar sensations. They may even try to control these feelings by scanning for them to make sure they are not happening. They might start to avoid whatever they think might trigger the sensations. But we cannot stop our nervous system from mobilizing us for action when it needs to and so this daily uncertainty can mean that many of us are in a constant state of anxious anticipation. From here it doesn't take much to send us up to the higher end of the dial of arousal where we then feel panicky.

Our central nervous system is great at helping us to detect and get ready for threat and danger, but it is also geared towards helping us to detect safety. Feeling 'safe' is a core emotion and is important for our wellbeing. Let's do an exercise now to activate this feeling.

Exercise: Have a think about a place where you feel completely content and safe. It could be on holiday, or in your bedroom, or in an imaginary place. Visualize this place where you feel safe and notice the image you see. What sounds are in this place? How does it smell? What can you touch? Notice where in your body you feel this sense of safety. What sensations you can detect, even if they are quite light, notice them. Remember this feeling of being safe. Notice when you don't feel safe and, if you need to, visualize your place of safety whenever you want to remind yourself of this feeling.

LEARNING TO FEAR FEAR

A panic attack is a frightening event, in which we experience the full force of our body's fear response, with a sudden rush of sensations such as a dizzying whoosh of adrenaline, thumping heartbeat, frantic, shallow breathing, racing thoughts, wobbly legs, dry mouth and thoughts or images signifying immediate danger.

The very first panic attack can often be a purely biochemical event that happens suddenly and without warning, especially during times of acute stress. The sensations can easily mimic a heart attack, so it is completely understandable that we can feel genuinely afraid that something life-threatening is happening to us. For some of us these sensations then become associated in our brain with fear. We learn to be afraid of them because we think they mean that we could be having a heart attack.

Because we fear these sensations, we will be wary of them happening again. We might start to scan our bodies just to make sure they aren't happening, but this puts us on guard. If we are on guard then we are in a heightened state of arousal (rising up through the dial). When we are in this heightened state, we will notice our dry mouth and our quick, shallow breathing and the thumping heartbeat. Our brain uses all of this information to predict that something bad is happening, and our fear level rises further.

Many things can become triggers too. Our brain stores information in a fragmented associative network. Small things like the type of day it was when the first panic attack happened, how hot or cold it was, whether it was night or day, the colour of the carpet, the place where it happened. Any of these can become triggers for the brain's alarm system and can provoke a feeling of unease.

An example would be a person visiting a shop that they haven't been into since they experienced a panic attack and had to leave suddenly. As they approach the store their brain is in hyperalert mode, predicting that it is possible they might panic again. This prediction will set in motion a process in their body to get them ready for action. There will be a release of adrenaline and cortisol, and an increase in breathing and heart rate, just in case they need to get out of there quickly. This rush of bodily activity might feel frightening and they may have the thought: 'Oh no! Am I going to have another panic attack?!' This ramps up the fear and preparedness for danger. The person will become more convinced that the catastrophe will occur.

This fear is called the 'fear of fear', because we learn to feel afraid of our body's own fear response. It's not unusual to experience this. An epidemiology study in 2011 estimated that panic disorder affects 1.7 per cent of the population. In today's numbers that would be approximately 112,000 people in the UK.

When it comes to fear and anxiety, our main coping method is usually a form of avoidance, because we want to stay away from anything that signifies danger to us. If our own bodily sensations set off our fear response, then we have to try to avoid feeling these. But you cannot get away from your own body. If you try to then you enter a state where you have to be on guard and on alert to your own body's activities. This is a state of stress which has been found to have real effects on our general wellbeing and the functioning of our immune system.

Avoidance keeps us fearing the thing that we avoid. In Chapter One we looked at how we can feel afraid of getting upset because of what we think it means about us. This fear of getting upset leads us to avoid seeing a therapist, even if we know rationally that it would be something that might help. In a way it makes sense not to want to be upset but trying to avoid this can make us more anxious.

In the example of our five-year-old having bad dreams about monsters in the bedroom, you will see avoidance behaviours manifesting themselves in delays in going to bed, asking questions and needing reassurance, mentioning that they are scared to go to sleep and asking to sleep in your bed. With children there is a balance to strike between offering comfort and helping them to learn not to be afraid of their feeling of fear. After successive nights of sleep with nothing bad happening, but importantly within a general context of feeling safe and comforted/soothed, their brains will detect that they are safe and that there are no monsters, and the fear will gradually extinguish. But if we do not comfort them they can remain in too high a state of arousal to be able to tolerate their feelings and may find a way either to shut off and distract or to act out. Likewise, if we reassure them and distract them too much, then they won't learn how to manage the feelings for themselves.

The way to extinguish a fear is through managed exposure, within a context of safety. Avoidance doesn't extinguish a fear. It reinforces it. We can use exposure to learn to reduce the fear of our emotions too. The first step is to consider that maybe they are not going to hurt you, that maybe they are not as dangerous as you have been told they are. The next step is to start to notice and label them. By this I mean actually notice what sensations you can detect in your body, as well as any thoughts that go through your mind, when you are in certain situations. Notice without judgement, if possible. This is easier said than done, because you might have an instant avoidance response. That's OK. Just notice what you can and label what you notice.

Use the tool below to help:

Tool: The three rules for clarity and managing an emotion:

Notice

Label

Accept, without judging

Do a quick scan. What small sensations can you detect, however tiny they are? The trick is to be curious and reserve any rush to judgement. It's all just information from your body and brain. You are safe right now to notice.

Is there a lump in your throat, a fluttery feeling in your chest or a buzzy feeling in your head? A twinge in your finger? Are there particular thoughts going through your mind? What impulse or action do you want to carry out? Notice these.

You could take it a step further and run through some of the emotion words to see what fits for you: angry, anxious, sad, excited, ashamed, withdrawn, guilty. Can you choose one of these for a ballpark and then refine it further by looking for other words that would fit better? See the Appendix for a list of emotion words or make up your own. For example, right now I am feeling a bit nauseous because I'm hungry and need lunch. I'm worried I haven't got enough work done for today before I have to pick my little girl up from school. I notice a tension in my head too just above my left eye. If I had to find words for how I feel, I'd say a little on edge and headachy from focusing so intensely.

Words can be hard to pin down for emotions though. Mainly because we can be used to just using the big ones for obvious unpleasant emotions. We don't tend to get a lot of practice at labelling pleasant or more middling experiences. Our mood can also be a complicated mixture that is hard to identify, and perhaps we are not just experiencing one mood, but a feeling-state that is made up of many pieces of information. It's also important to note here that the language networks in the brain can struggle to articulate feelings, because aspects of feeling-states come from different areas of the brain and body.

After we did the lemon exercise in the introduction, we went on to evoke three other memories and feeling-states. I used the words 'pride', then 'mild embarrassment' and 'contentment' to label these. If you did the exercise, was it easy? Or did you find it hard? Learning to tolerate and accept our bodily states – both the pleasant and the unpleasant ones – rather than avoid or suppress them, is an important skill in emotional regulation. Paul Gilbert, the founder of Compassion-Focused Therapy, believes that it can free us from the turmoil that results when we try to avoid our own emotions (Gilbert, 2010). Maybe you found this easy and you didn't need to distract yourself at all. But it isn't always easy to just 'let' an emotion be there, especially when it is a state we have labelled as unpleasant.

We do, however, have the ability to learn to manage and overcome fears that do not serve us, and construct new experiences. We can re-evaluate and change. This is the key to our continued survival: adaptation. Therapy can help encourage these adaptive processes, so that you can be the best you that you can be.

In the next chapter I will be looking at what can get in the way of us knowing how we feel. I also want to show you how to unpack what is upsetting you, so that you can start to see how to use therapy to help you.

CHAPTER THREE

Why Am I Upset? Part One

In the next two chapters I want to help you unpick what is upsetting you. I'm going to use a tool called a 'formulation' and show you how you can use this to uncover what happens for you in certain situations. This tool can be found in Chapter Four, but first I'd like to explain some of the reasons behind why we can find it surprisingly difficult to know what is upsetting us sometimes.

ATTENTION AND AWARENESS

In the lemon exercise we intentionally visualized a lemon, and then switched our attention from this image on to what was physically happening with our bodies. This deliberate shift in our focus of attention increased what we were aware of at that moment. We expanded our awareness.

In our daily lives it is normal for us to operate with limits on our awareness, only attending to a certain amount of information at any particular time. Our brain and body pick up and transmit a vast amount of information, much more than we can attend to. It makes the brain more efficient to have a limit on attention. If we were to notice everything that was happening inside our bodies and outside in the environment, we would be overwhelmed. For some people sensory overload is a moment-to-moment struggle, and their brains can have difficulties filtering out certain stimuli. I am one of these people with a sensory-processing sensitivity: lights, temperature and sound can all really grate on me and cause overload. It's a common issue for neurodivergent people and for

63

those who score highly on Elaine Aron's 'Highly Sensitive Person' (HSP) Scale (see Appendix for further information and self-tests). We can all differ with regards to how much sensory information we can comfortably attend to. Some people can be more sensitive to taste than others and be super-tasters. Some people score high for measures of 'sensation-seeking' (see Appendix) and find that this puts them into a comfortably aroused state that others would find intolerable.

The way that we process sensory information both within and outside us has an impact on how we feel emotionally too because, as we've seen in the previous chapter, there is a relationship between our emotions and our bodily sensations. For some of us this relationship can be a smooth one, whereas for others it can be unpredictable, or lead to overload, or maybe not be noticed at all. We all have our own baseline band of awareness that we are wired to function within.

Our brains have the job of filtering the two-way traffic from the brain, body and environment, so that we can operate efficiently. To do this job it needs to streamline the decision-making processes. This is one reason for learning and developing habits. If you do something repeatedly – for example, stop to get coffee from the same shop every morning – your brain will learn: *if* I want coffee (at that place and time), *then* I will get it from that shop. It will streamline the coffee-decision process such that the thought about coffee, or a sensation in your stomach in the morning, will be followed by a combined set of automatic actions in your brain and body that motivate you towards that shop. If it's been happening for a while, your brain will make its prediction quickly and efficiently. You may not even notice a thought about coffee, or a sensation. You might find you're already at the coffee shop without consciously deciding to go there at all. As Lisa Feldman Barrett has found from her research, the brain is a predicting machine. It predicts based on past experience. There is a lot of automatic activity going on outside our awareness.

We can see the negative effect of these automatic processes when they connect with things that we fear. An example here would be unpleasant thoughts that scare us and we try to push away. If a thought goes through your mind that you don't like, you might want that thought to go away. You might do something to try to make the thought go away, like distract yourself, carry out a ritual or tell yourself to stop thinking that thought. By doing any of these things you are teaching your brain: *if* that thought occurs, *then* I must 'do' (a particular action) to make the thought go away.

RITUALS AND BELIEFS

The thing that you 'do' in response to the thought will become part of the decision tree, especially if it is reinforced. Reinforcement is when something makes something else more or less likely to happen. If you carry out a ritual and the thought disappears, then your brain will remember this as a positive outcome, and will prompt you to do that same action the next time you notice the thought.

There are many different rituals that we might feel we have to do, for example, repeating something to ourselves, checking that plugs, taps or switches are not on, washing our hands, arranging things in a certain way. These actions become rituals when we come to believe that in order to get a particular outcome, we have to repeat them a number of times. They can become a problem when the number of times we feel we have to repeat them feels excessive but we cannot stop.

Rituals are common, and they can be effective in reducing unpleasant thoughts and sensations. A study published in 2016 by Alison Brooks and colleagues demonstrated that when participants carried out rituals personal to them prior to a performance, they reported fewer anxious feelings. One of the theories put forward for this is that the ritual helps to relieve some of the physical tension that we can feel as we are activated and ready to perform. It's our way of moderating that feeling of nervousness which we tend not to like and want to get rid of.

Our belief about the power of the ritual is part of it too, though. If we believe a particular ritual is responsible for stopping something bad from happening, for example a bad performance, we will carry out that ritual. If the performance goes well, we attribute it to the fact we carried out the ritual. It's reinforcement. The two become connected in our brain and will subsequently form part of our decision process in a similar situation in the future. It would feel 'wrong' not to carry out the ritual because of how it has become 'coupled' to that decision process. This is why we can become dependent on having to do the same ritual again the next time.

Our beliefs make a difference. If we believe a thought is 'bad' or means something 'bad' about us, or about others or the world, then we will feel anxious when we get that thought. If we believe that a ritual that we carry out is helping to stop that bad thing from happening, then we will keep doing it. The ritual will likely reduce some of our anxious feelings and thoughts, as Brooks and colleagues found in their study. This will make us more likely to carry out the ritual when we feel anxious again. It's a powerful feedback loop that can be very hard to get out of. The reduction in anxiety that we feel after performing a ritual is like a 'reward' for the brain. We have stopped a bad thing from happening, for now. The next time we have that thought, or a feeling associated with that thought, our brain will remember what worked last time and will prompt us to do the same thing again. The decision will have been streamlined. This works for other beliefs that we develop too, for example our beliefs about therapy or about our own emotions, which we explored in the previous two chapters.

SCANNING

Whenever we have labelled something as 'bad' or as something we want to avoid, it becomes 'flagged' in our threat network as something to watch out for. We are wired to be able to perceive threat swiftly, in order to take evasive action if need be. This is key to our survival. So if we sense danger, or label something as 'bad', or believe it is harmful (and this includes one of our own thoughts or feelings), then we will experience a strong drive to avoid this thing. This is why we can get an immediate urge to distract, or push away, an unpleasant thought or image.

Unfortunately, we are also designed to scan for or check for those things that we want to avoid, in order to make sure that it's not about to happen. Sounds helpful? Mmm, not really a recipe for a peaceful life, though, is it? Our brain is a predicting machine, and so it will predict based on what has happened previously. We saw in the previous chapter how people who struggle with panic attacks scan for the very sensations that they are fearful of. This is an automatic process that you may not realize you are doing. Have you noticed how much you 'scan' social media if you have a disagreement with someone? If you feel rattled by a comment someone's made on Twitter, it's a bit hard to ignore it, isn't it? You might try to, but then find you have to check back. Or have you ever scanned a spot in a room for spiders to make sure there isn't one? Or scanned a street for someone you want to avoid? The classic example is walking down a dark street and being alert to every moving shadow or sound. Every footstep behind you sounds too close and feels like a potential threat, as you scan for any signs of danger.

The purpose of scanning is to make sure we are ready to take action quickly if needed, but the vigilant state that it creates in us makes us more likely to interpret things as threatening, even if they are neutral and non-threatening (Van der Kolk, 2014). When we are in a vigilant state, we see worst-case scenarios more easily. This can make us even more anxious. The loop continues. Over time it can be hard to unpick exactly what has triggered us to feel anxious, because of these continuous loops we can get stuck in, which can lead us to feel on edge a lot of the time.

AVOIDANCE: SUPPRESSION AND DISTRACTION

One strategy that we often use with intrusive thoughts and anxiety is distraction or suppression. These are normal coping strategies that we may all have used at one time or another. For example, pushing back tears when you feel you might cry, or distracting yourself from worrying about why a friend didn't reply to your message. We have the ability to switch what we attend to, and this changes the way we respond to something. This can be helpful and adaptive at times, but it can also lead to us developing a fear response to the thing that we are trying not to do. For example, men and boys have traditionally been given a message to hide that they are upset. Maybe this started as an adaptive strategy to maintain a focus during dangerous times, during wartime for example. But the message has been reinforced so many times that it has become a social norm. We can see the fear underneath it when we look at the language that is used, for example 'be a man', 'don't cry', 'don't be a sissy' (Andrews, 2014). The message here is that something bad will happen unless you try to distract yourself from your own mind. *If* you don't suppress, *then* it is bad. This is the conditional response that our brain has learned.

This suppression, as well as being a social norm, can become a personal habit that over time leads to a fear of what will happen if we don't suppress. Will we be judged harshly by others, or by ourselves, or both? We may then come to fear any sign of emotion 'creeping' in when we don't want it to. Emotions become the enemy. But there is a price to pay when we suppress our body's natural processes. Emily Butler and her team at Stanford University asked a group of people to suppress what they thought and how they felt about a distressing TV show that they were shown. The group reported increases in blood pressure, and also feeling less positive and connected to the other members of the group. This was in contrast to the response for members of the group who were asked to respond naturally to the show. These members instead reported feeling positively connected to other group members, and felt they were sharing an experience. They showed no increase in blood-pressure measures.

We can suppress rather than express when we need to, but this takes resources and energy. Webb and colleagues in 2012 reported on a study that indicated how people can think that they are able to control an emotion, but still report high amounts of that emotion. Perhaps in trying not to have certain feelings we are setting ourselves up to notice more of those feelings. The scanning feature of our brains would be one way of making this more likely. I'd like to show you another one of the processes that can happen when we suppress and try to 'stop' a thought.

EXERCISE: THE PINK ELEPHANT

Imagine a pink elephant. It can be any shade of pink, with any background, three-dimensional or flat, tiny or as large as you want it to be. Have you got it? OK, make sure you can clearly visualize your elephant. Now tell yourself to stop looking at it, stop thinking about it. Stop thinking about the pink elephant. Stop it! If it pops up, try to get rid of the image, push it away, tell yourself to 'stop thinking about it'. Keep doing this for about a minute and raise a finger each time it pops up. Each time it does, immediately tell yourself to 'STOP THINKING ABOUT IT!'

How many times did it pop up? Just make a note of this number.

Now, let's try something else. This time call up your image of the pink elephant and try to make it stay there. Each time it goes away, bring it back up. After a minute, pause, breathe slowly in and out and then notice whatever thoughts or images pop in and out. Let them come, and let them go.

What did you notice? In the first exercise, how many times did the pink elephant pop into your mind when you were trying to make it go away? How did you feel when you were trying to stop thinking about it? Were you calm, or a bit activated? Was it easy to make the image go away, or a bit harder than you thought?

What happened for you in the second exercise when you were trying to make the thought stay there? Was this easier than trying to push a thought away? Or was it hard to make the thought stay there? At the end, when you were allowing your thoughts and images to come and go without doing anything, what was this like?

When I do this exercise with my clients, it can be a surprise just how much the image of the pink elephant keeps popping up when they try to make it go away. This is an example of 'ironic process theory' (Wegner, 1996), where trying not to think about something actually makes us more likely to think about that thing. This occurs because the brain has to keep in mind what it isn't supposed to think about in order not to think about it. This is one of the processes that can happen with worries at night-time. The more we try to switch our minds off and tell ourselves to 'stop it!', the more likely these thoughts will rebound. This can then have an impact on our sleep, as we become frustrated at not being able to stop worrying. This frustration means our bodies are in a state of higher arousal and activation. Unfortunately, this can make us more likely to have 'what if?' or anxious thoughts, and so we can get caught in another unhelpful cycle.

The ironic process theory is one of the mechanisms that causes distress when people struggle with intrusive thoughts and keep trying to push them away. This process also adds to the distress of post-traumatic stress disorder (PTSD), where we try not to think about the traumatic event. What can happen instead, though, is that through trying to push the memories away they can rebound back again. Because they are trauma memories, they can be confusing and distressing because they present themselves as 'flashbacks' rather than distant memories. These flashes of what happened can be images, smells, sounds, bodily movements or sensations. When a flashback pops up, it can feel like the event is happening right now. This is because traumatic memories often don't get encoded with time and date information like other day-to-day memories do (Siegel, 2011; Van der Kolk, 2014).

OVERCOMING AVOIDANCE

With flashbacks and intrusive thoughts, an important aspect of the therapeutic work is to provide strategies for helping the person to feel safe and grounded, whilst enabling them to gradually process and tolerate the experience of the thought or memory. The end point is to be able to let the thought, image or feeling pop in and out without having to apply the effort of suppression, which adds an extra layer of distress.

Sometimes we push emotions away because we don't feel safe to express them. Feeling angry for example can be a powerful feeling-state that we often moderate. Researchers such as Paul Gilbert, the founder of Compassion-Focused Therapy, believe that we suppress anger either to maintain our social relationships or avoid further threat (Gilbert, 2010). An example here would be not being able to express annoyance directly to our boss at work, but then going home and either withdrawing and going silent, or blowing up at our partner for something else. It can feel safer to express ourselves at home or in our cars, yet on reflection the things we explode over are often not the true source of our rage, just a safe trigger for us to discharge how we feel.

We spoke in the previous chapter about how we can learn that it isn't safe to express how we feel sometimes, so we find ways of suppressing our emotions in order to avoid further threat. This is part of what makes us social animals, able to fit in with our social group (Gilbert, 2010). We learn how to behave in order to be accepted. To be accepted is to feel safe as well as connected. It's what our social engagement (Porges, 2011) or affiliation system (Gilbert, 2010) is designed to motivate us towards.

It is interesting that we have this ability to prevent ourselves from expressing what we feel. It helps us to adapt and function during periods when it isn't helpful or safe to express a certain feeling. But this avoidance of our feelings can have a negative impact on us. It can result in us becoming distanced from and unable to identify and regulate our emotions as a result, as Mitmansgruber et al. found in their study of experiential avoidance in 2009.

I am also struck by how suppressed emotions do not seem to disappear. Where do they go? Emotion research cannot yet tell us, because there is no agreement about where emotions are located, and they may not be held in one place at all. In fact, in Lisa Feldman Barrett's recent book *How Emotions Are Made*, she points out that there is no conclusive evidence that emotions are located in any particular part of the brain.

Yet we can suppress them, and we can have them be activated, or reactivated, at a later time, so how is this possible? The way that our brains and bodies respond during trauma, and the way that traumatic memories are stored and subsequently triggered, gives us a potential insight into how this might be.

UNFINISHED PROCESSES: THE INCOMPLETE NATURE OF TRAUMATIC MEMORIES

Trauma memories are thought to be stored as fragments of information that are not integrated into our standard memory networks in the same way as other memories. For example, if you try to recall an event from the past week, say for example having dinner last night. The memory of this dinner is made up of chunks of information. *You* were in *that* place, at that *time*, with *that* person. As you recall the memory you might recall other pieces of the event as well, like where you were sitting, what you were looking at, what type of food was on your plate or how it tasted. But it wouldn't *feel* like the event was happening right now – unless something traumatic happened at that dinner, which I hope was not the case for you! If something did happen, then I'd like to invite you now to tell yourself (and your brain) that the event happened last night and is *not* happening right now.

When traumatic memories are recalled, we can feel a wave of emotion and our bodies can react as if the event is happening in the here and now. One of the theories about traumatic memories is that they are not stored with time and date information, and so are not completely integrated into our memory as something that happened 'back then'. As a result, when triggered by any reminder, we become 'activated' as if our body needs to deal with something right now. Our fight-or-flight response is set in motion, and we may act from this state even though rationally we may know that nothing is happening in the present moment.

Trauma researchers believe that our brain's associative networks store many different types of information about what happened during the event. For example, the position our body was in at a moment of impact, the time of day it was, colour or smell information, and importantly the appraisal or meaning that the event holds for us. Some researchers are looking at how the unfinished processes of our nervous system also become stored. For example, say you were startled by an aggressive bull whilst in a field, and you started to run away but your foot became trapped and you couldn't move. This unfinished potential energy of the movement that couldn't be completed could be stored in your brain's neuronal networks. If at a later date you have this network triggered, then the stored sensory-motor information could also be released. Your legs and body move in response, almost as if there is a need to discharge what was not able to be discharged at the time. This is the theory that has been put forward by Peter Levine, the founder of the trauma therapy 'Somatic Experiencing'. His view is also a central idea in the seminal book on how our bodies can and do reflect what we have experienced in life: *The Body Keeps the Score* by Bessel van der Kolk.

Our memory systems are complex associative networks where neurons connect to other neurons and the links are vast and multi-layered. It's why sometimes you can have odd reminders of past events with the slightest of triggers. In Levine's book *In an Unspoken Voice*, he discusses the fascinating story of the explorer David Livingstone, who suffered a life-threatening attack by a lion. The lion was shot, but not before it had seriously and very nearly mortally wounded Livingstone. In speaking about the incident Livingstone reported that during the attack he felt numb and somehow didn't feel pain or fear. This would have been due to the immobilization response which we can enter if we are in a life-threatening situation with no way out.

Livingstone recovered from the attack. However, every subsequent year, on the anniversary of that day, he suffered an inflammatory condition in the same shoulder that had been badly injured in the attack.

Medics would be rightly confounded at how this could happen. This type of presentation is not unusual though, and has been passed off as a psychosomatic issue, as if it isn't real somehow. We have had, and still do have to some extent, a perception that symptoms must be either psychological or physical. Modern neuroscience is able to show us that we do not need to take this limited view any more. David Livingstone's annual injury is a real event potentially being triggered by the neuronal network in his brain and body. Levine discusses how a trauma involves the whole bodily system and, as a result, the various 'memories' that can be triggered can and do involve our bodies – for example, the twitching of a muscle in the leg of someone remembering how they tried to run away from danger.

Our bodies are a significant part of our brain's associative network, and the vagal nerve has been shown to be a main vessel through which our body and brain communicate. It is no coincidence that our gut and heart are both now being found to be an intelligent part of this system, connecting as they do to the vagal nerve. They are a key part of our nervous system and have even been found to have neural (messenger) networks similar to the brain (Porges, 2011; Levine, 2010). See also the new book by heart surgeon Reinhard Friedl, who highlights some incredible stories of how our hearts are more than simple muscles (Friedl, 2021).

Taken together, all of this information that is potentially 'stored' in the associative network of our brain and body is relevant when it comes to the suppression and subsequent expression or disclosure of emotions in our daily lives. As we recall an event and start to feel an emotion about it, we are processing the felt experience, which can include various bodily sensations, and we are integrating or reintegrating the experience and the meaning of the event into our memory networks.

My point here is that our day-to-day emotional health is affected by the things that we have not yet fully processed or integrated into our memory networks. I am also saying here that these do not have to be huge traumas. They could just be the way that someone spoke to you, or an offhand comment that was made, or something that you've been putting off and not thinking much about at all.

DISSOCIATION

I need to make special mention of a process that can happen in traumatic circumstances which leads to further difficulties when trying to process a traumatic event.

The attack on David Livingstone shows us how in an extreme situation we can enter a state of shutdown, or tonic immobility. This state can make us feel somewhat numb or even separated from our body, but it also helps us to feel less pain and terror through actions such as the release of endorphins, the body's natural painkillers.

After the event, though, this can mean that the memories of the incident are blocked off from our conscious awareness and stored in a fragmentary way. Many things can trigger these fragments. A sound that is similar, or a smell, colour, shape or shadow that resembles something from the actual event. In Livingstone's case it was the date that triggered his inflammatory response. When something triggers a reminder of the event, it can cause us distress but feel like it comes out of nowhere. We can feel terror or pain for seemingly no obvious reason, and this can be a frightening experience.

Dissociation is a feeling of numbness, as if you are shut down or viewing life from behind a screen, unable to feel or connect to a feeling. This is the opposite of hypervigilance and hyperarousal, where we can feel on edge, irritable, nervous and ready to run from the starter blocks. Some people can have the experience of going from numbness to overwhelmed and not know why this is happening, whereas others may feel they are like a soldier in the midst of battle, always hypervigilant and on edge. Still other people may feel they live in a continual state of numbness, where they don't 'feel' much at all. All of these states are features of how our system has at some point needed to keep us safe from threat.

Trauma memories have a fragmented, frozen and unfinished quality to them, but when the threat has been life-threatening or the situation has kept us trapped, then these memories can be even harder to access or connect to. It is the trauma therapist's job to help a client process and integrate, within a context of safety, so that the person's brain and body learns that the danger is passed, they are safe, and the memory can be retrieved, processed, reintegrated and stored as a memory from the past.

But non-traumatic, day-to-day emotions and actions can also have this unfinished, fragmented quality to them. I often notice how a situation I thought had little to no impact on me at the time it happened can be recalled with strong feelings when I am talking to my husband or a trusted friend. Many times, I've heard myself say, 'Wow, I didn't know it had upset me that much.' There can be a need to retrieve, process and integrate the daily goings on in our lives sometimes, especially when we have periods of stressors, demands, unexpected events, or social struggles.

In this chapter we have looked at how there can be many reasons why you might be feeling upset, yet not know why. Our deep core fears and beliefs often filter the way we interpret the world, ourselves and others. Sometimes these can lead us into unhelpful patterns and cycles. We also have a default attention setting which can mean that we are operating on autopilot, not aware of what is bothering us until it becomes painfully obvious or distressing. We use suppression and distraction as normal coping strategies, sometimes repressing without awareness of doing this at the time. These strategies can become crutches, which can lead to emotions becoming the enemy. We may engage in rituals or other behaviours to stop us from experiencing certain feelings, but these can keep us trapped. If a thought or bodily sensation starts to emerge that we don't want, we may tell ourselves to 'stop it'. This sets up a loop in the brain that makes us more likely to notice that thing that we don't want to experience. This can make us more distressed and so the cycle continues.

In the next chapter we will look at a strategy for unpacking why you might be upset. But the most important thing I want to get across is that it's OK not to know why you feel the way you do. It is about so much more than the crude labels of being 'weak' or 'mad', as I hope you can see from this chapter, so let's put those to one side for a moment. There are much better ways of explaining what might be causing our upset.

CHAPTER FOUR

Why Am I Upset? Part Two

Therapy is a helpful place to be if you're having the thought 'I'm getting upset for no reason'. I believe there will be a reason, or many layers of reasons, but it can be very difficult to see these for ourselves, as we saw in Chapter Three. The explanation for why you feel the way that you do does not have to be a major trauma, nor does it mean that you're going 'crazy'. In fact, often the sensations, thoughts, feelings and behaviours all make sense when you see them in the context of how our brain and body work together to negotiate situations.

CLIENT EXAMPLE: 'I DON'T KNOW WHY IT'S UPSETTING ME SO MUCH!'

I'd like to show you one method that I use in my practice to respond to a client who does not know why they are upset:

Client (C): I don't know how to explain it, I just seem to be getting upset for no reason.

Therapist (T): When was the last time you felt like this?

C: Yesterday morning, I was on a training course and we had to drive to a meeting point, leave our cars and walk two miles into some woods where we were to spend the whole day, without a toilet or other facilities.

T: How were you feeling as you set off?

C: Apprehensive, on edge. But I wanted to get through it because I wanted to complete the course. I tried to think positive and tell myself, 'Everyone else can do this – why can't I?' I tried to keep focused on the satnav, but that just kept telling me how late I was.

T: What happened next?

C: Well, I got there fifteen mins late, feeling in a right tizz. I'd planned my route so carefully the night before, so I couldn't understand why I was so late! My heart was thumping. I saw the other group members getting into their cars. One of them quickly told me I was to go with the group leader in his car. I went to grab my bag and realized I needed the toilet, and this would be my last opportunity all day to use one. I had to go now while we were at the service station. I raced through the shop and was as quick as possible. But as I came back out, the group leader was in front of me looking very annoyed. 'Hurry up, you're holding up all the traffic!' he said loudly and then walked towards the cars. His words felt like an attack.

T: What did you notice when he said that to you?

C: I thought, 'Oh no!' felt a surge of panic, then looked at the direction he was walking in and saw a line of cars stopped on the road just after a roundabout. I felt so awful and backed away, thinking, 'I can't do this!' He was already at his car, so I had to half-yell, 'I can't do this; go without me.' He looked at me, but I waved him away. I walked as fast as I could back to my car, feeling the hotness and the tears. I can feel my heart racing now just thinking about it.

T: How did you feel when you got back to the car?

C: Upset. I was crying, head in my hands, feeling like a failure for not being able to do it after all that I'd gone through in preparing myself for this day. I'd been apprehensive for weeks leading up to it, but kept telling myself it was silly to worry about a toilet. So when it popped up I'd just put it out of my mind. I can feel the tears coming now just thinking about it. I was so disappointed in myself and was thinking, 'Why can't I communicate properly?', 'I'm useless', 'I can't do it', 'Why am I struggling with something everybody else finds so easy?', 'Why did he just walk away and leave?' Yesterday on the course, two of the other participants were an hour late, and they were treated so respectfully, not shouted at because they were holding everyone up. I had the thought: 'It's always me that has to help others if they struggle, but no one ever cares if I need help.' This makes me upset thinking this now. I feel so embarrassed. I'm not on my own any more, not like I used to be. I don't understand why I'm so upset about this.

T: Don't make any future judgements about what you can or can't do right now. There is a reason why you feel upset. Let's look at what you said there, because you mentioned several things that seem to be very good reasons. This is what I heard:

You were apprehensive before you got to the meeting point. This means that your brain and body were already prepared and in a state of vigilance. You may or may not have noticed sensations or a feeling-state of anticipation, with perhaps a heat in your body or head, a tightness in your chest and your heart pounding. These and other sensations are because your body and brain are readying for action. On the dial of arousal, you were perhaps already at the midway point, if not more. In this state you are likely to be easily triggered into irritation, or worry, or thoughts of avoidance.

You said that for weeks leading up to the event you had a thought about the toilet but dismissed it as 'silly' and 'not important', so you never really gave yourself any permission to take your concerns seriously. As a result, you didn't speak with the tutor about how you were feeling, and couldn't get his ideas on how best to manage, or make some kind of allowance for late arrival/early leaving, etc.

Despite this anxiety you kept going and aimed to get to the meeting point. This was persistence, not failure. You could have backed out, but you didn't.

Unfortunately, the events that followed served to further increase your level of anxious arousal, or nervousness. Because the group leader had no idea about your struggle, he didn't know he had to make any allowances for your lateness. You were told in a hurried fashion to leave your vehicle (your safety/means of escape) and travel in the group leader's car. You had no choice in the matter since you were late, so this had already been decided for you. You then needed the toilet, and this triggered anxious thoughts about not having access to one for the rest of the day. This was your only chance to go, so you did, except nobody else knew what you were doing. Nobody else knew how important this was for you that day. Whilst you were inside the service station toilet, you wouldn't have been aware that the other cars were lining up on the road just after a roundabout, waiting for you. When you came out of the toilet the group leader was angry and told you to hurry up because you were holding up the traffic. You were then faced with his anger and blame for holding up the other cars, and you perceived this as an attack. Your body then went into flight mode, and you backed away and told him to go without you. He didn't question this.

You escaped to your car for safety, but quickly felt upset at what had happened and how it felt like an utter failure after all the effort and the preparation that you had gone through to try to get to this event. Your brain's associative network went into overdrive with thoughts such as 'I can't do it, I'm a failure'. The network then retrieved other memories and residues from other times when you believe you had failed. Our memory network is set up in such a way that if we are in a certain state of emotional arousal, and in a certain place, we are more likely to recall memories of things that previously happened when we were either in that emotional state and/or in that particular context. It's called context dependency. What you learn in one state will be easier to recall when you are in that same state. So you then had more memories retrieved of previous failures and these confirmed your judgement of yourself as a 'useless failure'. This then made you feel even worse.

As well as labelling yourself as useless, you also interpreted the group leader's actions as a sign that he didn't care whether you were there or not. You thought about his actions with participants on the previous day and how he had seemed more understanding towards those people than he had with you. This led to having thoughts about no one caring if you struggle, which triggered off residues of times when you have struggled and been alone. This made the experience even more upsetting for you because these two negative core beliefs – 'I'm useless' and 'I'm alone and no one cares' – would have been activated on top of everything else that you felt in that moment.

What do you think when you hear me say all of this? Does it sound understandable why you might have been upset?

C: Yes, I see what you mean. It was a struggle, but I did my best, I guess. I didn't succeed in doing what I wanted to do, though, and I worry about whether I can ever do it again.

T: Indeed, because this was a difficult situation, your automatic response is to not want to experience this again. However, look at how much you did manage to tolerate. It was a big challenge to go as far as you did, but you attempted it and, more than that, you got quite far, considering how uncomfortable you were. You could decide never to try again, but that is not your only option. If you make small repeated attempts to 'push' yourself just enough, but not too far outside your tolerance levels, with a newer attitude of 'maybe I can do it', you will find that you will train yourself not to fear these situations in future and will build up your sense of 'I can', rather than reinforce 'I can't'.

If you are going to do this, though, it is important to choose challenges that have meaning for you: things that move you towards what you value, not those that you feel you should do.

This was a difficult situation that was bound to make you feel like you were outside your comfort zone. But it doesn't necessarily have to mean that you can't do things like this in future. It also doesn't have to mean that when you are upset there is no one there. If it happens again, you could call someone close to you for support, or perhaps you could have a word with the tutor in advance to let them know that this is a personal challenge for you, and you would be grateful for some support or extra time. Maybe even let them know how they could support you if you find it a struggle. You mentioned how you hadn't taken your concerns seriously in the lead-up to the event and had downplayed its importance, which meant that you didn't seek support and the tutor was unaware of your struggle. If you had made him aware, it's likely there could have been some considerations made for you, and you would not have felt left alone in your struggles.

WHAT IS THE STORY THAT YOUR BRAIN IS DEFAULTING TO?

Our brains can easily make up a story to fill in the blanks when our deeper emotions have been triggered. For example, 'It's his fault for not communicating properly to me; he shouldn't have treated me that way.' Look at the story that you tell yourself. It might just be your brain's way of trying to understand why you felt threatened and triggered. It may only be a fraction of the picture that you can see and not the whole truth. Pause, breathe and be curious about what you think is happening. Pay attention to your body and notice what it's doing. If you have been triggered, take a moment to help your body's arousal level calm down, and remind yourself that you are safe – if you can and if you are safe.

The above example demonstrates that, although it can feel like we cannot see the woods for the trees when it comes to why we're upset, there can be very good reasons why; we just need a way to unpack and understand them.

FORMULATING OUR STORIES

One of the ways that I do this in my practice is with something called a formulation. I've plotted the client example that we just looked at into one of these formulation diagrams in order to show you how we can unpack the different elements of what happens. You don't have to get everything in there, just start with what you know and build it from there:

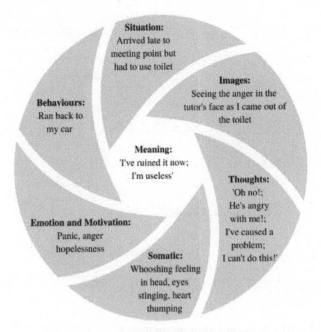

Fig. 4 – Client formulation example

By unpacking a situation into these different elements, you can start to see the links between what happens and the stories or interpretations that you might automatically jump to. This can then help you to target these areas in therapy in order to change what happens for you in future.

If you'd like to have a go at doing one of these for yourself, bring up the last time that something bothered or upset you. It doesn't have to be something huge.

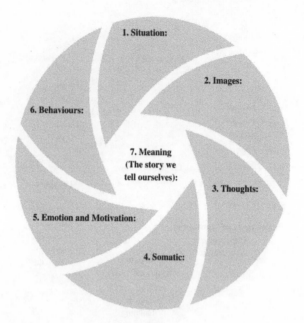

Fig. 5 – Blank formulation template

In the circle under No. 1 (Situation/Context), enter where you were or what was happening. Add anything that helps to set the context. As you think about this event or experience, notice if you are seeing an image of what happened. In No. 2 (Images, memories), put a word or phrase that sums up this image.

Notice what is happening in your body right now. Even if it is slight, can you detect anything? Maybe a gripping feeling in your gut, or a heat in your face, or the slightest of pains in your head. Bring the image back up into your awareness and notice any shifts or changes in your body. Put whatever you notice, even if it doesn't make sense, into No. 4 (Somatic). What label would you use to describe how you feel about this event? Put this into No. 5 (Emotions). As you notice this feeling and the things that bothered you about this situation, what thoughts go through your mind? What is the main thing that upset you about this situation? Put these into No. 3 (Thoughts). What did you do? For example, 'I went home', 'I said nothing but kept thinking about it'. Put what you did into No. 6 (Behaviours).

As you look at this, what do you think is the main story that you were telling yourself about this event? For example, 'I always mess things up', 'I can't trust anyone' or 'I can't cope'. Don't worry about not having the right words: just put whatever snippets come to mind.

Have a look at your circle, notice all the different elements that make up your experience in that situation. There are others that we could add here – for example, consequences of what you did, features of the space you were in at the time, past experiences with key people in your life. But we have to start somewhere, and this is a good place to start. As you look at this circle, notice all the different elements that you have unpacked, and the way that one relates to the other. For example, a certain thought makes you feel a certain way. Or when you feel a certain feeling, you tend to 'do' (a behaviour) a certain thing. Notice the way that the situation led to you seeing it in a particular way.

What you can do is complete one of these circles each time you feel upset or bothered by something. You will then have a collection and can look for patterns. Are there some meanings or stories that seem to pop up frequently? Do you notice that certain emotions always give you a particular sensation in your body? What tend to be the go-to things that you do when you feel upset?

For example, you could discover that certain situations always have a tendency to make you worry you are not good enough, or when certain feelings come up for you and you feel criticized, you always tend to ruminate and find it hard to shake the feeling. A therapist could help you take this further to see what significant people or events in your life have influenced these core ways of viewing yourself, others and the world, and help you to shift and change your stories and interpretations.

Sometimes what helped us at one point in our life can come to be something that hinders us in the present. An example would be a person who learned to be quiet and not speak up because, earlier in their life, they were taught to be seen and not heard. They were given the message that their opinion didn't matter. They learned that if they did speak up, they would be punished, so they suppressed their reactions and never learned how to be assertive. Anytime they felt the tingly, fluttery sensations in their gut or chest in response to being asked a question in a group setting, they would see this as a sign that something bad could happen if they spoke up, and so they keep silent and try other ways to manage the feelings of activation in their bodies. Or maybe they don't notice these sensations at all but instead have thoughts about how they can't speak or how others don't want to hear them, or worse.

Keeping silent served them as children and stopped them from being punished. However, in adulthood, this way of coping can become unhelpful, because it stops them from being able to set boundaries, assert themselves and ask for what they need. It also stops them from being able to contribute when in group situations and this prevents them from feeling accepted by others for what they believe.

Here's another example formulation circle:

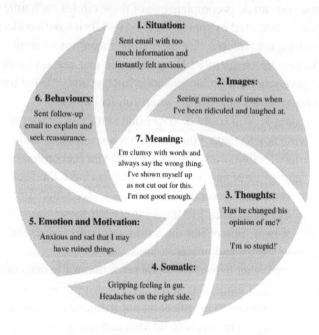

1. Situation:
Sent email with too much information and instantly felt anxious.

2. Images:
Seeing memories of times when I've been ridiculed and laughed at.

6. Behaviours:
Sent follow-up email to explain and seek reassurance.

7. Meaning:
I'm clumsy with words and always say the wrong thing. I've shown myself up as not cut out for this. I'm not good enough.

3. Thoughts:
'Has he changed his opinion of me?'

'I'm so stupid!'

5. Emotion and Motivation:
Anxious and sad that I may have ruined things.

4. Somatic:
Gripping feeling in gut. Headaches on the right side.

Fig. 6 – Client formulation example 2

In this example, I've noted down a time when I felt worried about saying the wrong thing (1. Situation) and felt anxious about what the other person's response was going to be (5. Emotion). As I waited for their reply and nothing came, my anxiety increased, and I noticed a tension headache (4. Somatic). I felt certain that I'd messed things up for myself (3. Thoughts). I kept ruminating, running over what I'd said in my mind and tried to figure out what to do. I sent a follow-up email to try to soften what I'd said and seek a reply that would reassure me that things were OK (6. Behaviour).

The story that my brain constructed for this event based on what it knows from my prior experience is a variation of impostor syndrome. The fear of being found out as not up to the job, not good enough. We filter the present through the lens of our past experiences. If we have secret fears – of not being as perfect as we wish to be, or of being judged by others – then these will be the things our brain looks out for.

Our brains are predicting machines, and they predict based on the evidence they are presented with. Often this can lead us to make swift judgements of right or wrong, good or bad, failure or success. It's partly an efficiency strategy to make a quick decision, but it isn't always correct. Like our threat system, which is geared up to assess threat quickly. Sometimes it sees a spider or a snake where there isn't one. This is normal, but if we don't stop to re-evaluate and process the conclusions we automatically jump to, then we can find ourselves stuck with judgements that keep us limited. When we process and re-evaluate our stories, we discharge the negative emotions held within these stories. In the next chapter I'd like to show you some methods for doing this.

With just about everything that we think, feel and do there is activity in the brain. When we alter what we do, we create change. This constant adaptation and change process is called *neuroplasticity* – the science of how certain processes in our brains can be altered and new connections made.

When it comes to our emotions, thoughts and behaviours, the first step towards change is to notice what is actually happening.

What is it you are struggling with? Therapy can help you unpack and figure out what this is. Maybe a certain situation tends to trigger a particular feeling for you? Perhaps there are unpleasant thoughts that you can't get rid of? Is there a habit that you just can't stop? Make a note of what you observe the next time it happens. Use a formulation circle if you like. The act of noticing and labelling is very powerful, because it alters and expands our band of awareness. This is one of the first steps in making a change.

We cannot alter the fact that our brain makes predictions, but we can start to change why it predicts things in that way, and we can decide how we interpret the effects of that prediction.

WHAT WOULD YOU LIKE TO RE-EVALUATE?

Therapy can help us to notice and re-evaluate patterns that no longer serve us. It can be hard to do this for ourselves though, and it takes time, because we are incredibly complex machines. Our brains are constantly relating one thing to another, creating meaning and making predictions. We can see this busyness in action when we try to meditate or do a mindfulness exercise. There can be so much happening that we often don't know where to start.

An emotion isn't just a thought, or a word such as 'angry'. It's an image, a firing of several thoughts, sometimes a smell or sound, and a set of physiological actions in your brain and body. It's a motivation to 'do' something, an impulse, a desire. It can be triggered by things within and without; a memory, a sound, a thought or our body's own physical sensations. What should we start to notice first?

Science is beginning to show us that there is an ongoing interplay between our brain and body in relation to our emotions, and by starting to notice the felt sense of what is happening in our bodies we can tune directly into an emotion.

Check in with your body throughout the day. If something happens at work or at home – for example, you get a message on your phone that irritates you or makes you feel criticized – notice where you feel this in your body. Is your gut twisting or clenching? Do you have a pain in your head? Notice whatever it is and see what happens as you bring this into your awareness. Your thinking brain will be predicting what to do next. Notice that, then bring your attention back to your body and notice what is happening. Then switch your attention to your environment. Notice the things that tell you that you are safe and supported right now. You can deal with this threat in your own time; there is no immediate danger. Now go back to your body and listen to what it wants to do next. Shake out any tension, go for a brief walk. Now that you know you are safe, your brain can predict what to do next.

If you are feeling criticized or rejected, or in the midst of a disagreement on social media, Brené Brown's advice from the book *Dare to Lead* (2019) can be helpful. Know that you have support from the inner circle of people whose opinion matters to you. Those on the outer rings of the circle can disagree or criticize. Notice the feeling you get when you think about the people who matter to you. Where in your body do you feel this? Notice it. Bring your awareness to it. You are strengthening the sense of connectedness by giving this feeling your attention.

CHAPTER FIVE

Will Talking about My Feelings Make Them Worse? And if So, What Can I Do to Make It Easier?

Imagine a dog on a beach barking at the waves as they splash towards him. The dog jumps and spins around on the damp sand, as if driven mad by the whoosh and hiss of the waves. He darts towards them, then back again, to a safe distance, and barks with the whole of his body to warn them off. But the waves don't stop, and the more the dog tries to fight them, the bigger the swell of anger grows inside him.

If he could stand back and watch the waves, he would see that they come, but they also get smaller and slip away. If he could let the water touch him, he would see that he could tolerate it eventually. He might need to practise standing quite far back at first, to get used to the feeling of the water on his fur. But this would be less of a struggle than trying to make the waves go away.

One of my clients gave me this wonderful image of a dog on a beach barking at the waves. It mirrors for me the struggle we can have with emotions when we try to push them away. But if we stop struggling and stop trying to run away from them, we can feel so much better. Russ Harris, a doctor and therapist who has become a popular speaker in the Acceptance and Commitment therapy movement, calls it turning off the 'Struggle Switch' (Harris, 2008).

I often hear new clients say that they are worried they will feel worse if they talk about their feelings. This belief that emotions are made worse by talking about them keeps people silent. When we are silent, we cannot process our experiences. If we do not process our felt experiences, then we cannot truly learn enough about our own emotions in order to manage them. You wouldn't manage a sports team by having no idea of the individual skills and abilities in your players. You'd have no control over how a game would play out if this was the case, and it would feel unpredictable and uncertain. It's the same with our emotions. By suppressing them and pushing them away, we never get to learn enough about our own processes in order to manage them better. Because we don't know enough about them, we find them unpredictable and we feel out of control if they become triggered. We don't want to lose control, so we push them away. This avoidance keeps us fearing them, and the cycle continues.

EMOTIONAL SUPPRESSION

As humans we have a natural ability to be able to suppress, repress or express. Sometimes we knowingly suppress, sometimes we unknowingly repress. An example of repression is not knowing that something has bothered you until you later talk about it and feel upset, perhaps saying something like 'I had no idea that bothered me so much'. This is normal, but do we balance out our natural tendencies to suppress, with setting aside time to process? In day-to-day life I don't believe we do, because we desperately do not want to get upset. But this emotional suppression has a cost. It can make us feel even less in control of our emotions, and it also has an impact on our physical health.

A study by Gross and Levenson, published in 1997 in the *Journal of Abnormal Psychology*, found that when participants were asked to suppress either a positive (amusement) or negative (sadness) emotion, the act of suppressing the emotion produced increased activation in the 'sympathetic nervous system' (SNS). The SNS is the part of our nervous system that sets off the 'fight or flight' response and gets us ready for action. Along with the release of stress hormones, it increases our heart rate, blood pressure and breathing in order to tackle the task at hand. If this type of activity is prolonged it takes us into a state of chronic stress. So if we suppress either positive or negative emotions this has an effect on our body similar to that that occurs when we are dealing with something stressful.

Somehow, we have been given the message that it's wrong, weak or crazy to notice and express our sensations and our feeling-states. But the research is clear that suppression as a strategy for managing our emotional health is not helpful. Peter Levine, in his book *In an Unspoken Voice*, discusses a study in which emotional suppression was correlated with higher rates of heart disease in men. James Pennebaker and Joshua Smyth's research into expressive writing and emotional disclosure found a link between poor immune system functioning and emotional suppression (Pennebaker & Smyth, 2019). There have also been many other studies that have documented the effects of suppressing emotions. See for example the study by Webb and colleagues in the References section.

All of this tells us that if we stop trying to avoid our feelings, we might feel better. But how do we actually do this?

THE ALTERNATIVE TO SUPPRESSION: PROCESSING EMOTIONS

Expanding our awareness of what an emotion is

Mindfulness practices show us that we have the ability to expand what our brains are able to be aware of. We can consciously decide where to focus our attention. We can bring ourselves back to the 'now' and away from thoughts about the past or the future. But we can also 'expand' what we are aware of. Daniel Siegel, the author of *The Neurobiology of 'We'* (2011), writes about a 'Wheel of Awareness': a hub-and spoke model with our awareness at the centre, which can be directed towards the different spokes of the wheel. The spokes are organized into sections: the five senses (touch, sight, sound, taste, smell); interoception and the interior of the body; mental activities (thoughts, images, memories); and our sense of interconnectedness with others. Siegel talks about how we can learn to expand the current boundaries of our awareness, and how we can change the flow of information in our brain, and our wiring, by our use of mindful awareness practice.

The practice of expanding what we are aware of is important when it comes to emotions. One of the spokes in Siegel's model refers to 'interoception'. Interoception is the sense of what is happening inside our body. It's the sensation of fast breathing as you run up the stairs; it's the lurching feeling in your stomach when you're on a rollercoaster. It's the fluttery feelings you get when you are talking on the phone to a particular person. It's all of these and many, many more sensations. It is this interoceptive awareness that I believe plays a key role in our feeling-states. So where do we start with it?

Notice

This is the first step. It might sound obvious, but it is central to being able to gain mastery over what is happening for you. There is a part of the brain that is involved in 'noticing' and in becoming aware of what you experience. You can enhance it, and some scientists would say that you can increase the size of this area through long-term mindfulness practice.

Curiosity

The next thing I'm going to ask you to do is to set an intention to be curious about the sensations in your body that you notice. Maybe you are used to immediately doing something to distract yourself from the fluttery feeling of anxiety, or that quick whoosh of adrenalin. Whatever it is that you notice, how about seeing where the sensation goes if you let it be? Yes, you can distract yourself if you want to, but that isn't your only option. Could you allow yourself to be like a scientist and be curious about what you notice? Could you try to embrace the uncertainty rather than push it away? The sensations in your body are not going to harm you. You do not need to fear them. If you let them be, they will come and they will go. Like waves on a beach.

When or if you feel angry or anxious, you might also notice lots of thoughts or maybe images flashing up, wanting attention. Your brain will be trying to figure out what's going on and what to do. That's OK. Notice what is happening in your body. You do not have to answer the thoughts right now, let them be there. They will come, and they will go.

Observe without judgement

Try it now. Check in with your body. What posture are you holding? What position is your spine in? Is it slumped, or twisting to the side? Imagine straightening it a little bit, and actually let your spine move to where it wants to. Then notice your stomach: are you holding it in? Let it go, let it flop out. Adjust yourself if you notice any twists or tenseness anywhere else. Take a big breath in and let it flop out like a big sigh. Now, do a scan to see what sensations you notice. Is there a tingly feeling, or any niggles or pains anywhere? Just notice them and see what happens as you observe them, with curiosity and without judgement.

Take a breath in and slowly breathe out, trying to make that out-breath last for a count of six. Do this again, then once more, and now take a big breath in and let it flop out like a big sigh.

FINE-TUNING OUR EMOTIONAL AWARENESS: EMOTION-FOCUSED INTEROCEPTIVE AWARENESS

We have just practised noticing what was happening in our bodies and aimed to observe without judgement. Now I'd like to ask you to notice your bodily sensations the next time you notice an emotion. I'm going to call this *emotion-focused interoceptive awareness*, because it involves noticing this felt sense as part of your emotional state. Whether you are feeling angry, frustrated, worried, tired, sad or disgusted, try to turn your attention to what your body is actually doing, inside and out. It can be hard. I know, because I've trained myself to do this and it took me a while. Either I didn't notice anything or I was taken over by an emotion and forgot what to do. It takes practice to develop a new pattern, but we can do this. Our brains can create new neural connections if we practise enough. As we saw in Chapter Four, this is called *neuroplasticity*.

It's much easier to do this if we can overcome our fear of getting upset though. That's the first step. Have you ever felt tears coming and then swallowed hard to push them away? Or have you ever cried and then said 'I'm sorry', or tried to hide your tears? Why do we apologize for this activity in our bodies? What are we afraid will happen if we don't push the feeling away? Really. What do we think is going to happen? It's like we have to feel safe to get upset, and maybe we have learned that it isn't safe to get upset. Our past relationships and attachment patterns teach us what to do if we are upset. If we have never felt safe around those close to us, then we will have learned to be vigilant for what might happen. We may never have felt that it was OK to cry. This is where therapy can be very helpful: in providing a protected therapeutic relationship where people can feel safe enough to let their bodies express upset. To allow their nervous systems to *stand down* from the watchtower and discharge its weaponry for a brief moment. And afterwards to feel that rare feeling, of *relief*.

But we can teach ourselves to know when we are feeling safe enough to let our systems express upset. The thoughts that go through your mind will tell you a lot, but your body will give you so much information if you listen to it. Notice the way that you feel calm, warm and content in certain situations and with specific people. This sense of not only being *safe* but feeling *connected* in a secure way to another person is vital for our health. Notice the people and situations where you feel this way. Take note of the situations where you do not feel safe, where you might experience a churned-up feeling in your stomach or a fluttery feeling in your heart. Observe what happens in your body as you go about your day and notice the slight changes as you speak to certain people on the phone or over Zoom. Notice the way that you feel more activated when there is a knock at your door, or when your phone interrupts you. That feeling is your nervous system getting you ready for action. Notice this, and notice how it calms down again afterwards, or not. If it doesn't calm down, then your system still thinks you need to be activated. Notice this, not with worry or frustration, just curiosity. Then if you don't think there is anything that needs your attention right now, tell yourself this and do some slow breathing to help your nervous system know that it can stand down.

Emotion-focused interoceptive awareness is a blend of mindful body awareness, focusing-oriented therapy, polyvagal theory and somatic psychology. It is informed by current findings in neuroscience, particularly the work of Sarah Garfinkel and Lisa Feldman Barrett and the occupational therapist Kelly Mahler. It is about homing in on what is happening in our body in relation to how we feel emotionally and how activated our nervous systems are. My view is that increasing our interoceptive awareness is an important part of processing and regulating our emotional state.

Here's an example. Imagine you have been rushing through the day, from one thing to another, feeling irritable and not happy, but no time to work out why. Then you get home and try to sit down and relax, but your mind won't stop whizzing as thoughts and worries pass through. A friend calls and wants to ask your advice about a difficult issue, then your child spills their dinner on the floor. The cumulative stress from the day takes you out of your window of tolerance, and so you shout. It's not your fault. Take a look at what was happening in your body throughout the day. See it in terms of a dial, with each rush onto the next thing taking you a notch further. With each stressed or negative thought, the activation in your body increases. You didn't stop to notice or level off this activation, you inadvertently kept it going until you maxed out. You were not *aware* of what was happening. Then the final straw came, and you exploded. Because you were not aware, you didn't see the shift into the expression of anger until it happened. Your thoughts and beliefs about the situation will also have been interacting with the activation in your body. For example, 'This shouldn't have happened'; 'She shouldn't need to…'; 'Why does everything always go wrong?'

You can change the anger by amending those thoughts, but if you also get to know what is happening in your physical body, you will get a fuller picture of your *feeling-state*.

Let's say you wanted to try this emotion-focused interoceptive awareness technique. How would it change things? Well, you'd still have a busy day, doing everything you needed to do. But imagine you have me in your head asking you to pause at moments throughout the day, not for long, just thirty to sixty seconds. Maybe when you are brushing your teeth, or getting into your car, or before coming out of the toilet. Or before you set off in your car to come home. Do a body scan. Check all of the sensations that you notice right now. The thumping in your head, the churning in your stomach, the clenching of your toes or something else. Notice it. Bring to your awareness the tension, stress, irritability, niggles or feeling of being on edge. Whatever it is, notice this activation in your body, without judgement. Label it. Own it. Take a few slow breaths in and out. That's all. Pause, notice, label, breathe. Whatever you notice I want you to know that you do not have to push it away.

Although this might seem like you aren't doing very much, actually you really are. You are stopping to check in with your body and notice what is happening. This 'checking-in' expands what you are paying attention to. You get to be involved in the dialogue between body and brain over whether you need to pause or keep the pace going. You get a chance to rearrange your posture, to breathe and to label what is happening for you. Labelling helps us to regulate our emotions. Try putting words to what you notice in your body right now and try not to judge what you notice. It's tricky, but the more you practise it the easier it will get.

The next time you feel stressed, irritable, worried or sad, aim to notice what is happening in your body. Whatever you notice, aim to see it as 'information' rather than being upset by it or trying to avoid it.

DISCHARGING AND PROCESSING EMOTIONS

We all suppress our feelings sometimes and this is a socially accept-able thing to do in certain situations. However, we also need to learn when we need to tackle this suppression and process what has been buried or repressed. There are many strategies that we can use for this such as talking to a therapist, expressive writing, crafting, playing sport or talking to friends. I believe it is important to find ways to regularly and effectively discharge and process emotions in order to clear or recharge ourselves. This concept is not new, and the current 'It's OK to talk' campaigns are aimed at directly tackling the unhelpful 'bottling it up' culture that has dominated as a social norm in many cultures. Once we have become more aware of what we are feeling, by pausing to notice what is happening in our body, we can start to find the best method for us.

Talking therapy

Talking to a therapist is one approach you can take, and there are many positive things about processing emotions in this way. The safe, validating and attuned therapeutic relationship makes it easier to learn how to gradually tolerate the more difficult emotions. The therapeutic relationship in therapy is a key factor in what has been found to be helpful about counselling and psychotherapy. Being accepted, validated and heard by another person is healing in itself.

Expressive writing

But there are other methods you can use aside from talking. Putting our feelings into words can be therapeutic when those words are written, not only when they are spoken. One of my long-term coping strategies is expressive writing. I use a blend of James Pennebaker's Expressive Writing technique (Pennebaker & Smyth, 2019) and Julia Cameron's 'Morning Pages' (Cameron, 1994). I do my 'pages' at night, before bed. I know that Julia states morning is better, but I have no spare time in the morning. Plus, I like how nightly pages are a more helpful alternative to scrolling on my phone before bed, which only tends to activate rather than relax my mind. This is especially true if I accidentally come across an unpleasant news story or image. On that note, why do people like to post pictures of the massive spiders they've discovered?!

Nightly pages help me to work through issues before I go to sleep, so they're not playing on my mind through the night instead. When I first started doing the pages at night, I did worry that they would trigger me and stop me from sleeping, but that hasn't happened. They clear my mind. I aim to write three A4 pages, longhand. I start with whatever comes to mind, even if that is 'I don't know what to write!' I'll just write that and then maybe a 'blah blah blah...', and I keep doing this until something comes, and something always comes. Usually about halfway through is when I notice myself seeing patterns, or seeing that something bothered me more than I thought it did, or seeing myself writing about something I didn't know was even connected.

I find the process fascinating because something seems to happen at the halfway point where I find I am writing from a deeper level. Often, I need to write through a lot of surface 'stuff' first, and this can feel like a chore some nights. But I am always glad I pushed through and did the pages. They are my brain dump, my way of processing, my way of seeing what I couldn't see at the time, and my way of discharging and clearing.

I do notice a difference if I've gone for a time without doing these pages. It feels like I have a lot to process in my head. I feel backed-up, busy, unfocused. Like that feeling you get when you've been at a conference for too long and just crave a dark, silent room to unwind and sort through the mass of information in your head. Or is that just me?

I don't always know how I feel about some things until I get them out onto the page. There have been many times that I've doubted this technique over the years because it seems hard to fathom how it could possibly work. But then I do it and immediately know and resolve to keep doing it. It's an important part of my emotional health. That being said, even I can't do them every night. But I do them often enough to know they help me.

Exercise: Tonight, instead of scrolling through your phone before settling down to sleep, take a notepad and write out whatever comes to mind. Keep writing until you've covered at least one side of paper. The aim is to write three sides of A4 just noting whatever comes to mind. But you can just write one page to start off with. Notice what sensations you detect in your body – however slight they are. If you find your mind is blank, just write that your mind is blank until something comes to mind. Whatever comes up, write that and follow it. When you've finished lie down and go to sleep without looking at your phone. Make a note of how your sleep was and how many hours sleep you got. Do this for five nights. Notice what happens with your sleep and how you feel emotionally.

James Pennebaker, the originator of the *expressive writing for health* movement, suggests that we can use this technique in a focused way to specifically write about things that have troubled or distressed us. His research has found that this *emotional disclosure* shows strong benefits not only emotionally, but also with people's physical health and immune system functioning. James's co-researcher, Joshua Smyth, used an adapted version of the nightly pages to help with his insomnia. Smyth took a Dictaphone and recorded into that prior to sleeping, as a way to offload thoughts and feelings and clear his mind and body.

Informal processing strategies

It's possible that you may be doing your own form of clearing or processing without being aware of it. Some of the ways that we naturally do this are by talking to friends, going to a football match, going to a club, watching movies, singing, crafting, creating or journaling (a form of expressive writing). These activities are potentially vital to our mental health because they may counteract the effects of emotional suppression. However, when life gets busy or stressful, these are the things that can often get pushed down the list of priorities, and we then do not have an outlet to help us process stress. It is at times like these that we desperately need a healthy way to manage what is happening for us inside.

Cognitive reappraisal

Another strategy that has been found to be helpful is 'cognitive reappraisal'. This might sound like a purely thought-based exercise, but it actually starts with mindful awareness and noticing what our bodies are doing and what our brains 'think' is happening. The next step in the process is to re-evaluate what we think is happening and remind ourselves that a catastrophe isn't occurring, we aren't in imminent danger, and it is safe for our arousal system to calm down.

Here's an example of the difference between suppressing and reappraising an emotion:

You're out and about, and you see a friend across the street walking quickly. They seem to look at you and, just as you raise your hand to wave, they look away and keep walking, not acknowledging you at all. You think, 'Why doesn't he want to speak to me? He doesn't like me,' and then feel upset, dejected, embarrassed. Then you either blame yourself or the other person – 'I didn't want to speak to him anyway, what a jerk', or 'It's just like at school: I'm always ignored' – and this might make you feel even worse, but you might push away this feeling and try to distract from it or discount it or battle with it. This would then mean you are battling with something and would likely lead either to more annoyance or withdrawal and ruminating.

Reappraisal would involve noticing the thoughts and feelings, such as a dropping sensation in your gut and the thoughts 'he's ignoring me; it's just like at school when I felt alone'. Then looking for other ways to interpret the situation. For example, rather than rushing to the most extreme interpretation, considering instead that the person maybe didn't see you, perhaps they were in a hurry or preoccupied. Maybe they were feeling embarrassed or having a bad day and didn't want to be recognized.

When you look at all of the possible reasons – whilst also taking on board your feeling-state and the fact that there is no immediate danger to deal with – you will feel your bodily arousal calm itself and be free to choose whatever answer serves you best.

A study by Megías-Robles and colleagues in 2019 found that people who used reappraisal strategies scored higher for emotional intelligence than those who used only emotional suppression as a strategy.

For reappraisal to work, it needs to include more than just changing our thoughts. The process has to include our felt senses too. This is the part that many of us can be shut off from, and as a result it can be difficult to be faced with them in therapy. In cognitive-behavioural therapy, if the focus is only on changing thoughts, then clients can often report a sense of 'It makes sense rationally, but I just don't feel it'. This is the mismatch between logic and emotion when we try to change how we feel by only looking at what our thoughts are doing. A good CBT therapist should always look at the interplay between thoughts, feelings and behaviour. 'Feelings' here encapsulates the physical 'felt sense' as well as the emotional label such as anxiety or anger that the person might be feeling.

How therapists process emotions

As a therapist, I have to hold my own emotions during a session rather than express them. I have to create a space for my client that is untainted by my personal thoughts and feelings. This doesn't mean I have to behave as if I don't feel anything and be some kind of robot. It means I need to moderate my own feeling-states and be aware of the impact, if any, on my client. A client could be talking about an event that triggers memories for me, and I will notice my thoughts and the sensations and movements of my body, but I must not let these colour the client's story or our relationship. I have to be able to manage this 'parallel process' that is taking place for me. I have to expand what I am aware of in that moment and keep a mindful overview of these processes throughout the session.

Every therapist, from trainee to senior, has to have something called 'clinical supervision', which is usually a monthly appointment with a senior therapist who has completed training to practise as a clinical supervisor. It is where our clinical work as therapists is discussed. It is an essential requirement in order to be an accredited therapist and aims to ensure that therapists are practising safely and within their capabilities. If we are CBT therapists accredited by the British Association of Behavioural Cognitive Psychotherapists (BABCP) for example, then we have to have our clinical supervision with a BABCP-accredited CBT therapist/supervisor who can appropriately oversee our CBT practice to ensure we are not offering therapy to clients that is outside the remit of CBT – not practising a therapy that we are not qualified for, in other words.

But another important feature of clinical supervision is to acknowledge the parallel processes that are taking place within us as we help our clients. As well as being triggered about issues that connect with us, we will also have thoughts and feelings about our clients and the difficulties they bring to the session. These are important to be aware of in case they inadvertently affect the therapeutic relationship that we form with a particular client.

I recall two of my previous clients, a period of four years between them, who each presented with a trauma that seemed to mirror a traumatic experience that I had also been through. In a way this was an easier parallel process for me to identify, because as soon as they mentioned the topic of what had happened, I knew I had to be extra mindful of my own process. I recall having a flash of my own memory and then the thought 'OK, I need to watch myself carefully in this session'. I remember the way my awareness seemed to expand in that moment to take in all the many pieces of information. I noticed slight shifts in my posture and the way my head was tilted. I spotted my own memories popping up in response to my client's desperate attempt to not see her images. I noticed the stillness of the room we were both in and how shielded we were from the chaos of our memories. I wanted to let her know that she was safe now, in this moment, with me. That nothing was happening right now, and that her threat system could stand down a little. I felt like a watchtower, noticing and labelling everything that came to my attention. This 'labelling' was very important. It enabled me to sort through and categorize what was mine, what was ours, what was hers and what I needed to do next.

I recall feeling very tired after these sessions, but I also knew that the heightened awareness had helped me to manage this parallel process in a careful way, respecting both me and my client. Without this I could easily have been operating blindly from the filter of my own experience.

The training that we have as therapists enables us to use our awareness to be mindful of what is happening for our clients, and what is happening between us and our clients, and also what is happening inside us while we are working with our clients. We train ourselves to notice where there might be blind spots. Yet even we can find that we still have emotions to process from our personal lives and need to have strategies for these feelings.

In this chapter we have looked at how the fear of getting upset creates extra layers of anxiety and frustration, because it makes us struggle against our own emotions. This fear has traditionally led us to believe that we need to work harder at suppressing our emotions. But we don't need to do this, and in fact studies are showing us that this is not healthy. What we could do instead is accept that it is normal to suppress, but that this activity needs to be balanced out with a processing or discharging activity, for example talking to a therapist, or expressive writing.

One way that we can learn to do this is by seeing emotions as real physical events. They are real sensations in our body. They are the result of activation in our nervous system. This is all activity that we can notice, and when we start to develop our interoceptive awareness we can see the subtleties of our own feeling-states. We also get to see what our body and brain are predicting is going to happen, and we get a say in how this plays out.

CHAPTER SIX

When Should I See a Therapist?

Another comment I have heard from clients is over whether they are feeling upset enough to be seeking therapy. I have often heard remarks from clients such as: 'I feel like I'm making a big deal out of nothing and wasting your time' and 'You must have others to see who are much worse than me'. Such comments are usually spoken by a person who is clearly upset and has every reason to be. These reasons are not always apparent to them initially, as with the client in Chapter Four who stated they were getting upset 'for no reason'. But together we unpacked what was happening for them and discovered that their brain and body were actually dealing with quite a lot behind the scenes. When we can see things at this level, there is always a reason for what is happening.

There should be no shame in not knowing what is wrong and seeking help to unpack it. But speaking to a therapist isn't as easy as consulting the relevant expert, such as a plumber or a surveyor, in order to fix a problem in our home. We have been taught to fear expressing upset, and this gets in the way of us being able to seek help. There is this pervasive idea that we should somehow know everything about how our brains and bodies work, even though we're not supposed to pay attention to our upset. And if we get stuck, we can't show that we are struggling. Imagine calling out a plumber, but when he gets there you hide the water leak and tell him there's nothing wrong and that he should go and find a bigger emergency somewhere else!

In our school systems and throughout our life we are not given an instruction manual for how to operate and manage the powerful machines that we carry around within us. We have been taught to be afraid of our emotions and not 'look in the cupboard'. We have been given the message that 'feeling' is in some way unimportant or weak. This has shut us off from the science of ourselves. Our mainstream education curriculum has traditionally lacked courses that could teach us how to manage being ourselves. Alain de Botton queries this in the book *The School of Life* (2019):

'We are left to find our own path around our unfeasibly complicated minds – a move as striking (and as wise) as suggesting that each generation should rediscover the laws of physics by themselves.'

Of course, this is how things have always been, but we do not have to keep them this way. There are glimmers of hope. I know of primary schools where pupils learn about stress and mindfulness and are taught about how to calm and soothe themselves. There are mindfulness colouring sessions in some schools, and lessons about feelings such as anger and sadness, joy and pride. In the psychotherapy field, we now have conferences which blend neuroscience, psychotherapy, yoga and theatre. Thousands of books are available to us to help us understand ourselves. It may all be fragmentary at the moment and not formalized and structured, but we are getting there. In time, I hope this will lead us to feeling less confused and embarrassed about being upset, because we will understand more about feelings and how to let them come and go; how to discharge and recharge in a healthy way. This will have important implications for reducing mental health difficulties.

But how do you tell when things are getting to the point where you need to see a therapist?

First, I want to say a bit about risk and what to do if things have become so bad that you can't see the woods for the trees.

SUICIDAL THOUGHTS

If you are feeling hopeless and making plans to end your life, then it is clear that you have been through some very difficult times. The fact that you have endured so much already and got this far means that you are already courageous. Before you take that final step, email jo@samaritans.org, or call 116 123, if you are in the UK. I have given a more detailed list of organizations and crisis support in the Appendix. Go there now if you are feeling this way.

If you don't know what to say over the phone, tell the advisor you don't know what to say and let them guide you, or use one of the prompts in this chapter. If you prefer to write out how you feel, then you may want to choose one of the prompts below and start with that.

In any case, use the phone call, email or piece of paper as a way to dump all your thoughts, feelings and experiences. They don't have to make sense at the moment; just get them out.

Then, take yourself to a different space. It can be a park, or a different room in your house. Ideally green space, where you can experience nature and trees. Like we did earlier, I'm going to ask you to notice your body rather than your thoughts. Give your mind a rest at the moment and take your body somewhere different. Even if it is just for twenty minutes. Walk or lie on the ground if it isn't too cold. Notice the sensations that you feel right now.

If you cannot get out, see if you can search for a video of a forest or beach on your device. As you watch, notice your body. Switch between your senses: close your eyes and listen, move your head and body to get your movement sensors going. Is there a smell that you like, such as a candle or fragrance? Bring that into your space. Or use music to stimulate your hearing and the movement sensors in your ear.

In the Appendix there is a link to a safety plan template that you can use to make a note of the things that feel helpful for you. If the critical part of your mind tries to downplay what you are doing or how simple some of these strategies seem, that's OK. Thank it for looking after you, because maybe you've needed that part to be on guard to look out for you previously. But it doesn't have to run the show right now. There are strategies it may not be aware of that could help you feel better. Can you give that part of your mind a break right now?

DON'T WAIT

Even if you are not at the point of despair or taking your own life, I would urge you to please not wait until things get really bad. The earlier you start to offload and process your experiences, whether that be with a friend, through a daily journal or with a therapist, the better. In my experience the earlier we do this, the more likely we are to prevent a lot of mental distress and chronic illnesses further down the line.

You may worry that by contacting a therapist you will have to sign up to endless weekly sessions. That is not the case. It is absolutely fine to look for a counsellor and say, 'I just need a bit of support with something that's upsetting me,' or 'I just need to offload,' or 'I need some help to get back on track.' I have had many clients who have just needed that first session to express how they feel in a safe private space. There are of course psychotherapies that are longer term, but not everybody needs that. An experienced therapist will always take it at your pace and will provide the space and the relationship to help you feel supported and in charge of the process.

NHS THERAPY AND CASENESS

In the UK, there are some complications when it comes to getting therapy provided through the NHS or accessing other free therapy services such as those provided by your employer. Because of the way these providers are set up and funded, they have to gather statistics to demonstrate to funders and taxpayers that they are providing an effective service. Because of this, you will have to complete an assessment by filling in a questionnaire. Depending on the score, you might be offered a certain type of therapy and a certain number of sessions.

The NHS uses a term called 'caseness' to decide if someone scores over the right cut-off point on a questionnaire. They need to have this because they have finite resources and have to draw a line somewhere. If you have been through the NHS therapy service, then you will be familiar with both the Patient Health Questionnaire (PHQ) and the Generalised Anxiety Disorder questionnaire (GAD) (see Appendix). These measures are used to give an indication of low mood and depression, and problems associated with anxiety.

PRIVATE THERAPY

In order to access private therapy, you do not have to meet these 'caseness' criteria, although unfortunately only those who can afford to pay have the luxury of being able to get the help of a therapist outside the NHS. Even so, there are ways for those of us who are not wealthy to make private therapy work for us without having to struggle financially. There are cost-effective options, such as breaking the cost down, or only using therapy as and when. Perhaps private therapy could be a personal utility. After all, therapy can make a difference to your outlook on life, your relationships, habits you want to break, thoughts and images that distress you, feelings you don't like, decisions you struggle with, patterns you keep finding yourself in, and your hopes and dreams for your future. Seen in this way, it is an important life utility.

In Chapter Eight I will talk more about the process of therapy and how to get the best out of it for you. But let's look at what signs might tell you that it could be helpful to see a therapist.

There are some questionnaires in the Appendix for this chapter that can help to give you some ratings for how you feel. But remember that self-assessments are no substitute for seeking actual help. The PHQ and GAD are broad measures and cannot give you a specific answer as to what is happening for you.

WHAT SORTS OF PROBLEMS DO PEOPLE GO TO SEE A THERAPIST WITH?

Here is a list of the things that I have heard over the years that clients have struggled with. Can you identify with any of these at all?

Thoughts and images

'I'm not struggling as much as others; maybe I'm not feeling bad enough to see a therapist.'
    'Why can't I stop these images and thoughts?'
    'I don't deserve to feel better.'
    'I'll feel worse if I talk to someone.'
    'I can never tell anyone about this.'
    'I'm stuck and cannot make a decision.'
    'I can't get it out of my head.'
    'I want this memory to disappear.'
    'I'm worried I'll be criticized.'
    'I'll never get over this.'

Feelings and bodily sensations

'I feel hopeless.'
    'I feel useless.'
    'I feel worthless.'
    'I feel lost.'
    'I feel alone.'
    'I feel sad.'
    'I feel empty and cut off.'
    'I feel shut off from life.'
    'I feel flat and have no energy.'
    'I'm in pain all the time.'
    'I feel stuck.'
    'I'm tired all the time.'
    'I've got no interest in things any more.'

Panicky and on edge

'I'm feeling helpless or powerless.'
    'I'm feeling so out of control at the moment.'
    'I feel so vulnerable when I go out nowadays.'

'I'm always scared.'
'I'm scared to sleep because of bad dreams.'
'I'm anxious and on-edge most of the day.'
'I'm scared of speaking in the team meetings.'
'I can't tolerate it anymore.'
'I feel so irritable all the time.'
'I get angry for no reason.'
'I'm so annoyed at myself.'
'I'm feeling upset for no reason.'

Behaviours

Ruminating and looking for answers
   Carrying out rituals and finding it hard to stop
   Being unable to stop certain habits or behaviours
   Avoiding or trying to avoid
   Checking light switches
   Scanning body for lumps
   Scanning social media feed of an ex-partner
   Being unable to sleep
   Waking up during the night and being unable to get back to sleep
   Having no motivation to do anything

If you can identify with any of these, then maybe it would help to note down on a formulation circle like the one we used in Chapter Four. For example, if you find you are having arguments all the time or getting angry more than usual, then put the angry feeling into the 'Emotion' section, and 'having arguments' into the 'Behaviour' section.

It can be tricky to find the right words for how we feel. Part of the reason for this is how little we are taught about emotions as a subject. We tend to use the same core words repeatedly (anger, sadness, anxiety). So I've started a list of emotion labels in the Appendix in an effort to start building a bigger vocabulary of words we can use to describe emotions. I would love you to add your words to the list. There is some evidence to show that there are benefits to be gained if we are able to manage our emotions better and have more of what Barrett calls 'emotional granularity' (Barrett, 2017). Our feelings are not black and white. They can vary in intensity, in how pleasant they are and how we feel about them. There is a wide spectrum, so let's find some more words to describe these events. As we find more words we will be noticing more of these feelings. The more we look the more we will see. The more we see the more experience we get with tolerating our feelings. The more we do this the more mastery we will have at understanding and managing them. As we manage them better we will feel better. We will 'feel' better.

Here is another list of when it might help to see a therapist:

Feeling like you have things you are unsure of and want to process
    Wanting to understand yourself better
    To offload
    When training to be a therapist
    When you have lost someone close
    To help come to terms with a change
    To improve relationships with those around you
    To know yourself and your emotions
    To 'feel' better.

To 'feel' better could mean to be able to tolerate your felt senses, and your own body, or it could mean to get a sense of balance back to your emotional life if you are feeling overly negative, flat, stressed or irritable.

Feeling better is about getting to know what a feeling 'feels' like for you. When you get to know this, you can label what is really going on for you, and if you can do this without judging or hating what you notice, then you are on the way to being better able to regulate and control your emotions. You will be more in control of what is happening for you than if you try to avoid or suppress. If you avoid or suppress then you will always be on the run, battling with yourself. It doesn't have to be that way.

Have a quick check-in now with your body. What sensations do you notice? Over the next week, repeat these occasional check-ins with your body just to see what you notice. I would also recommend trying the expressive-writing technique that we looked at in Chapter Three as a daily brain dump, either in the morning or in the evening before you go to sleep.

Everyday life is busy. There is a lot to process. Give yourself some time and space to offload and process.

In the previous chapters we talked about the techniques of emotional suppression and distraction that we all have to employ, and how we rarely allow ourselves to offload or discharge. This is partly due to conditioning about being afraid to become upset for fear of what may happen. But research is showing us that it is not healthy to only suppress emotions. Given this it seems important for us to find ways to discharge and recharge, so it makes sense that we should find ways to do this. Therapy is one way, but it is not the only way. I will be looking at alternatives to traditional talking therapies in Chapter Ten, but in the next chapter I would like to help you to find a therapist. I'll take you through what to look for, what the difference is between counselling and psychotherapy, psychology and psychiatry, and where to go to find the right therapist for you.

CHAPTER SEVEN

Finding a Therapist

WHO SHOULD I CONTACT? THERE ARE SO MANY OF THEM!

In this book so far, we have been preparing to see a therapist. But the next step is how to know which therapist to see and where to find them. This is a bit tricky, because there are many different types of therapy, so there are a lot of therapists out there. With the rise in online therapies there has also been a huge growth in companies wanting to signpost you to therapists on their site. It is great to have so much choice in one sense, but too much choice can sometimes mean we get stuck making decisions. In this chapter I am going to take you through the different therapies available and what things to look for. I also want to help narrow down your choices and show you how to find a therapist.

RAPPORT AND TIMING

If you allow yourself a bit of trial and error in finding the therapy and therapist that are right for you, it will make things easier. Therapists are people, and it has been demonstrated repeatedly in research that the relationship between therapist and client is a vital part of the success of therapy. It is important that the therapist you speak to is someone you feel you can build a working relationship with, so if you don't feel like you are 'clicking', then do try to mention this. As therapists we are trained to have this discussion, because we know how important the 'fit' is, so your therapist may even be expecting this topic to come up. Perhaps they will raise it first, but in any case, the therapist should aim to make the discussion as easy for you as possible.

Nevertheless, I know it can be difficult. What to say? What words to use? You could say 'I'm not sure this is working for me right now' and let the therapist guide you from there. It's a hard thing to do, and as a result one of the most common outcomes is that, rather than have the discussion, clients just don't come back. This is normal and can often mirror how we deal with other relationships in our lives. What can happen though is that we either blame ourselves or the therapist for why we don't want to go back to the session. I'd like to offer another possibility if you have this experience. Maybe you and this type of therapy or therapist just didn't 'fit' at this point in time. It doesn't mean you did anything wrong, and it doesn't mean the therapist did.* It just wasn't right for you and that is OK. You can move on without carrying this with you.

I'd like also to suggest the possibility that if something isn't right for you right now, that doesn't rule it out from being right for you at a different point in time. I have experienced for myself how we can find it hard to connect with a person or with a certain style of working at a certain point in our lives, but then find we come back to them at a later date. Sometimes the timing just isn't right for a certain piece of information to mean anything to us. Life can become stressful and complicated, especially after traumatic experiences, so there can also be very little time or space for therapy. I have had several clients throughout the years who have had to take a break but have come back to me when they were ready. If you can say, 'This isn't right for me right now,' you are leaving the way open to come back should you ever wish to.

---

* I want to add the following caveat here: if you feel that the therapist spoke or did anything that felt inappropriate, then please do raise this. If it isn't possible to raise it with the therapist themselves then please do go to the registration or accrediting body of the therapist.

SHOULD I SEE MY GP FIRST?

If you are in the UK or Republic of Ireland, a first question is often: 'Should I go to the GP or find a private therapist?' It can be important to go to the GP first if you are experiencing symptoms which you are unsure of, so that you can have a medical check-up to make sure there is no underlying condition that requires medical treatment. This is especially true if the symptoms you are noticing have appeared suddenly. Some conditions I am thinking about in relation to this are thyroid disorders, diabetes and hormone changes that occur during perimenopause and menopause. Also, sudden, unexpected flashes of aggression, impulsive behaviour and memory loss can be due to certain conditions in the brain which may need further investigation.

If you do see your doctor, they will hopefully offer you some support options, for example self-help information (Step 1), or a referral to NHS therapy services. There is usually a wait for these therapy services, but they are free. You may be offered options such as six sessions with a psychological wellbeing practitioner (PWP), a group education programme or an online guided self-help programme. This is termed 'low intensity' (or Step 2) therapy, and it aims to give you information about common psychological symptoms such as anxiety or low mood and help people at as early a stage as possible. If you have some individual sessions with a PWP they will find out more about what you experience and offer some strategies to help you manage your anxiety and low mood.

In NHS therapy services, 'high intensity' (or Step 3) therapy is when you are referred for sessions with a CBT therapist or counsellor and are usually allocated 6–12 sessions. You will have an assessment, and an individual treatment plan will be agreed between you and the therapist. But it differs from low intensity therapy in that a more detailed formulation of your issue will be carried out in order to understand what is happening for you. For example, in low intensity (or Step 2) therapy for panic attacks, the practitioner will provide education about panic and anxiety and provide strategies for coping with and managing your anxiety, along with some exposure-based exercises to help reduce the panic attacks. But in high intensity (Step 3) therapy the CBT therapist will gather details about what exactly happens for you when you have a panic attack and understand what triggers them and what may be underlying them. This is called a 'formulation', which can be very detailed depending on what happens for you.

You would of course be referred straight to Step 3 therapy if the problems you are having are moderate to severe, and would not have to go via the low intensity option if that is the case.

IMPROVING ACCESS TO PSYCHOLOGICAL THERAPIES (IAPT)

The Step 2 and 3 therapy services mentioned above are part of what is called 'IAPT'. In England, IAPT is another name for primary care mental health services. It began in 2008 and aimed to increase access to psychological therapy for people who were suffering from mild-to-moderate anxiety and depression. In many parts of England, you should be able to refer yourself to the local IAPT mental health service. Northern Ireland, Scotland and Wales have slightly different arrangements and names for their services, but they are broadly based on and influenced by the IAPT model. I've provided links in the Appendix for you to find your local service.

IAPT is structured around a stepped-care model:

Step 1 – watchful waiting, wait and see, signpost to relevant self-help website.

Step 2 – guided self-help, computerized CBT, 6 sessions either individually or as part of a group of psychoeducation-based and goal-directed sessions with a 'low-intensity' practitioner, called a 'psychological wellbeing practitioner'.

Step 3 – 6–12 sessions with a CBT therapist or counsellor. For trauma (with either a CBT therapist or EMDR therapist), the number of sessions can be extended up to 18.

Step 3+ – this exists in some services where clients have more complex difficulties but still might be seen in primary care services first rather than have to wait for secondary care services.

Step 4 is usually outside of IAPT/Primary care and is managed by Secondary care/Community mental health teams. It is for those clients whose needs are complex and need more than 6–18 sessions. For example, those who need more time to be able to trust and open up to a therapist, or who need extra time to be able to stabilize and manage their emotions or certain behaviours. They may also need help and input from other services such as social work and/or psychiatry and as such will need a multidisciplinary approach and a care plan that is coordinated so that services work together to help the person.

In reality, people do not fit neatly into these stepped categories, and when I worked in an IAPT service it would be normal for me to see clients from steps 2–4 in an average week. Lack of funding from government for IAPT services has often meant that secondary care services (Step 4+) lose out and can have much longer waiting lists and staffing issues as a result. The split between primary and secondary care isn't always helpful in practice, because clients do not fit neatly into little boxes, nor should they have to. There can also be difficulties when clients have to be referred between these 'steps'.

With the development of IAPT came a new type of worker; a 'psychological wellbeing practitioner' (PWP) who could deliver CBT interventions that were deemed not to need the input of a CBT therapist. However PWPs are highly trained and many have psychology degrees on top of the intensive 'Low Intensity' training courses that they have to complete. It is fairer to say that they are low intensity therapists because they are very focused and accomplished at providing these interventions. In many NHS services the term 'psychological therapist' is used to include both PWPs and CBT therapists/counsellors.

The rationale for developing the PWP role was that more people could be helped if therapy sessions were shortened to thirty minutes, and brief interventions were offered. Some examples of the type of interventions used by PWPs are: psychoeducation, which is information about what anxiety and depression are techniques for how to notice and challenge negative thoughts and simple exposure programmes. A 'graded exposure' programme for panic, for example, would aim to help a client gradually tolerate the bodily sensations of increased anxiety, without neutralizing or avoiding them. Our instinct is to avoid what makes us anxious and fearful, but with panic this avoidance keeps us fearing our own bodily sensations.

IAPT has completely restructured the way therapy is delivered, from changing the usual therapy hour to thirty minutes for Step 2 sessions to bringing in more group sessions and providing access to online self-help. It has also introduced 'blended therapy', which is a mix of face-to-face or telephone support whilst working through a computer-based programme. SilverCloud is an online CBT programme that often has therapist support by telephone as part of the intervention.

The demand for therapy services is always high, and as a result staff often have targets for the number of therapy sessions they have to deliver in a week. In the IAPT service where I worked – and I know this is not unusual – PWPs would have to deliver around eight thirty-minute sessions with clients every day, with a target of 35–40 cases per week to achieve. For CBT therapists and counsellors there are also targets for their hour-long sessions – sometimes up to twenty-four clients a week. This work is intense because staff aim to provide a therapeutic space and emotional support for people who are upset but are also trying to do this whilst completing questionnaires with clients, work on individual treatment plans, carry out interventions and track therapy goals.

Unfortunately, the waiting lists are still painfully long in many IAPT services and also in IAPT-equivalent services in Wales, Scotland and Northern Ireland. The same is also true in secondary care services, which include psychiatry, psychiatric units and longer-term or specialist therapy services.

QUESTIONNAIRES AND SELF-REPORT MEASURES

If you see a therapist as part of an NHS therapy service, you will usually have to complete 'Self-Report Measures' for each appointment. In England these tend to be the Patient Health Questionnaire (PHQ-9), Generalised Anxiety Disorder scale (GAD-7), Work and Social Adjustment Scale (WSAS) and Phobia Scale. I have included these in the Appendix along with an explanation of how to interpret the scores in case you want to score yourself. These measures help services to categorize by need and assess change. It is important for monitoring a client's progress, and it helps the therapist and their clinical supervisor pick up on no change or worsening of symptoms. NHS services are funded by commissioning groups who want to see the numbers on how many people have treatment, and how many are improving or not. The statistics are important to keep the service funded and free for clients.

In private therapy you do not have to complete these measures, although you may want to for your own reference point. Sometimes it does help to give you an idea of how varied your symptoms can be and how many areas of your life are affected. Some clients have reported that seeing all the different symptoms and experiences written out on a questionnaire helped them because it shows that others must be experiencing those symptoms too, and this makes them feel less alone. Some clients do not find them useful and some therapists feel the same. But the questions can also help clients articulate what may feel hard to put into words. It is the way that these tools are used that can make them a help or a hindrance. In the Appendix, along with these main IAPT measures, I have provided links to other questionnaires that I have used and found helpful. It is important to mention though that questionnaires cannot capture the richness of your overall experience and by their nature they are limited. You may be having symptoms that are not on the questionnaire at all. So it is important to not base too much on these scores but to use them as a guide in conjunction with what you and the therapist discover is relevant for you.

COST

If you see a therapist through the NHS or via your employer, then this will be free, but there will usually be a wait, especially in NHS services. If you look for a private therapist you can see a therapist of your choice at a time to suit, but you will have to pay. When you first look at private therapy fees it can look very expensive, especially in some cities. However, if you look at how to space this out and what you can get from that cost it can be more than worth it.

The general therapy model tends to be weekly sessions, with a range that can vary widely depending on whether you are seeking short-term (6–8 sessions) or mid-longer-term therapy (12–48 sessions, and sometimes more than this depending on the issue). I believe that you have to start somewhere and that it is helpful to begin with a budget for ten sessions of therapy. You may need less than this, and you may need more than this, but if you budget for this amount you will be giving yourself a realistic chance of trying therapy without feeling you have to rush and be better after one or two sessions. If you start therapy feeling anxious about needing to get change quickly, it will be counter-productive for you and the therapist. Of course, you want to feel better quickly, and you may very well feel a great deal of relief after the first session. But it is important to try not to race ahead too much and stay instead with what you are experiencing in the moment. Change happens because of the choices you mindfully make right now. Be curious, rather than judgemental, about what you notice, if you can.

Paying for therapy could be seen like budgeting for a training course or conference, or as essential maintenance, like car repairs, or even like buying a new bed. It is an outlay, but the life-changing benefits can have knock-on effects for the rest of your life. We can spend quite a substantial amount of money maintaining our cars, our houses and upgrading our technology, and we are worth spending money on too, and not just for temporary cosmetic reasons, but for longer-lasting change.

You could also break the sessions up into chunks or arrange fortnightly sessions. This spreads the cost and gives you more time to reflect and process in between. Some types of therapy may not offer this, but it is always important that you speak with your therapist about what would make it work for you. Sometimes fortnightly sessions can give you time to process, reflect and make changes over a longer period of time. People differ with regards to how much time they need between therapy sessions, but it is important to maintain the momentum of therapy and not leave too long a gap. If you are on a set budget but you are motivated to engage and try therapy, it is worth discussing this with your chosen therapist. Some therapists can offer a sliding scale of fees for an agreed period of time, especially for people who are motivated and want to help themselves.

It is important to note here that there are some psychotherapies, for example psychoanalytic psychotherapy, that may offer you twice-weekly sessions rather than weekly or fortnightly sessions. This is normal for some insight-focused therapies.

In the private sector you can see a therapist for as long as you need to. If you start to experience benefits, then you will feel better; if you feel better then you are likely to see how therapy can help you and will be more likely to budget for subsequent sessions. How you feel and think is integral to your everyday life, so it can make a real and lasting difference when therapy works.

Therapy isn't wasted money. It is a way to make your day-to-day life feel better for you. It can help you get through those blocks that stop you from getting what you want, from being confident in situations that currently make you feel intimidated, from stopping that pattern of behaviour that you just can't get out of.

When you pay for therapy you are paying for someone to help you to change something for the better. Therapy can be challenging but also life-changing if you allow it to be.

CHOOSING A THERAPIST – NHS, EMPLOYER-FUNDED OR PRIVATE?

If you go through NHS therapy services or via your employer, then the person carrying out your assessment will try to match you with the right therapist. You won't have too much choice over which therapist you see, but you can be sure that the therapist will be registered/accredited and fully checked and vetted.

NHS

In the appendix for this chapter, I have listed the links to NHS psychological therapy services in the United Kingdom.

Through your employer

Some companies have their own in-house counselling services, while some subcontract counselling services to organizations known as Employee Assistance Providers (EAPs). This information should be given to you when you start working for an organization, but if you are unsure, do speak with your manager or occupational health department. You may be able to access therapy at no cost to yourself via these services. Often there can be a range of services available, from supportive counselling to CBT or trauma-focused therapies such as EMDR and TF-CBT.

Charities and Organizations offering therapy, some at low cost or free

There are some free, low-cost or sliding-scale-fee counselling services offered by some charities and voluntary organizations. Always check that the therapist is registered with a therapy body though. There is a list in the Appendix you can use to cross-reference.

Private therapy

For private therapy you can choose the therapist you see, but you do need to check that they are registered and/or accredited. I have included a list in the appendix of the main therapy bodies that you are likely to see listed on therapists' profiles. With private therapy you will have a great deal of choice available to you. On some sites and directories the therapist will have posted an introductory video, or at the least have a photo of themselves, so that you can get a feel for what they are like and a sense of whether or not you can work with them.

I have also provided links to the websites and directories where you can find a private therapist, but as you will see there are a lot of therapists and an extensive list of therapies out there. It can be bewildering trying to choose. The first questions you are likely to be asking yourself are: 'What type of therapist should I choose and what type of therapy?' We will look at these areas in turn now.

WHAT TYPE OF THERAPIST – COUNSELLOR, PSYCHOTHERAPIST OR PSYCHOLOGIST?

When you are looking at fees you might notice that there tends to be quite a wide range of charges for therapy depending on whether you choose a counsellor, a psychotherapist or a psychologist. Here are the main differences between these three titles (although a psychotherapist may also use short-term counselling methods in their practice, and a clinical and counselling psychologist will usually have training in more than one psychotherapeutic theory).

COUNSELLOR

In general, a counsellor is someone who works with clients on a short-term basis and supports them in the present. They provide a confidential and supportive space for current issues. They can also offer strategies for managing how you feel. Sessions can be weekly and usually last no longer than six months, although this can vary. An example would be bereavement counselling.

For registration and accreditation purposes there is often a requirement of a diploma or undergraduate degree or Levels 4–6 of the national qualification framework in the UK (or Level 7 in Ireland) (www.gov.uk/what-different-qualification-levels-mean/). You can also have a look at these two websites to understand the qualification requirements:

See also www.cpcab.co.uk/qualifications/

And www.apcp.ie/accredited-counsellor/

PSYCHOTHERAPIST

A psychotherapist is someone who has been trained to look in depth at how the past impacts on how you feel currently. They will work with you to understand patterns of thoughts and behaviours, past relationships and why you feel, think and behave in the way you do. An example would be a course of trauma-focused therapy to help deal with the impact of traumatic experiences.

For registration and accreditation as a psychotherapist there is usually a requirement of training to master's level, or level 7 (or level 9 in Ireland) of the qualifications framework. There are more details of psychotherapy qualifications on the following websites:

www.psychotherapy.org.uk/psychotherapy-training/

Or www.apcp.ie/accredited-psychotherapist/

For both counselling and psychotherapy you will know if your therapist has met the requirements if they are registered/accredited with a recognised therapy body - more about this below.

CLINICAL OR COUNSELLING PSYCHOLOGIST

Clinical and counselling psychologists will have trained in at least two different psychotherapeutic methods and can practise these alongside being able to offer psychological testing. They are usually also involved in or have been involved in research and have studied psychology to doctoral level. They will usually but not always have the title of Dr, or the terms PhD, PsyD or DClinPsy after their name. The titles 'Clinical Psychologist' and 'Counselling Psychologist' are protected under law, and only psychologists registered with the Health and Care Professions Council (HCPC) may use these titles. Clinical and Counselling Psychologists will usually also have chartered membership of the British Psychological Society (BPS), which enables them to use the CPsychol abbreviation after their name. They may also have associate fellowship membership abbreviations from the BPS as well. Two fictional examples would be Dr Brown, CPsychol, AFBPsS, and Mr Brown, DClinPsy, CPsychol, FBPsS.

PROTECTED TITLES

The title of 'Psychologist' on its own is not protected. That being said there are therapists who will have an undergraduate degree in psychology that has been approved by the BPS as conferring them graduate membership of the BPS. This allows them to use the abbreviations 'MBPsS' after their name. This experience is very valuable to have, but a psychology degree on its own does not make someone a therapist. Make sure that your therapist has had appropriate therapy training and check if they have registration or accreditation from a recognized counselling or psychotherapy body.

The titles of 'Counsellor' and 'Psychotherapist' are not protected by law. However, there are some therapists who do have titles protected by the HCPC. These are art psychotherapist, drama therapist, music therapist and occupational therapist. It is confusing, isn't it!

ACCREDITATION AND REGISTRATION OF COUNSELLORS AND PSYCHOTHERAPISTS

Whether you see a counsellor or psychotherapist, it is vital that they have the appropriate therapy qualifications and training, and that they are registered and accredited by a recognized body. This shows that they have been vetted and appropriately assessed to have the training, experience and personal qualities to be an effective therapist. It also provides you with an organization you can go to should you have any concerns about that therapist's practice. As part of their registration, they will be expected to uphold strict standards and guidelines for practice. Some of the standards therapists must ensure they work to are:

Working within their scope of practice. For example, if they are a psychodynamic therapist, they will practise this method and not another that they are not qualified in. If they are a CBT therapist, they should not practise psychodynamic therapy if they are not qualified to do so.

Having regular clinical supervision. Clinical supervision is essential for all therapists regardless of level of experience. Newly qualified and experienced therapists must have a set number of hours of clinical supervision to maintain registration and accreditation. Clinical supervision is where we discuss our cases (confidentially) to ensure we are working according to our training. Ethical issues, if they arise, are also discussed, as are any difficulties that the therapist may be experiencing with clients. We are always learning and always have questions to bring to supervision. No therapist is an expert on every client or every therapeutic method. This reflective practice is essential to our ongoing learning and development.

Working ethically and confidentially. Our conditions of registration and accreditation are based on us upholding strict ethical and confidential procedures with regards to our clients and the issues they bring to therapy. We work to the code of conduct set out by our accrediting bodies.

Continuing professional development. Another requirement of our accrediting bodies is that we set aside a set number of hours per year for 'continuing professional development' (CPD). This is usually attending training courses to update or learn new skills, reading journal articles or books, or writing relevant information. This requirement aims to ensure that we are maintaining and updating our knowledge where necessary.

Professional indemnity and public liability insurance. Therapists working in private practice must arrange their own private insurance. The aim of this insurance is to protect the public from any wrongdoing or harmful acts by the therapist.

Disclosure and Barring Service (DBS) certificate. The DBS certificate used to be known as the Criminal Records Bureau check. There is a Basic and an Enhanced level of DBS certificate. The Enhanced shows details of all criminal records, if any. It shows any cautions or warnings given, and any reprimands as well as spent and unspent convictions. It will also show if the person is prohibited from working with children and vulnerable adults and is on the 'barred list'.

Counselling and psychotherapy are not on the list as needing an Enhanced check according to the British Association for Counselling and Psychotherapy (BACP), but providers who employ therapists will often seek an Enhanced check, and it is good practice to have this if possible.

Apart from the type of therapy, these are the criteria I look for when I choose a therapist:

Accreditation and registration by a recognized therapy body. Have a look at the list in the Appendix to see if your therapist is on one of these lists.

Insurance and DBS certificate.

Number of years' experience.

Professionalism of profile and online persona.

HOW TO NARROW THE SEARCH

THERAPY MODE

The first step to narrowing down your search is to have in mind whether you are looking for individual therapy, couples therapy, family or group therapy. This will help you to narrow down the bodies and directories that you search in (the middle column of Figure 7). After this, have a think about whether you are looking for short- term support or would you like to work on issues that you have struggled with for some time. For the former look for short-term CBT or counselling, and for the latter look for longer-term CBT/psychotherapy.

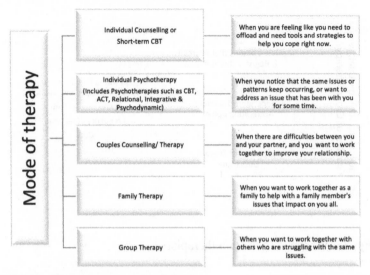

Fig. 7 – Choosing a mode of therapy

Once you have this narrowed down, have a look at Figure 8 to select where to look first.

WHERE TO LOOK

If you are looking for a private therapist then you will have many therapists to choose from and will be able to select the one that you feel suits you best. You could use a search engine to find a therapist in your area or via keywords. For example, 'CBT Therapy near me', or 'Family therapist near me'. This is likely to bring up many pages of search results. Another option is to use the directory search on either an independent therapy directory or from a therapy body that is recognized and also responsible for accrediting and registering therapists.

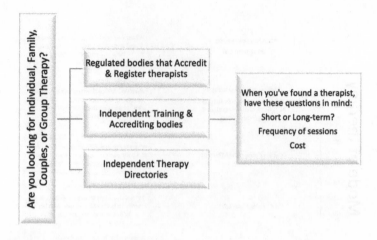

Fig. 8 – Where to look for a therapist

Regulated bodies that accredit and register therapists

This is a good first port of call. Although the terms 'counsellor' and 'psychotherapist' are not protected titles, therapists in the UK will usually be registered and accredited with a particular body. Some of the most well known (though not the only ones) are BABCP, BACP, NCS, UKCP. I have provided a link to these bodies in the Appendix. These sites will usually have a 'find a therapist' search facility.

Independent training and accreditation bodies

An example here is the British Psychoanalytic Council and the British Association for Behavioural and Cognitive Psychotherapies. These bodies usually accredit practitioners that are specifically trained in their approach. These sites will usually have a 'find an accredited therapist' directory. There are a very large number of these training bodies and I have provided a list of them in the Appendix. This can be a good place to look if you know the approach that you want to try, e.g. AEDP, Brainspotting, CBT or EMDR therapy.

Independent therapy directories

These have usually been set up by private companies to offer therapists a place to list themselves and be found by potential clients. The most well known of these are Counselling Directory (CD) and Psychology Today (PT), but new ones are appearing quite frequently, so there is a lot of choice available.

Some of the directories offer the ability to book the session directly with the therapist via their site. They display the therapist's profile and an availability calendar, and you choose the slot you want and book the session without leaving the site. For other directories, such as CD and PT, you choose who you want to contact and then you can email or phone the therapist directly to set up a convenient appointment for you both and find out more about them and their therapy prior to booking.

Where these directories work well is in offering clients a wide choice of therapists who have all been checked and vetted to have the appropriate insurance cover, DBS certificate and accreditation or registration with a credible therapy organization.

Therapists will pay a combination of flat fee plus commission to be listed on these sites. They also pay to be listed on the directories of their registration and accrediting bodies, which can be a substantial amount in some cases. As a result, it is unlikely that you will see the same therapist on all of the sites.

The main benefit of being in a directory is to be found when a client searches for a therapist on a search engine. It takes a lot of money and work to appear at the top of Google's search rankings in certain areas. This is outside the reach of many therapists, and so they choose sites that help them to be found by clients. There are so many sites now, though, so the question is, which one to choose? This is a dilemma for clients too.

When you are looking for a therapist in these directories you can drill down using the search filters, such as type of therapy, the issues you are struggling with, the location, whether they offer online therapy. Even so, this can still yield quite a lot of therapists for you to trawl through, so it does help if you have an idea of the type of therapy you are looking for prior to searching.

When you are looking at therapists in these directories, do aim to look for registration and accreditation with recognized counselling and psychotherapy bodies. The site should tell you if it approves only those therapists who are registered and accredited with a recognized body. The list of bodies you can use to cross-reference for yourself is in the Appendix.

Another issue to be aware of is the information that the directory asks of you. For most 'find a therapist' features on websites you can look at the therapists available, choose your preferred one, then contact them yourself by phone or email. However, on many of the current therapy directory platforms, you can have a more interactive experience. There are questionnaires that you can complete to be matched with a therapist, you can book and carry out the session on the site using the company's payment and video-calling platform. It is important to be aware that the more you can do on a site, the more of your data is needed to enable you to carry out these functions, so you need to know who is looking after this data and that they will keep it protected and secure. Companies need to have a clear privacy policy on their websites to show how they manage and secure your data if they ask for personal information from you. For sites such as Timewith, for example, you can take a helpful questionnaire to narrow down the choice of therapist, but it does ask for quite a lot of personal information. This is not a problem when a company is clear on how they protect and keep your data safe and have a clear policy on their site, with contact details. According to the guidance set out by the UK's Information Commissioner's Office (ICO), you can ask for your data to be deleted, or limit the way that a company uses your data. You are also entitled to ask for copies of the data held by you, and the organization should not charge you for this. Here are the links to the rights you have over your data:

ico.org.uk/your-data-matters/

ico.org.uk/your-data-matters/your-right-to-get-copies-of-your-data/
what-to-expect-after-making-a-subject-access-request/

In the UK and the European Union, the law that companies have to uphold in relation to data protection at the time of writing is called the General Data Protection Regulation (GDPR). In the US for personal health data there is the Health Insurance Portability and Accountability Act (HIPAA). If a company processes the data of residents of the UK or European Union, then they should comply with GDPR, even if the company is based in the US. This may be subject to change now that the UK has left the EU, but the company should still abide by a privacy policy that protects your data, and this should be specified in the 'privacy policy' link on their website.

Look for their privacy policy page. It should specify a person to contact with data and privacy concerns. Check what the site states it will do with the data it collects from you. It is also useful to check that the company has a registered address and isn't a faceless entity with only an email address.

WHAT TYPE OF THERAPY SHOULD I CHOOSE?

Once you have a broad idea of the area of therapy you are looking for, e.g. couples counselling, psychotherapy, family therapy or counselling, the next decision is which type of therapy would you like to try? This is not an easy decision, because you have a lot of choice! To help with this task I wanted to give you an outline of as many therapies as possible in the hope that when you do look at the directories you will recognize some of the names and abbreviations listed on the therapists' profiles.

There's a helpful book by Ariane Sherine called *Talk Yourself Better*, which describes the main modes of talking therapy available in the UK today and gives a brief overview of that therapy from both the client and therapist's perspective. It's a well-researched book, but even this doesn't include all the therapies available, because new ones are being added all the time. A recent estimate states the number of therapies at over a thousand (Rost, 2019).

Therapists usually train in one or two 'core' approaches and become registered/accredited in these approaches. Many have core mental health training as a psychiatric nurse, occupational therapist, social worker, or clinical or counselling psychologist prior to specializing in a particular therapy.

In addition to providing an alphabetical list of types of therapy below, I have also categorized them according to the main theoretical approaches; for example, within cognitive behavioural therapy (CBT) there are sub-types such as ACT (acceptance and commitment therapy), REBT (rational emotive behaviour therapy) and TF-CBT (trauma-focused CBT). This extra category information is in the Appendix. Below is a description of as many psychological therapies as I could find in the UK as of September 2020. I have included a URL for the UK training or accreditation association for that therapy (where available).

There are many different types of talking therapies, so it is a case of finding what works for you. At its heart, therapy is a space, and a relationship with a person who frames your difficulties in a particular way in order to help you find some clarity and a way of working through those difficulties. If one approach doesn't seem to fit for you, do try another one.

ALPHABETICAL LIST OF PSYCHOLOGICAL THERAPIES

Acceptance and Commitment Therapy (ACT) – contextualscience.org

ACT is known as a 'third-wave' CBT approach, but it differs from CBT in a few ways. One of the main differences is that instead of challenging thoughts and getting tangled up looking for the evidence against a negative thought, an ACT approach would be to accept the thought and 'lean in' to the experience, rather than push against it and avoid. Mindfulness, compassion and acceptance are important aspects of an ACT approach.

Accelerated Empathic Therapy (AET) – iedta.net/edt/about-edt/types-of-edt/aet

Developed by Michael Alpert, AET is similar to focusing-oriented techniques in that it is an approach to recognizing and tuning into what our body is doing when we feel certain emotions.

Accelerated Experiential Dynamic Psychotherapy (AEDP) – www.aedpuk.com

AEDP was developed by Diana Fosha and is an experiential therapy (meaning it doesn't only rely on talking but 'experiencing'). It aims to blend a focus on experiencing emotions within the context of a healing relationship in order to bring about change. AEDP is an approach that takes into account contemporary research into interpersonal neurobiology, attachment, neuroplasticity and affective neuroscience. AEDP therapists have to be registered/accredited in a core mental health profession prior to training.

Accelerated Resolution Therapy (ART) – acceleratedresolution-therapy.com/what-is-art/

ART was developed by Laney Rosenzweig, a marriage and family therapist. It is a blend of EMDR, CBT, Gestalt and brief psychodynamic therapy. It aims to help clients rapidly reprogramme trauma memories.

Advanced Integrative therapy (AIT) – www.ait-uk-europe.com/about-ait

Developed by Princeton professor and psychotherapist Asha Clinton, AIT is an integration of psychodynamic, CBT, object relations, energy psychology, Jungian and transpersonal theories. It is a trauma-focused approach to unblocking and healing the energy of the body and mind.

Adlerian therapy – www.adleriansociety.co.uk

Developed by Alfred Adler, one of the 'big three' fathers of psycho-therapy alongside Sigmund Freud and Carl Jung. Adler termed his approach 'individual psychology'. The Adlerian approach aims to blend the study of the individual with their wider societal context.

Affect Phobia Therapy (APT) – www.affectphobiatherapy.com

Affect phobia therapy was developed by the psychologist Leigh McCullough in the 1990s. It is a variant of psychodynamic psycho-therapy that now integrates elements of short-term dynamic therapy, CBT and experiential therapies. It focuses on the fear of feelings as a central aspect of many psychological difficulties. Similar to AEDP, APT-certified therapists have to be registered/accredited with a recognized body prior to training.

Attachment-Based Therapy – thebowlbycentre.org.uk

This is an approach that involves understanding an individual's early relationships with caregivers and how these influence the person's subsequent relationships. It is based on psychoanalytic theory.

Attachment-Based Intensive Short-Term Dynamic Psychotherapy (AB-ISTDP) – iedta.net/edt/about-edt/types-of-edt/ab-istdp

AB-ISTDP uses neurobiological findings in combination with an attuned therapeutic relationship to help clients with developmental and attachment-based traumatic experiences.

Behavioural Activation (BA) – babcp.com

Behavioural Activation is a technique within CBT that is usually used for depression. It focuses on helping to get motivation back by utilizing actions that help to activate feelings of reward, achievement and pleasure.

Bereavement counselling – www.cruse.org.uk

Grief is a process that is natural although it can involve stages which are painful to move through, especially when we lose a loved one and find ourselves alone. A bereavement counsellor can provide support for you through this difficult time.

Body Psychotherapies – eabp.org and ismeta.org

In body psychotherapy and somatic psychology, the brain-mind-body are seen as integral and not separate. The focus is not only on talking and language but also on what information is stored in your body and how your body is part of the expression of yourself and your feelings. This is a list of some of the therapies that tend to come under this heading:

Bioenergetic Analysis –
www.bioenergeticanalysis.net/whatisbaeng.html
Biosynthesis – www.europsyche.org/approaches/biosynthesis
Bodynamic – Somatic Developmental Psychology – www.bodynamic.com
Embodied-Relational Therapy – erthworks.co.uk
Energetic integration – energypsychotherapyworks.co.uk/practitioners and www.fieh.co.uk
Hakomi – hakomiinstitute.com
Integrative Body Psychotherapy – ibmt.co.uk
Interplay – www.interplay.org
Lifespan Integration – lifespanintegration.com
Pesso Boyden System Psychomotor/Psychomotor therapy – pbsp.com
Sensorimotor Psychotherapy – sensorimotorpsychotherapy.org/about/#what-is-sp
Somatic Experiencing (SE) – www.seauk.org.uk
Somatic Stress Release Technique – www.drscottlyons.com/somatic-stress-release
Total Release Experience (TRE) – treuk.com
Trauma Relief Unlimited (TRU) – traumareliefunlimited.com

Brainspotting – www.bspuk.co.uk

Brainspotting therapy was developed by David Grand in 2003. David had trained in Somatic Experiencing and EMDR and had blended these two therapies into a technique which he called 'Natural Flow EMDR'. He then developed this further into 'brainspotting'. It is an approach that uses the key role of a healing relationship between client and therapist (called the 'dual-attunement framework'), in association with the processing of traumatic material whilst 'holding' a specific spot in the client's visual field. Brainspotting uses various eye positions or 'gaze spots' either when processing distressing material or for strengthening places in the body where clients feel calm and safe. Brainspotting therapists have to have core mental health training prior to being certified in this technique.

Cognitive Analytic Therapy (CAT) – www.acat.me.uk

Developed in the 1980s by Anthony Ryle, CAT is an approach that integrates elements of psychodynamic therapy, attachment therapy and CBT. It is a time-limited approach that is also available in many NHS services.

Cognitive Behavioural Analysis System of Psychotherapy (CBASP) – www.cbaspsociety.org

CBASP is a therapy that is used with chronically depressed clients. It blends elements of CBT with interpersonal and dynamic therapy. Through an in-depth situational analysis of a problem the therapy aims to show how our behaviour can create the problems we then experience.

Cognitive Behavioural Therapy (CBT) – babcp.com

CBT incorporates a range of behavioural and cognitive therapies that share the principle that how we feel, what we think and what we do are related and that we can change how we feel by altering how we think and what we do. It is a psychotherapy that has gathered a large amount of evidence and has been adapted for brief and short-term interventions as well as for online and self-help interventions. In CBT an issue is broken down into its elements in order to assess what is driving the problem and maintaining it. Different strategies are then used to make changes and alter either thought patterns or behaviour patterns. There are a range of protocols that have been developed in CBT for various difficulties, such as David Clark's Panic Disorder Protocol.

If you are looking for a CBT therapist, do look for either BABCP accreditation or chartered psychologist status. If not then do check they are accredited or registered with a psychotherapy body that is recognized or are a Chartered Psychologist. The standard CBT qualification is a Postgraduate Diploma in CBT or an MSc in CBT. On these university courses there is a mixture of theory work, practical and supervised client work, placements, observed live sessions and regular clinical supervision. Home study and short distance-learning courses cannot provide the depth of training needed to qualify someone as a therapist. Check through the person's listing and see what qualifications they state.

Cognitive Processing Therapy (CPT) – cptforptsd.com

CPT is a form of trauma-focused CBT that is used for PTSD. It focuses on the meaning of the traumatic event and offers techniques for processing and altering this negative meaning that is keeping people stuck. Those who use CPT will already be practising/registered therapists who go on to take this extra training for their trauma work.

Coherence Therapy – www.coherencetherapy.org/discover/what.htm

Coherence therapy (previously called 'depth-oriented brief therapy') was developed in the 1990s by Bruce Ecker and Laurel Hulley. The overarching principle of this approach is that rather than signalling pathology, the memories, thoughts, feelings and behaviours that we experience have a 'coherence' and are there for a reason. Therapy involves the bringing into awareness of patterns and expressions, in the context of an empathic and attuned therapeutic relationship.

Compassion-Focused Therapy (CFT) – www.compassionatemind.co.uk

CFT was developed as a theory and approach to therapy by Paul Gilbert. It blends elements of evolutionary psychology with CBT and neuroscience. CFT works with three systems: the drive and achievement system, the social engagement system and the threat system, with the aim of gaining a balance and regulating emotional disturbance.

Comprehensive Resource Model (CRM) – comprehensiveresourcemodel.com

Created by Lisa Schwarz, CRM was initially developed for clients suffering with chronic PTSD, attachment disorders and dissociative disorders, but it is being more widely used with other difficulties. It is an approach that blends elements of neurobiology with relational and somatic work and spirituality.

Contemplative Psychotherapy and Core Process Psychotherapy – www.acpponline.net

These psychotherapies blend an understanding of Western psychology with Buddhist philosophy to understand how to access our core state of openness and joy.

Couples Therapy – tavistockandportman.nhs.uk/care-and-treatment/treatments/working-with-couples/

There are many different approaches to couples therapy, such as Collaborative Couples therapy (CCT) and Discernment & Divorce Counselling.

Behavioural Couples Therapy - tavistockrelationships.ac.uk/
iapt-couple-training
Encounter-Centred Transformation - hedyschleifer.com/
The Gottman Method - www.gottman.com/
Imago Therapy - imagorelationships.org/
Relationship Enhancement Therapy - nire.org/research-
on-relationship-enhancement-and-filial-methods/
the-relationship-enhancement-model-and-the-10-re-skills/

Deep Brain Reorienting (DBR) - www.deepbrainreorienting.com

DBR is an approach to healing trauma and especially attachment-based trauma. It was developed by Frank Corrigan and is based on his neurophysiological work. The approach aims to heal the shock, horror and bodily residues of traumatic experiences and adverse interpersonal experiences.

Dialectical Behaviour Therapy (DBT) - sfdbt.org

DBT is a therapy that was developed by the psychologist Marsha Linehan in the late 1980s. It is based on CBT but extends CBT principles to focus on several core components: emotional regulation, distress tolerance and interpersonal difficulties.

Dynamic Emotion-Focused therapy (DEFT) - iedta.net/edt/about-edt/types-of-edt/iedp/

DEFT was developed by Susan Warren Warshow. It is a psychodynamic therapy that focuses on shame-sensitivity and the inhibitory nature of shame as a main difficulty for clients. The therapy uses the attunement and empathy of the therapist as a main vehicle through which clients can start to break through the walls of shame that keep them blocked.

Dynamic Interpersonal Therapy (DIT) – www.bpc.org.uk/professionals/kite-mark-therapist/dit/

To practise DIT therapists have to be already qualified and trained in psychodynamic therapy and have a number of hours of supervised practice. DIT and interpersonal therapy (IPT) are both used in NHS services, especially for clients who struggle with depression and for which CBT is not recommended or helpful. NICE guidelines recommend this therapy along with CBT, couples therapy for depression and counselling for depression.

Eye Movement Desensitization Reprocessing (EMDR) – emdrassociation.org.uk

EMDR is a therapy that is recognized by NICE and the WHO as an effective therapy for trauma although it can be very effective with other difficulties also. It was developed by Francine Shapiro, a clinical psychologist who noticed that whilst she was thinking about something personally traumatic to her, her eyes were tracking side to side. Through the use of dual attention and bilateral stimulation (eye movements, music or tapping), the therapist aims to help the client reduce the overwhelming distress that some memories and feelings produce.

Emotional Freedom Technique (EFT) – eftinternational.org/about-us/about-eft-international-efti/

EFT has been considered a psychological form of acupuncture as it involves tapping meridian points on the body to alleviate psychological distress. It has been found to be as effective as CBT and EMDR in a recent meta-analysis and has been utilized within some NHS services. See Sebastian and Nelms, 2017.

Emotion-Focused therapy (EFT) – www.iseft.org/What-is-EFT

Developed by Leslie Greenberg in the 1970s, EFT places our emotions at the heart of therapy. Therapists take an experiential, humanistic approach, gently guiding the client to be able to experience and understand their emotions and reactions.

Emotionally Focused Therapy (EFT) – iceeft.com/what-is-eft/

Emotionally focused therapy was developed by Sue Johnson originally as a couples therapy technique. It is an approach that utilizes attachment science research to focus on helping us develop better relationships. The approach is structured and time-limited and works on changing cycles of interaction that cause us difficulties.

Emotional Schema Therapy (EST)

Emotional schema therapy is a new technique within CBT that has been developed by Robert Leahy.

Existential Psychotherapy – existentialanalysis.org.uk

Existential therapy takes a philosophical approach to therapy and incorporates wider questions about the human condition and what it means to be alive and how questions of meaning affect us individually. It was developed by Viktor Frankl, who also devised 'logotherapy', a type of existential therapy

Family Therapies

Attachment Narrative Therapy – aft.org.uk
Dyadic Developmental Psychotherapy (DDP) – ddpnetwork.org
Family & Systemic Psychotherapy – aft.org.uk
Family Constellation therapy – thecsc.net
Filial Therapy – nire.org
Parent Child Interaction Therapy (PCIT) – pcit.org
Relationship Enhancement Therapy – nire.org

Focalizing Therapy – www.theinstitute.org/what-is-focalizing

Developed by Michael Picucci, 'focalizing' is a therapy that aims to help clients overcome blocks with the use of an intensive form of body-focused meditation along with specific exercises.

Focusing-Oriented Therapy – www.focusingtherapy.org/for-clients

Focusing is a therapy technique that was developed by Eugene Gendlin. It involves turning one's attention to the momentary 'felt sense' and inner knowing that one can have but find hard to put into words.

Functional Analytic Psychotherapy (FAP) – societyforpsycho-therapy.org/functional-analytic-psychotherapy-fap-using-awareness-courage-love-treatment

FAP is an integrative approach to therapy that uses the therapeutic relationship as the medium through which to see what is happening for the client and help them change patterns that are no longer working for them. It blends research from the areas of social-cognitive, behavioural and neuroscientific research.

Flash Technique – flashtechnique.com/wp/

The Flash technique was developed by Philip Manfield. It is an addition to the standard EMDR protocol and a way to help clients whose traumatic memories are too painful to access.

Group Traumatic Episode Protocol (GTEP) and Recent Traumatic Episode Protocol (RTEP) – emdria.org

These protocols are used by EMDR practitioners for recent traumatic events as part of an early intervention strategy.

Gestalt Therapy – gestaltcentre.org.uk

Gestalt is an integrative psychotherapy that aims to help clients focus on the here and now and see how their patterns of relating to themselves and others affect them holistically.

Hakomi Mindful Somatic Psychotherapy – hakomiinstitute.com

'Hakomi' is a Hopi Indian word that broadly translates to 'Who am I?' This method of psychotherapy was developed by Ron Kurtz in the 1970s. It uses mindfulness and attuning to the body and emotions whilst uncovering and addressing core beliefs that keep us stuck.

Havening Technique – www.havening.org

The Havening technique was developed by Ronald Ruden. It involves recalling a traumatic experience and using distract-and-soothe techniques to concurrently distract your awareness from the trauma and soothe and calm your system down. There are no randomized controlled trials of Havening to help us understand how it might compare to other trauma therapies as yet.

Holographic Memory Resolution (HMR) – www.healingdimensions.com/about/HMRDescription.htm

HMR is a technique developed by hypnotherapist and addiction therapist Brent Baum. It combines elements of hypnotherapy, energy healing, colour therapy and somatic psychology into a brief trauma-focused approach.

Human Givens Approach – www.hgi.org.uk

The human givens approach was developed in 1997 by a group of psychologists and psychotherapists who decided to research what actually works in psychotherapy and how to blend these factors into an effective therapy. Human givens is a short-term, present-focused therapy that blends a variety of therapy techniques.

Humanistic Psychotherapy – ahpp.org.uk

Humanistic approaches to therapy such as person-centred therapy, client-centred therapy and Rogerian therapy focus on helping the individual to move towards their potential rather than seeing pathology and disorder. It is a non-directive therapy; the therapist allows the client to take the lead but provides the core conditions of warmth, empathy and unconditional positive regard within which self-healing can take place.

Hypnotherapy – www.cnhc.org.uk/hypnotherapy and see www.bscah.com

On the Complementary and Natural Healthcare Council's website (link above) you can check if the hypnotherapist you are seeing is registered with them. With so many different types of hypnotherapy training available it is important that the practitioner you see is appropriately trained. Hypnotherapy as an approach has been found to be effective for many conditions. It aims to encourage a natural state of focus and relaxation from which to work through difficulties.

Internal Family Systems therapy (IFS) – www.internalfamilysystemstraining.co.uk

IFS therapy takes the position that we all have an undamaged, core, compassionate self that can be accessed, whilst also having other parts within us that protect us, defend us or even act against our best interests sometimes. Therapy aims to access the central, core self and integrate the other parts of our system so that we are functioning from an integrated whole system.

Integral Therapy – citintegral.com/integral-psychotherapy

An approach developed by the philosopher Ken Wilber that uses a five-element model that aims to bring together ideas from the main psychotherapy orientations into a 'meta-orientation'.

Interpersonal therapy (IPT) – www.iptuk.net

IPT is a time-limited therapy that is used in the NHS for clients struggling with depression. It aims to help overcome relationship difficulties by seeing how these link with our mood.

Intensive Experiential-Dynamic Psychotherapy (IEDP) – iedta.net/edt/about-edt/types-of-edt/iedp

Developed by Ferruccio Osimo, IEDP was based on ISTDP, but places more emphasis on an exploration of the relationship between the therapist and patient.

Intensive Short-Term Dynamic Psychotherapy (ISTDP) – www.istdp.org.uk/about-istdp

Developed by the psychiatrist and psychoanalyst Habib Davanloo in the late 1960s, this adaptation to traditional psychoanalysis aims to provide the benefits of psychoanalysis but in a shorter time frame, for example 40 hours rather than 250–600 hours.

Jungian Analysis – www.jungiananalysts.org.uk

A deep analytical psychotherapy formed from the work of Carl Gustav Jung, a Swiss psychiatrist who was a contemporary of Sigmund Freud. Jungian analysis usually involves more than one session weekly and can include up to five sessions a week. It involves the gradual bringing into conscious awareness of deeper unconscious processes, sometimes with techniques such as dream journaling, art and music. Jungian analysts have to have previous experience in mental health prior to their advanced analytical training, which involves thrice-weekly personal therapy during their training.

Logotherapy – www.logotherapymap.com

Developed by Viktor Frankl as a form of existential analysis, logo-therapy (from *logos*, the Greek word for 'meaning') is a therapy that focuses on individual responsibility and finding ones true meaning and reason for living by looking at the things that block you from achieving this.

Meta Cognitive Therapy (MCT) – mct-institute.co.uk/treatment-advice

MCT was developed by Adrian Wells and Hans Nordahl and grew out of traditional CBT. It has been found to be effective for depression and anxiety and aims to work on the beliefs that keep people in a state of repetitive worry and rumination.

Mentalization-Based Treatment (MBT) – www.bpc.org.uk/professionals/kite-mark-therapist

MBT is an attachment-focused therapy that can be carried out either individually or in a group setting. It aims to help people understand their own thoughts, feelings, impulses and behaviours, as well as those of other people, in order to improve relationships.

Mindfulness-Based Cognitive Therapy (MBCT) – www.bangor.ac.uk/mindfulness/mcb.php.en

MBCT is a blend of the mindfulness work of Jon Kabat-Zinn and the cognitive science and psychotherapeutic work of Zindel Segal, Mark Williams and John Teasdale. It has been shown to be effective for depression as well as a range of other issues.

Narrative Therapy – www.theinstituteofnarrativetherapy.com

Narrative therapy was developed by David Epston and Michael White. It is an approach that considers us within our sociocultural and familial context as well as the differing contexts which make up our identity. The approach focuses on helping us to 're-author' our stories.

Neuro-Linguistic Programming (NLP) – anlp.org

NLP has been around since the 1970s and is an approach which aims to show us how we use language to understand ourselves and the world around us. Within the approach there are a range of techniques that can be used to help change the way that we think and perceive.

Personality-Guided Relational Therapy (PGRT) – iedta.net/edt/about-edt/types-of-edt/personality-guided-relational-therapy

A form of psychodynamic therapy developed by Jeffrey J. Magnavita that focuses on the processes and conflicts within four subsystems of personality: biological-intrapsychic, interpersonal-dyadic, relational-triadic, and sociocultural-familial.

Positive Psychotherapy – (PPT) – www.positum.org

PPT is a short-term therapy that blends psychodynamic, transcultural, CBT and humanistic approaches. It was developed in Germany in 1968 by Nossrat Peseschkian and is based on three principles: Hope, Balance, Consultation.

Psychoanalytical Psychotherapy – psychoanalytic-council.org

Psychoanalytical therapy is an in-depth therapy that usually takes place more than once weekly for a year or more. The psychoanalytical therapist will create an empathic but neutral relationship space for the client's unconscious patterns to come into conscious awareness. Psychoanalytical therapy was developed by Sigmund Freud.

Psychodrama – www.psychodrama.org.uk/index.php

Developed by the psychiatrist Jacob Levy Moreno in the 1920s, psychodrama is an approach that uses dramatic action and role play within a group therapy setting to bring issues into 3D space so that they can be worked through.

Psychodynamic Psychotherapy (PPT) – psychoanalytic-council.org

Psychodynamic therapy uses the same principles as psychoanalytical therapy but it tends to be briefer and can be utilized either as an individual therapy or as part of group or couple therapy.

Psycho-Organic Analysis (POA) – www.europsyche.org/ approaches/psycho-organic-analysis

POA was developed in 1975 by Paul Boyesen. It is a blend of psychoanalytic theory and body psychotherapy.

Psychosexual Psychotherapy – www.cosrt.org.uk/ psychosexual-therapy

Psychosexual therapists are usually trained not only in counselling and psychotherapy but in anatomy, physiology and pharmacology. This type of therapy blends the physical with the psychological in order to help clients in a highly specialized way.

Psychosynthesis – psychosynthesistrust.org.uk

Psychosynthesis therapy was developed by Roberto Assagioli as an extension of his psychoanalytical training in the early 1900s. Assagioli was influenced by theology and philosophy and this therapy aims to bring these extra dimensions into therapy. Psychosynthesis aims to incorporate the spiritual aspects of ourselves into therapy. It posits that we are many parts and that some of these parts have been repressed or denied. Therapy aims to help us get in touch with these lost parts of ourselves and become an integrated whole.

Rapid Transformational Therapy (RTT) – rtt.com/whatisrtt

RTT was developed by Marisa Peer and is a brief approach which utilizes specific strategies from CBT, hypnotherapy and other psychotherapy approaches.

Reality Therapy (RT) – www.wgi-uk.co.uk

Reality therapy is a counselling method that is based on William Glasser's 'choice theory'. The method focuses on how to fulfil our various needs within the context of maintaining healthy relationships with those around us.

Rational Emotive Behaviour Therapy (REBT) – www.arebt.one

Developed in 1955 by Albert Ellis, a clinical psychologist who initially trained in psychoanalysis, REBT can be thought of as the first cognitive-behavioural therapy and was a strong influence on Aaron Beck's development of cognitive therapy. In REBT the work involves targeting unhelpful beliefs that can influence our behaviour. For example, 'I'm useless' can be a belief that people feel about themselves deep down, and so they try to avoid feeling this, yet some situations can activate this feeling and cause difficulties.

Redecision Therapy –
theberne.com/redecision-therapy-training

A blend of transactional analysis and Gestalt therapy developed by Mary and Robert Goulding. It aims to help clients change the core messages that they may be carrying with them from childhood.

Regression Therapy – www.ibrt.org

Regression therapy is typically a blend of psychoanalysis and hypnotherapy. The main principle of the approach is that there are several core layers to our consciousness and therapy aims to help the person uncover the influence of past experiences. Some therapists look at past 'lives', but not all regression therapists include this as part of their practice.

Rewind Technique – www.humangivens.com/college/rewind-technique-training

The 'rewind technique' was originally called the 'visual-kinesthetic dissociation technique' and was used in neuro-linguistic programming (NLP). It was later developed into a protocol for treating trauma memories by Human Givens therapists Joe Griffin and Ivan Tyrrell.

Schema Therapy – schematherapysociety.org

Schema therapy was developed by Jeffrey Young and was a development of his work with Aaron Beck, the founder of cognitive therapy. Young saw that for some clients, the cognitive therapy model needed to go further in helping them with what he later termed 'maladaptive early schemas' – what would be called 'core beliefs' in CBT. Young focused on these schemas and discovered ways of helping clients understand how these core schemas affected their lives and led to certain coping styles. Schema therapy has become a recognized method for helping clients with longstanding difficulties. Practitioners need to be registered psychotherapists at master's/doctoral level in order to train as schema therapists.

Solution-Focused Brief Therapy (SFBT) – ukasfp.org

SFBT (also called solution-focused practice, as it is used in many settings, such as in coaching and business) grew out of the work of Steve de Shazer and Insoo Kim Berg at the Brief Family Therapy Center in Milwaukee in the 1980s. It is an approach that focuses on what is going right for you and how to harness this to achieve your goals.

Somatic experiencing – See 'Body Psychotherapies'

Sophrology – www.sophroacademy.co.uk

Sophrology is a self-help method where the focus is on certain 'dynamic relaxation' methods to help produce feelings of calmness, focus and relaxation.

Sensorimotor therapy – See 'Body Psychotherapies'

Systemic Psychotherapy – See 'Family Therapies'

Tara Rokpa Therapy – www.tararokpa.org/therapy/about/index.php

An approach that blends Western psychotherapy approaches to the mind with Buddhist traditions. It was developed by Akong Tulku Rinpoche over thirty years ago. The Tara Rokpa association is an accrediting member of UKCP.

Transactional Analysis (TA) – www.uktransactionalanalysis.co.uk and theberne.com

Transactional analysis was developed by Eric Berne in the 1950s as a way of understanding personality and the interactions between people. One of its main ideas is that we have three core ego states: Parent, Adult and Child, and that these show themselves in our communication patterns.

Theraplay – www.wp.theraplay.org/uk/for-parents

Theraplay is a child and family therapy that focuses on the parent-child interaction and helps to create positive change within this relationship for both parties.

Thought Field Therapy (TFT) – www.thoughtfieldtherapy.co.uk

TFT is a tapping technique similar to EFT but uses a more involved set of steps and algorithms in its process.

Transference-Focused Psychotherapy (TFP) – istfp.org

This approach is an adapted form of psychoanalysis which is used in the treatment of borderline personality disorder.

Transpersonal Psychotherapy – www.transpersonalcentre.co.uk/index.php/transpersonal-psychology

Transpersonal therapy aims to help us not only to understand our psychological struggles and reach a state of psychological health, but also to embrace and explore our spiritual self and the wider spiritual context within which our different states of consciousness operate.

Trauma-Focused Cognitive Behavioural Therapy (TF-CBT) – tfcbt.org/about-tfcbt

TF-CBT is a specific evidence-based protocol that was designed to be used with children and young people in association with their parents.

CHAPTER EIGHT

What to Expect from Therapy

FINDING AND ARRANGING THE FIRST APPOINTMENT

When I was looking for a therapist not so long ago, I got so caught up in the search that when I had found someone, sent the message and arranged the first appointment, I then stopped and felt a swirl in my gut and thought, 'Oh God, I've done it now, what am I going to say?!' I wanted to message her back and cancel the appointment. I had thoughts of 'I don't need to see a therapist, it's not that bad'. I realized in my mild panic how my clients must feel when they make an appointment to see me. What advice would I want to give to them? What could I say that would help them, and what could I say to myself to make sure I didn't cancel the therapist I booked to see?

'It's OK to be apprehensive. It doesn't mean you have to cancel.'

'Try it and see how it goes. You don't have to continue if it isn't right for you.'

'You deserve to give yourself this space to tell someone how you feel.'

'Maybe the fear is part of the problem: bring it with you to the session, drag it in kicking and screaming if you have to.'

'Tell the therapist how difficult it is to talk.'

I can see how in my anxiety I had the thought: 'It's not that bad, so I don't need to see a therapist.' But things do not need to be really bad to see a therapist. In fact, it's better to see one much earlier, before it gets to that point. Except that's not usually how it goes is it? We don't realize that we are struggling until we are *really* struggling. The NHS therapy services unwittingly add to this perception because you have to complete questionnaires to show how 'bad' things are for you before you can be assigned a therapist. But with the 'step' system that is in place at the moment, you should still be signposted to self-help, smartphone apps or a PWP. The message about early intervention is growing, and we all have a role to play in this. This was what I told myself in order not to cancel my therapist. To the part of me that worried I wasn't feeling 'bad' enough, I said, 'You don't need to wait until things get really bad, that's the point: it's about doing what you can to keep floating rather than waiting until you're nearly drowning.'

THE INITIAL SESSION

I was still apprehensive coming up to that first session though. But the way that I deal with this nowadays is to be curious about what is going on in my body when I have this activation. I pause and breathe; I tell myself that it is normal to be apprehensive just before I'm about to talk to a stranger about very personal things.

Apprehension is a state in which your nervous system is activated, and your body is getting ready for action. We all react differently in the lead-up to an event. For some there might be slight nausea or needing to go to the toilet a bit more, for others a feeling of irritability or poor sleep, or just feeling a bit like you're under a cloud. You might get worries about what might happen, or thoughts about cancelling – with your mind throwing up many reasons to justify doing so because of the uncomfortable feelings. Don't let this stop you, though – bring this uncomfortable feeling with you to the session. Tell the therapist how it feels. Tell them that you don't know what to say. They will know how to respond to this. Just turn up to the first session and take it as it comes, maybe even let the therapist know that you felt like cancelling. This honesty really does help in therapy.

EXPECTATIONS

The therapist may ask what you hope therapy will help you with. They ask this to get a sense of what your expectations are and to start a conversation about how to help you. There can be different reasons for accessing therapy, and in some cases people go to therapy because someone else has advised it, not because they themselves want to. This is important because if you are doing it for someone else then this will affect what you get out of therapy. If, deep down, you don't really want to do it, then you are already starting off on the back foot. If you are seeing a therapist because a court wants you to, or a social worker wants you to, or because you hope it will help with a claim for benefits or compensation, then this is a key part of your motivation and needs to be discussed openly. There can be many reasons why we are seeking therapy, and it is important to be able to have this discussion with your therapist so that you are both clear from the outset. If you and the therapist are not working to the same agenda, then this can cause frustrations and mixed messages and possibly affect whether therapy actually helps you or not. An example here would be if you saw a CBT therapist in the hope of getting rid of anxiety and never feeling it again. The therapist in question – if they haven't fully checked your expectations or you haven't been able to have that discussion together – would be hoping to help you gradually to tolerate anxiety and work with it. You would continue to do your best to push feelings of anxiety away and distract from them, while the therapist tries to keep the focus on exposure techniques: you feel you can't do it, and as a result the therapy doesn't work. The tragedy of this is when the client ends up feeling like they have failed, and it puts them off seeking therapy again.

HOW LONG IS A SESSION?

The traditional therapy 'hour' is between 50 and 60 minutes. Many therapists operate a 50-minute hour, where they see their client for 50 minutes and then write up their notes in the remaining minutes.

But not all therapists work like this: some see the client for the full 60 minutes. There is no consensus on where this 'therapy hour' came from, or what should be standard practice. The key message that I want to get across here though is that, whatever type of hour the therapist operates, that time is honoured as your time. If a session is booked for 2 p.m. until 3 p.m., then it starts at 2 p.m. and finishes at 3 p.m. You should not find yourself having to wait past your appointment time for your therapist unless there is an unexpected occurrence. Likewise, your therapist will expect you to be ready at 2 p.m., if that is when the appointment starts. The time is part of the boundary of the session, and boundaries are very important in the therapeutic relationship. Boundaries in therapy are there to give you a space that is reliable, safe and as predictable as possible. So, if you do arrange a session, make sure you are on time and preferably a few minutes early so you aren't feeling rushed. It is also helpful to give yourself an amount of time after the session before rushing back to work or on to whatever you have to do next.

EXCEPTIONS TO THE STANDARD THERAPY HOUR

In some therapies, for example EMDR therapy, there can be a need for some 90-minute sessions during the period when you and the therapist are processing traumatic experiences. This is to give adequate time for preparation, processing of traumatic memories and post-processing 'grounding and stabilization'. Within trauma-focused therapy it is vital that the therapist spends time on helping the client to reorient and ground themselves to the present prior to the end of a therapy session. It is potentially harmful to clients to leave them feeling activated and flooded with memories and emotions at the end of a session without knowing how to manage this activation. This work is called 'grounding and stabilization' and is an important part of trauma therapy work. It is important that therapists have been appropriately trained to carry out trauma-focused work with clients.

In NHS IAPT services, the 'low intensity' sessions are 30 minutes long, but are somewhat different in shape to a psychotherapy session. In a low-intensity session, the client and practitioner will review the tasks that were set in the previous session and any problems that came up and then work on the next goal. Low-intensity therapy is about providing information about mental health and emotions and setting some achievable short-term goals and learning new strategies to achieve these goals.

This is one of the areas where technology is forcing us to expand what can be offered when it comes to psychological help. Not everyone needs an hour-long in-depth therapy session. For some people, just to know a bit more about what they are experiencing and what strategies could help them cope is enough. A good example here is with worry and intrusive thoughts. For many of us that have a worry or a thought we don't like, the instinctive response is to want to block it out and not think about it. But this sets us up for a rebound of more of these thoughts because of the ironic process theory, most famously illustrated by the 'pink elephant' experiment that we have mentioned previously. A few sessions either online or face-to-face with a 'low intensity' practitioner can help to give information on how thoughts and anxiety work and how best to manage. For some people this might be all that they need. Seeing someone at an early stage like this can be vital to the prevention of more serious problems further down the line.

HOW MANY SESSIONS DO I NEED?

I am often asked, 'How many sessions will I need?' Clients want to know how long therapy is going to take, and how many sessions to budget for. The brain wants certainty, it wants to predict what's coming. But the answer is rarely if ever clear at the outset, because therapy is a very personal experience.

But it is a very valid question, especially when you consider the cost. Therapists will usually find it hard to give you an exact number if you ask in the first session, but most will ask you to commit to at least 3–6 sessions and then review. Of course, if you feel that you just don't click at all with the therapist in that first session and don't feel you are a good fit for each other, you may want to leave it at that. A good therapist should be aware of and pick up on whether you both feel you can develop a rapport with each other, and will offer you some alternatives to help you to find another therapist if this is the case.

What I would also say though is that the first session can be a time when you are feeling apprehensive – and research shows us that when we feel like this, we can interpret non-threatening and neutral things as unfriendly and aversive. So our first impressions can be more negative if we are anxious. Bear this in mind when you make your judgement.

There is some data available to show that for some clients just 1–2 sessions are enough to help them offload and focus on what the issue really is, and they then go away and deal with it. Research by the clinical psychologist Michael Hoyt estimated that the figure of clients who do not return after the first session could be between 20 and 40 per cent (Dingfelder, 2008). There are some practitioners who are starting to use the single-session model devised by Windy Dryden, where they offer clients a session as and when this is needed, rather than asking clients to sign up to a set number of sessions. Some university and college services operate in this way (BACP, 2020).

Although there is no clear rule on how many sessions you will need, I can give you some ballpark figures based on my own personal clinical experience. These are purely based on my practice, and other practitioners may think differently.

I would suggest 2–3 sessions to see if you can work with this person and this mode of therapy; 6 sessions to start to see the possibility of change and how therapy could help; 8–18 sessions to experience changes in your emotions, thoughts and behaviour; and 18 sessions or more for deeper work. These are my figures based on the way that I work, and I use EMDR, brainspotting and CBT as my main modalities. I have had clients experience deep, significant changes at session 10, and those that have felt better at session 6. I have also had clients who have completed intense deep work and experienced profound changes by session 18. It depends on the person, the issues, our relationship and the type of therapy, so unfortunately even I can't give you a one-size-fits-all number here. In other types of therapy, such as psychoanalysis, the deeper, insight-focused work would be carried out over a longer period of time. It's just a different way of working; neither is right nor wrong.

But what I would like to get across here is that whilst you shouldn't have to feel it will take forever, you also can't expect it to be a quick fix. It is always a good idea to let your mind process what happens in each therapy session at its own pace rather than trying to pressure yourself to get it over quickly. To use a home-improvement analogy, we should see therapy and looking after our emotional health as regular ongoing maintenance rather than a one-off, expensive extension that we have to gear ourselves up for and feel daunted by. The more committed you are to being curious and non-judgemental, and the more used you get to tolerating uncertainty, the quicker your change will be.

WILL I FEEL WORSE BEFORE I FEEL BETTER?

This is an important question. The answer is yes and no. You might notice negative feelings, but you also might experience that rare emotion called 'relief' too. But like with many things in life, it isn't as straightforward or as black and white as it appears. Therapy is about learning to notice, understand and manage yourself within the context of your relationships and your environment. The terms 'relationships' and 'environment' here can also include the wider places, people and lives that you feel connected to.

As you start to bring into awareness and examine your feelings, thoughts, behaviours and relationships, you may react to what you notice. It is in this space that you can then start to feel overwhelmed, confused, frustrated or even hopeless about what you become aware of. You might have thoughts about the process of noticing your thoughts itself. For example, 'Noticing my thoughts is just making me more aware of them and this is making me feel worse'; 'I don't like this feeling in my chest, so why would I want to be more aware of it?'; 'I don't want to talk about it, I just want it to go away. Why would I want therapy if it's just going to make me focus on something I want to ignore?' These are all real comments, real thoughts. They are what makes therapy such a double-edged sword, so important yet so tricky.

Therapy requires us to notice what we want to ignore and look at why we want to ignore it, in order to show us that it isn't going to harm us. Trauma-focused therapy, for example, is about showing you that you do not have to be tormented by a memory. You can learn to see it as a memory and not as a sign that the trauma is happening again. Trauma therapy helps you to process the very real physical activation that happens in your body, that makes you feel like you are reacting to that same event in the here and now. The outcome of the work should mean that you are able to have a memory triggered, and know that it happened, without having your body react as if that event is happening again right now. Your brain knows the event happened in the past and stores the memory with this time and date information too. This work can be life-changing for people, especially those who have had to avoid many things in their lives because of the uncomfortable feelings that seem to be triggered unpredictably.

Successful trauma therapy frees you from having to live in fear and avoidance. But to achieve this, the therapist and client have to work together on how much the client can tolerate. The 'window of tolerance' model is a useful way of thinking about this. We all have our own tolerance level for arousal before we feel either angry, panicked and overwhelmed, or, at the other extreme, not stimulated enough and feeling bored, flat and demotivated. This differs for everybody and it is normal. For some of us, just starting a therapy session and saying 'hello' to the therapist takes them right up to the top of their tolerance window. That is OK. It's about noticing what this feels like. It might manifest itself in a thought such as 'I can't handle this; I want to stop'. It might be a rush of a physical sensation like a whoosh of adrenaline rushing up to your head. It might be a pounding in your chest as your heart beats faster. Whatever it is, notice it. Pause. It's OK. You're at the top of your window. It's OK to say, 'Hang on, I just need to pause a moment.' Learning to feel better is about learning to let yourself 'feel' without being afraid of those emotions. Therapy is about helping you to create a space in which to do this.

FEAR OF CHANGE

Another common issue is that people to want feel better but find it extremely hard to make changes. This can show itself through subtle avoidance, or perhaps immediately dismissing something the therapist discusses with us. It can also show itself in forgetting or procrastinating over trying things agreed during a therapy session. The fact that we haven't done it then triggers thoughts and feelings of disappointment in ourselves or the therapy and we may give up. We can then feel hopeless about trying again because we see it as a failure.

It is always a good idea to consider any worries you might have about doing things differently or what would happen in your life if things did change for you. What would change look like? If you are someone who spends a long time on rituals to manage feelings of anxiety, what would you do with all the time you had available that is currently taken up with the rituals? Sometimes that can feel like a massive dark hole of uncertainty and chaos, and so it can feel easier to give in to the certainty of the rituals rather than face what might come to the surface if you don't carry them out.

It is worth thinking about how life would be different for you if things changed. Would your partner, friends and family react differently to you? Would they notice? What do you do if your changed behaviour brings you into conflict with the people around you?

An example here is a woman who struggles with very severe obsessions and compulsive rituals. She constantly needs to check that she has turned her cooker and taps off and has locked the front door at night. Her actions also affect her partner, whom she lives with. He has now become used to reassuring her that she has turned the cooker or taps off, and that she has locked the door. She repeatedly asks him, and this has become part of her ritual. His response 'reassures' her, which means that it calms her anxiety, until this anxiety is triggered again, and so begins another cycle of reassurance-seeking. It makes the woman's partner feel like he matters to her and he likes how she listens to him. He feels wanted and the dynamic of their relationship is that he is the more confi-dent one and she is less confident and trusts him more than she can trust herself.

The dynamic of their relationship is heavily influenced by the woman's anxiety and her partner's reassurance of her anxiety. In some relationships this can become very damaging, because the person with the power can use it to control the other person, either knowingly or unknowingly.

As therapy progresses and things start to change for this woman, she learns to trust herself and tolerate anxiety without seeking imme-diate reassurance from her partner. He initially experiences relief, but then starts to feel like he is not needed any more. Her increasing confidence makes him feel like he is losing her. He starts to feel less confident just as she is feeling more confident in herself. This is a point where the change in dynamics in the relationship could cause problems for the couple. But it doesn't have to. Just knowing that things might change, that the woman will be testing out different strategies and ways of being and that this doesn't mean she doesn't care for her partner can help him to support her in her journey.

HOW TO GET THE MOST OUT OF THERAPY

If you are paying for private therapy, there may be a discrep-ancy between how many sessions you can afford and how many sessions you ideally need. But there are a few ways you can get the most out of your sessions even if you do have this tension to manage.

PREPARATION

Jot down in whatever way works for you (doodle, voice note or text) the things that you are struggling with. Don't worry about grammar or making sense or having a neat list. If you want to you can use the formulation diagram from Chapter Four to order what you notice, but this isn't necessary. Make a note of what you would ideally like therapy to help you with, even if it seems impossible right now.

If you feel uncomfortable whilst doing this, notice where you feel that in your body. Pause. Take a break if you want to. It is just a feeling in your body: it doesn't have to mean anything bad is happening. Notice, label and accept. It is normal and it is OK to feel this.

Lower your expectations for the first session. Just aim to get there. Don't worry about how you express your thoughts or how things come out. Even if it feels like you don't know what to say. Bring all of this confusion with you and let it come out into the space between you and the therapist.

PROCESSING

It is normal for us to go through life without stopping to process what we are feeling and thinking. It's OK not to have the words to explain what you feel at first. This will come as you start to notice and make sense of your own system.

Outside the sessions, give yourself some time and space to process what you spoke about. Life does get in the way, but therapy works best if you don't just let the effect of that session disappear as soon as you leave the room, only picking up the thread of what you were talking about at the next session. This is easily done, though, so don't give yourself a hard time if you do. Perhaps aim to note down straight after the session the themes that stood out to you, or anything that you feel is important. Or give yourself some time to reflect later that day if you can. I tend to suggest a notebook, A4 file or journal to use for therapy, as a way to keep all the notes you make as you go through the process. This can help to be an objective marker of what was said, and some things that may not make any sense or seem to 'fit' can be things you come back to as you proceed further through your sessions. The journal can also be an important marker of change for you and can also be a helpful reminder of strategies to try during stressful periods in life.

ACTION

In CBT, the 'doing' is an important part of change. Changing behaviours is about actually trying new behaviours and experimenting to see what happens. This is an important part of other therapies too. It is the experiential part of the work. But it can become easily overlooked, and avoidance is very good at getting in the way. In CBT there are usually 'homework' or out-of-session tasks that the therapist sets in order to help clients meet this natural procrastination and avoidance head-on.

Goal-setting can be very helpful, but a modern twist on this is to work towards values instead. This is a main part of Acceptance and Commitment therapy (ACT). To do this you identify the things that you value – for example, 'family', 'good relationships with friends' and 'doing something for the community in which I live'. For these values you then identify something you could do that would be in line with one of these values, for example, arranging a day out with your family where you can all spend time together.

The 'experiential' or 'action' aspect of therapy is important for change. It's the difference between knowing something rationally and feeling it or having experienced it. I often think of grief as an example here. The lived physical experience of a wave of grief at the loss of a loved one is a very different thing from cognitively thinking about what the stages of grief are.

PACING AND THERAPY BREAKS

If weekly sessions are too much for you, do let the therapist know rather than leave without saying anything. People process differently, and I often have either fortnightly or tri-weekly appointments with some of my clients as they start to feel able to manage things on their own. Therapy should be a dynamic process that adapts to you. Make it work for you and discuss how to do this with the therapist. Taking therapy breaks is also useful too. I have had clients who have worked intensively with me and then taken a break of either a few months or a year or two, and then have come back to do some further work. They have made significant changes and have lived with these changes and 'bedded' them in before taking on further work. This can be a very effective way of working and one that creates longstanding and sustainable change.

ENDINGS

I have noticed a difference between my work in an NHS IAPT service and my work in private practice, especially when it comes to having a defined course of therapy. Because of the way that therapy works in the NHS, many clients will have a defined start and end point to their therapy, but this isn't always as clear-cut in private practice. The financial aspects of this are often a primary factor, but in general private practice clients tend to dip into and out of therapy more than they can in NHS services, and there is nothing wrong with this. It is, however, good practice to discuss the question of endings and make a plan for this rather than just stop going to therapy from one day to the next. Most if not all therapists will want to ensure you do have a planned ending to therapy. Endings can be just as important in therapy as the first session. Issues can come up in the ending of therapy that may not have arisen at all in the course of the work, or may have been discussed, but only keenly 'felt' when the actual ending occurs. As I mentioned above, there is a difference between knowing something intellectually and having a felt experience. Endings bring up feelings of loss and separation, as well as fears for the future or fears about relapse. These are important to work through, but you can do this more easily than you might think. If you are feeling anxious about the end of therapy, please mention this. It is normal to feel this way.

CHAPTER NINE

The Trouble with Therapy

A CLIENT'S VIEW OF A BAD THERAPY EXPERIENCE

I sat in front of this man who was sitting opposite me, but because it was a big room it felt like he was quite far away. He was wearing jeans and his long legs were stretched out, with one crossed over the other. He didn't say anything. I felt so uncomfortable and confused. What was I supposed to do? What should I say? Where do I start? Do they just want people to feel immediately confused and annoyed in this therapy just to see how people react?! How can that be helpful?!

I was snippy when I said, 'I don't know what to say.'

He looked at me as if he didn't like me very much.

'Well, you're here for an assessment. Your doctor thinks that you have difficulties with eating, but have also experienced other things too, like a voice at your window. What would you say to that?'

Yeah. It's true.

'Do you want to say anything about the difficulties you have with food?'

I shrug. 'OK, I suppose. Sometimes I binge and then drink loads in order to make it come back up again. I eat foods in a certain order so I can tell when I've got it all back up again. Sometimes I don't eat at all – depends on what phase I'm in.'

I don't recall the rest of the session. I just remember how cold he was.

He wrote a letter to my doctor to say that I wasn't suitable for his type of therapy, and, in the paragraph where he mentioned my eating, I will never forget how he misinterpreted what I had told him in the session. He wrote 'she drinks alcohol excessively'. It just seemed obvious to me that drinking loads to help me purge the food meant drinking water or juice or milk, but to him it meant alcohol. He had made an assumption about me that was not true. If he had really listened, he would have heard that as someone desperately concerned with calories there was no way I would drink alcohol. I was on a mission to reduce calories at all cost. Alcohol was empty calories so was simply out of the question. To me it was a horrible chemical that I detested for other reasons too. It destroyed my parents' marriage. This therapist didn't know any of this but still recorded his assumption in my notes, and I knew that I couldn't challenge it, because who would take my word over his? I was just a psychotic psychiatric patient to them.

The message to therapists here is to be mindful of how uncomfortable the initial session is for clients and to help them ease into the session. Always check your assumptions, especially if you are writing in the person's medical notes, check the accuracy of what you are saying and check your attitude to the client as you are writing the notes.

Be mindful of how you come across. Modern neuroscience tells us now that clients who have suffered from adverse childhood experiences (ACEs) are wired to live in unpredictable and threatening environments. In order to cope they become vigilant for threat. This hypervigilance can make even neutral environments seem threatening. Have you ever noticed that when you feel anxious, your senses are sharper, and you can be quicker to assess and judge things? Like how you can feel absolutely fine about turning the lights out and going to bed one night, but then the next night, after watching a horror or thriller, you turn the lights out and suddenly the darkness seems immediately threatening and you quickly rush to bed.

When we feel anxious, even a neutral expression on someone's face can be misinterpreted as threatening.

CAN I SEE A THERAPIST IF I'M FEELING SUICIDAL?

This sounds like a strange question really, doesn't it? You might think that if you are struggling so much and feeling suicidal that of course you should see a therapist. Except that there are therapists who would say that you are not suitable for therapy if you are feeling suicidal, because therapy is hard work and you need to be stable to undertake it. If you are seeking NHS therapy you have to score a certain amount on a questionnaire to show 'caseness'. However, if you are suicidal and in crisis then you will be directed to the crisis team and not therapy. In one sense it is right that people need to be supported through a crisis. This immediate short-term support is different to working on specific issues in a detailed way in therapy. But what too often happens is that crisis services are overstretched and offer a minimum of support. They often don't employ therapists who can offer a place for clients to safely offload and talk through what is happening for them. Therapists and counsellors are told to risk-assess and refer suicidal clients to crisis teams and can struggle to help a client access crisis support. Instead of a smooth, calm, confident and helpful route to managing suicidal clients we instead can have a panicked, urgent struggle.

The ideal would be smoother transitions between crisis support and therapy services, as well as more therapeutic support available in crisis teams. But we also need an overall emergency mental health service structure that can put an end to people being brought to A&E when they are struggling emotionally. The other side of this is that we need to do better at making support and therapy available to people earlier, rather than having people wait until they are thinking about ending their lives.

As of 2019, prior to COVID-19, suicide was the leading cause of death in men under the age of 50. In 2019 there were 5,691 suicides registered in England and Wales. The figure only included those whose death was recorded as suicide, and the true number is therefore known to be higher, as many suicides are recorded as 'accidental death' or 'misadventure'. An inquest has to determine that a person intended to kill themselves, and it is often very hard to know someone's intent. Often people who kill themselves will not notify anyone of their intent before the final attempt. Of the 5,691 deaths that were registered as suicides, three quarters of that figure were males (ONS, 2020). Every one of these deaths is a tragedy in its own way. I find it incredibly sad when I see a snippet of a news item about someone found dead in a certain place and then I read the sentence: 'here are believed to be no suspicious circumstances.' This tells me that the person may have died by their own hand. But there is usually no more said, nothing more reported about this person, unless they are a celebrity, in which case there is much curiosity about why that person died. But what about the unknown people who have slipped away from life while in the midst of their own pain, believing that nothing and no one could have helped? Should we just forget? Aren't their stories important to try to piece together somehow? Maybe, but how can we when the person isn't there any more? I think we need to do better at asking people earlier, at hearing people's stories.

This is an area where many therapists can struggle, and is often a weak spot for therapy services, as can be seen above in the therapist's example. The British Association for Counselling & Psychotherapy (BACP) has set out guidelines for working with suicidal clients (BACP, 2018), and their guidance does provide some advice for therapists on what they can do to provide tangible help for suicidal clients. It includes the standard elements of risk assessment, such as assessing intent and prior history, any protective factors that help keep a client alive and working with the person to draw up a safety plan. But it also importantly highlights giving the person a space to talk about and explore their thoughts and feelings and the meaning of these thoughts for them, without feeling they will be judged.

Whilst it is true that you wouldn't commence a course of trauma-focused therapy with a suicidal client, there are things that you can do to work with the client to manage how they feel and help them to stabilize themselves. I believe that we should not turn clients away and tell them they are not suitable. We should have the skills to be able to support them at their lowest point. There are exceptions, of course, such as when a client is actively suicidal and needs urgent help right now, or a therapist feels out of their depth and has not had the appropriate training in how to work with a suicidal client – although, frankly, this training should be mandatory for therapists.

Suicidal thoughts and feelings can make us panic and not know what to do. As a result, the person who has these thoughts can feel worried about making others panic and will then keep how they feel to themselves. This is the space where isolation can make the person feel even more lonely and cut off, and their feelings can worsen. It is no coincidence that men can find it hard to talk about their feelings, and men have higher suicide rates than women. The fear of talking is deadly.

THE DOUBLE STIGMA THAT AFFECTS HEALTH PROFESSIONALS AND PUBLIC FIGURES

On a gusty October morning in 1998, my partner Richard and I sat at the bottom of the stairs in our rented house. Him on the second step, head in hands, and me on the floor with my back to the wall. We were waiting for a phone call.

'I think I'd like to work in a shop.'

'Yes,' I smiled, trying not to pressure him with my hopefulness. 'You can.'

'I can't, though – I'm supposed to be a doctor.'

Just six weeks after this conversation, he took his own life.

Richard had been suffering with depression and OCD since the age of fourteen. His intelligence, personality and family tradition led him into a job that ramped up his already weighty sense of responsibility and desire always to do the right thing. His father, mother and brother were all doctors too. The pressure was real for him. But the invisible cages we become locked in can often be more harmful. Nowhere is this more painfully true than in depression. Depression is many things. It is a bundle of variable signs and symptoms, it has numerous causes, it can affect all groups of people, and each one of us can travel a very different road into and out of it. But the one defining feature of the killer inside depression is its ability to make us believe that there is no hope. This is when it takes the lead. This is when the thought 'what's the point?' becomes a belief that there is no point, that things will never change. That even if things do change, it doesn't matter anyway, because the depression will come back, and you will never be free of it.

This is more than just a thought. This belief becomes a real physical feeling that shuts you down physically and psychologically. But what we do not know at these times, and what depression forbids us from seeing, is that feelings change. Yes, there will always be problems, but there will also be a whole range of other things too: good, bad, life-affirming, awesome, neutral, irritating, inspiring, loving and all things in between. Under normal circumstances, the way that we *feel* about what is taking place in our lives can and will change, but when we are depressed, we tell ourselves that we will always feel depressed. Depression needs absolutes because it cannot tolerate uncertainty.

If you notice this feeling, please know that depression is talking to you from a dark place where it can see no light. Please let someone know. If the fear creeps in to tell you that you can't tell anyone how you feel because of what they may think, or what it may mean, or that something bad will happen, please know that fear is not the enemy here. Fear is where your energy is.

Imagine picking up the phone right now and calling the Samaritans. Do you think 'I can't do that!' or 'I don't know what to say!'? Notice that rush in your centre, notice that gripping feeling in your gut. Notice what is happening in your body right now. That is activation in your nervous system. It is energy. Follow the ball of uncertain energy. Pick up your phone and unlock it, then put it down. Pick it up again, unlock it, then dial the number. It could be the Samaritans or someone's number that you have been given to call. Tell them that you are struggling. Tell them that you feel embarrassed. Shame keeps us silent and struggling, but shame cracks when we speak its name. Notice what is happening in your body right now. The twisting, gnawing sensation in your gut, or the pain in your heart. Notice that. It is activation; energy. Just notice it and sit with it without giving it a negative label.

I know it isn't easy, and I also know that everyone's situation is different. What I have just written will not feel relevant to everyone who reads it. But in the hope that somebody needs to hear this right now I believe it is important to say: you are worth saving. Don't deny yourself the help that you would gladly offer to others.

It is OK not to know, it is OK to be uncertain. Depression believes that things will never change because it hates uncertainty. But uncertainty is not an enemy. Things do change and sometimes we cannot do anything about that. Let it go, don't try to control what you cannot change.

As healthcare professionals we are great at giving the message to others about how important it is to seek help: 'Don't suffer in silence'; 'It's OK not to be OK'; 'Talk to someone.' But it is far easier to say this to another person than it is to do it ourselves. I have this conversation with my clients frequently. They tell me how they tell their friends it is OK to talk, but for them it feels different. It feels like they can't talk, they can't tell anyone, no one would listen, or they wouldn't know what to say. Or their job would be affected.

We need to tell ourselves that it is OK.

Our judgements about what mental health is and isn't are relevant here. Due to a fear of being called crazy or weak, we are afraid to talk about how we feel. Because of this fear we catastrophize emotions, and we panic if people are struggling. We resort to a default of avoiding and distracting ourselves from emotions until things build up inside and explode. Some of us disappear into alcohol or drugs, some into OCD, some into eating disorders, and some cope by playing sport. We all find our way to work through our inner conflicts, and things keep going in this way. We never confront the elephant in the room: emotions, and how to actually manage them.

That is a general statement, I know. There are many healthcare professionals who do seek help, and there is more understanding and support available now. But for many professionals, especially, though not exclusively, in healthcare, asking for help feels like something they tell others to do but cannot do themselves. As Dr Clare Gerada stated in her article about doctors and mental health, 'help me' can be extremely hard to say. Dr Gerada has headed up the NHS Practitioner Health Programme since 2008 (www.practitionerhealth.nhs.uk). The programme aims to provide psychological support and therapy to doctors and was set up following the death of Dr Daksha Emson and her baby daughter Freya in 2000.

A report by the Society of Occupational Medicine in 2018 found that doctors were at greater risk of suicide and poor mental health than the general population. But they looked further into some of the reasons for this. They found that poor work-life balance and long hours, coupled with excessive workloads and sometimes bullying and harassment, led to a culture where doctors felt they had to 'put up and shut up', otherwise they'd be considered weak, a failure and unable to cope. All of this pressure keeps doctors silent and struggling until it is too late. The chartered psychologists who authored the report were keen to point out that although it focused on doctors, they believed the findings were relevant to other professions also (Kinman & Teoh, 2018).

The 'Surviving Work' and 'Surviving Work in Healthcare' websites (survivingwork.org and survivingworkinhealth.org) have reported findings of a recent survey of IAPT workers. It found that the wellbeing of IAPT workers is being affected by high caseloads and pressure to produce results.

The expectations that we can have on others and on ourselves can force us into a state of feeling like we have to cope with the pressure, and if we don't then that means we are weak, and that we have failed. This is not acceptable. When workloads are unmanageable, and when staff are feeling stressed, this is when we need to look at our expectations, and at the workload, rather than giving lessons in 'time management' and telling people they need to be more resilient. Collectively it is time to have a conversation about the fact that as humans we have limits on what we can process and cope with in a day, and these limits will also vary according to the person.

For those working in responsible positions and who feel they should know what to do and should somehow be immune to difficulties: you are human, you are not immune. The suicide of Gregory Eells in September 2019 is a reminder of this. Eells was Head of Counselling and Psychotherapy at the University of Pennsylvania. He was not immune. None of us are.

The psychotherapist Stacey Freedenthal who has written about her own struggles when she felt suicidal (Freedenthal, 2017), is not immune. None of us are.

The 5,691 people who died by suicide in 2019 were not immune either. None of us are. In the appendix for this chapter I have gathered together a list of all the mental health resources I could find that offer help to people in specific occupations.

MENTAL HEALTH IN THE PUBLIC EYE

In 2019 in the UK, on ITV at primetime, Ant and Dec stopped their show to make a statement about the importance of looking after our mental health. This came around the same time that Prince William and Prince Harry were also opening up about their struggles. This was a major TV channel, with two well-known presenters, and two figureheads of the royal establishment, talking about a subject that used to be taboo. This was and is important in our sociocultural concepts of what mental health is and whether we can mention it. These people were standing up to say that we can talk about it. We need to keep hearing this message until we can put into practice what it is really saying. This is the difficult part. It is much easier to say 'it's OK to talk' than actually talk about how you feel.

In September 2020, TV presenter and ex-England cricketer Freddie Flintoff spoke on BBC1 at 9 p.m. about living with the eating disorder bulimia. In the documentary you could see the conflict within Freddie as he spoke about his 'coping strategy' and about how he started to think about the possibility of change. It was clearly very scary for him, but this is how it can be for many of us. We have heard the message that you can get help and you can change, but in practice when you look at stepping off the train it can feel like you are about to lose your footing and fall into an abyss. We could hear this fear in Freddie's words: 'I know the best thing is to get help, so why am I not doing it?'

Fear. It is fear. It is very definitely not weakness. It is a fear of being vulnerable and losing control, but it is quite the opposite of weakness. What we have done though over the years is equate vulnerability with weakness. We have become collectively afraid and we have shamed ourselves and others. Freddie was already publicly shamed by the tabloid newspapers for his weight when he was a cricketer. The thought of opening up to someone in order to talk is terrifying after this.

As Freddie says, 'The strength is being able to say something.' Strength is looking right into the fast-moving swirl of what might happen if you let yourself get upset and doing it anyway. You are not alone. You are not wrong. Don't let shame keep you locked in silence. Call it out.

It does help to hear famous people's stories, like Freddie Flintoff's, David Harewood, Dwayne 'The Rock' Johnson, Vinnie Jones and Emma Stone, to name just a few of the well-known people who have spoken out publicly. As we hear more people talk about their stories, we can see that we are not alone with ours. There is someone else out there who has felt how you feel now, who has struggled like you are now, who felt that they had to keep silent. You are not alone in feeling this way, so don't isolate yourself. Even if you have had an unhelpful experience with therapy, or you are a therapist yourself. There will be a group of people out there whom you can share this with. There will be others who have felt the same way. Most importantly, even if you are scared about what might happen, a therapist will help you to find your voice, step by step. Just take the first one.

With COVID-19 and lockdown restrictions, mental health has hovered close to the surface as something that we are all aware of as we struggle to juggle and accommodate extra demands and pressures. Coupled with this is the dramatic shift in the spaces within which we live and work. This topic deserves more than a chapter in itself, as it is well known in environmental psychology that our wellbeing is intricately linked with our environment and the places and contexts within which we operate. For now, I'd just like to say that the physical spaces we work and operate within are part of our psychology too. If you work in the same room that is usually a walkway or transient space, such as a hallway or bathroom for example, or even a hotel room, then it will have this transient and anticipatory effect on you. This might help you to feel activated enough to work, or it might be an addition to the activation and apprehension that you already have to deal with. Context is important. Spaces are important.

Our brains have had an incredible amount to accommodate in 2020 and beyond. I hope that we can take account of this at some level and at the least keep mental health at the forefront of our minds in our daily lives and in our communications with others. We can be so quick to judge, so sharp in our assessments, especially – as we mentioned above – when we are anxious. Let's be mindful of this if we can and notice the judgements that we are making of ourselves and others. Most, if not all of us will have things to process as a result of recent events.

THERAPEUTIC HELP IN PSYCHIATRIC UNITS

When people are admitted to psychiatric units, it is at a time in their life when they are in utter crisis, often at the lowest point they could get. Yet the consensus seems to be that they are in crisis and so are not appropriate for 'therapy'. This is somewhat true. However, this is taking a rather one-sided view of therapy and what it is. A therapist, particularly a trauma-focused therapist, could help the client to ground and stabilize and manage how they 'currently' feel. They could give the person a space to talk about what is happening for them currently and the chaos that they feel in their lives at that moment. The therapist could help them 'frame' what is happening for them right now, and notice what makes things worse or better, along with what coping skills they have that could help, and what support and resources could help them. Psychoeducation and coping strategies are important elements of therapy too. Therapy should not just be for when clients are 'stable'. Crisis therapy is vital too. This is when people are at their most desperate, some with very few reliable support networks to call on. A therapeutic relationship at this point could make a huge difference. Too often the stories we hear are of traumatic experiences with inpatient admissions or people left alone whilst at their most vulnerable. This should not happen. We need to help clients to be better informed about what is and is not right in therapy. We need to empower people to speak out about their experiences, and above all we need as therapists to fight for better therapeutic services for people, especially those in crisis and in psychiatric units.

Therapy for psychosis

An area where we see this tension the most is with those people who are experiencing psychotic symptoms. Whilst it is important to ensure that as therapists we are working within our capacity, sometimes the system can make us label people as 'unsuitable' for therapy when this does not do anything at all to help that person. The view that people who experience psychotic experiences are not suitable for therapy is not helpful. Yes, there are some clients who have a drug-induced psychotic illness that clears once they have been through a therapeutic withdrawal from that drug, but for others we have more than enough data now to show how their lived experiences do have meaning. The dominant model in psychiatry has involved diagnosis and medication, but this is being strongly challenged at the moment. Two projects that are currently in operation are the Open Dialogue project and the Power Threat Meaning Framework.

The Open Dialogue Project – www.nelft.nhs.uk/aboutus-initiatives-opendialogue

This is an approach that was pioneered in Finland but is currently being tested in the NHS in the UK. All staff involved in the care of clients are trained in family therapy and psychological skills. The approach aims to work with the network that the person is within and not just seeing issues as only that person's problem. It takes a systems approach in order to help in a holistic and sustainable way.

The Power Threat Meaning Framework

Over the past five years a group of clinical psychologists have been working to produce an alternative way of understanding people's difficulties as a way of challenging the medical model in psychiatry. The framework set out by Lucy Johnstone and her colleagues is called the 'Power Threat Meaning Framework' (PTMF). The PTMF aims to be a realistic alternative to the current medical model of psychiatric diagnosis and medication. It puts a psychological and psychotherapeutic focus at the heart of a client's suffering.

In many ways the PTMF echoes what Thomas Szasz called for over 50 years ago.

- What happened to you?
- How have these experiences affected you?
- What did you do to cope?
- What strengths do you have?
- What sense do you make of all of this and what is the story that you tell yourself?

(adapted from Johnstone & Boyle, 2018)

The authors hope that the PTMF, which has been endorsed by the British Psychological Society, will be adopted by clinicians working in mental health settings, and provide an alternative to the dominant model which pathologizes and labels people.

OTHER ISSUES WITH THERAPY

Here are just some of the issues that we can come up against in therapy:

FEELING OVERWHELMED AFTER EACH SESSION

If you are leaving a therapy session feeling overwhelmed and in a high state of arousal, then this is not how things should be. It is important that your therapist paces the session appropriately for you and helps you manage any subjects that come up so that you are not feeling too overwhelmed like this. Of course, there can be sessions where something unexpected comes up towards the end of the hour, but if this is the case the therapist should help you to manage and regulate the emotions that come up for you. If you are finding that this is happening frequently, and the therapist does not seem to know how to help you cope with this, then it is important this is discussed with the therapist. If you do not feel that your concerns are being addressed, then please do speak with the therapy body concerned.

NOT SURE ABOUT THIS TYPE OF THERAPY

Some types of therapy involve very different ways of working. Where a CBT therapist would be quite active, directive and problem-focused, a person-centred therapist would go with what you wanted to discuss and aim to be non-directive as an important part of the therapy. These two types are quite opposite in that sense, and as a result you may find that you just don't get on with a certain style of therapy. There is absolutely nothing wrong with this. So tell yourself it is OK and let the therapist know that at this time you're not sure that this type of therapy is hitting the spot for you. You can always come back and try that therapy again. This brings me on to my next point.

FEEL LIKE I'M NOT GETTING ANYWHERE. IT'S LIKE A COFFEE MORNING WHERE I DROP IN FOR A CHAT

The 'non-directive' and person-centred counselling that we mentioned above can feel quite unstructured, because it is meant to be. It is about helping you to talk about what matters to you right now, and for the therapist not to interfere with their directions. There can be times when this type of therapy is advised and times when it isn't. If you have experienced trauma, then a trauma-focused therapy is advisable, so look for this in your therapist's description of their skills. That being said the therapeutic relationship is a vital component of successful therapy. For some clients who feel alone or disconnected, it may be the case that a safe, supportive place to offload is just what they might benefit from.

TOO MUCH GOING ON IN MY LIFE, NOT ENOUGH SPACE FOR THERAPY

I have seen many clients who have gone through actively traumatic events in their lives, for example those who have escaped from violent regimes to a foreign country, away from family and children, and who are still in danger. Sometimes there can be so much going on that there really is no time and no space psychologically or physically for therapy. This is OK. We spoke earlier about crisis therapy and the need for a provision for this type of holding space for clients, to help them find ways of grounding and stabilizing what is happening for them. This is not always available, sadly.

Basic needs come first. We have to get a roof over our head, find food and water, warmth, clothing and family first. But it is important to be aware that if you want to start therapy, you should try to make the space and time for it. You are important. Prioritize yourself if you can.

FEEL LIKE I'M THINKING ABOUT THE THERAPIST TOO MUCH. AND IS IT NORMAL TO HAVE INTIMATE THOUGHTS ABOUT MY THERAPIST?

Yes, this is part of something that is called 'transference'. Not every therapy will refer to it as this or see it in the same way, but it is common for you to start to think about your therapist as a person, as a man or a woman, and relate to them as you might relate to other similar figures in your life. There could be many facets to this. They might remind you of a schoolteacher, in which case this might bring up feelings and thoughts and memories from when you were at school and how you felt when you were in that teacher's presence at school. They might remind you of one of your parents, in which case you might find yourself relating to them in a specific way because of this. Or you might find yourself feeling attracted towards them or think about certain things that they said or did in the session. This is normal and it can be very helpful if you notice this and tell yourself that it is normal. It can be helpful if it is brought into therapy, especially in psychodynamic therapies. Transference, and its counterpart, 'counter-transference' – when the therapist finds themself relating to the client in a particular way – are important in helping us figure out what triggers us and what patterns we are getting caught in. Therapists bring their experiences of 'counter-transference', or 'parallel process' as it is also called, to their clinical supervision.

I DON'T LIKE MY THERAPIST

This problem is similar to the previous one. If you are having strong feelings of dislike towards your therapist, then it is possible that you and they are not going to be able to work together. The therapeutic relationship is vital to the success of therapy, and you cannot work effectively together if you don't like each other! However, that being said, it is possible that it could work. If for example the therapist reminded you of your mother, with whom you did not have a good relationship, and you were able to tell the therapist this, and the therapist helped you work through these feelings – without treating you in the same way that your mother did – then this could be a very helpful therapeutic relationship. But it is all about that rapport between you; if you do not have that then it will be very hard work for you both.

HOW MUCH SHOULD I SAY ABOUT MY THERAPY SESSION TO MY PARTNER, FRIENDS AND FAMILY?

Outside your therapy session you may want to tell those close to you how you are getting on in therapy, and this can often be very helpful. It helps to break down myths about therapy and enables people to find out more about how it is helping you. But you shouldn't feel like you have to talk about your sessions. They are your private space to talk and reflect on how you feel, so it is up to you how much or how little you say. The therapist you see will not discuss any details of the sessions with anyone other than their clinical supervisor (and cases will be coded in supervision so that no identifying details can be traced to you). Confidentiality is a vital component to therapy. You have to feel that you can trust the therapist to keep what you discuss private. However, there are some exceptions when confidentiality may be broken and these should be made clear to you at the start of therapy. This is if there is a risk to yourself or others, or if there is concern about the welfare of a child, information about money laundering or acts of terrorism or serious crime.

WHAT SHOULD I DO IF I FEEL I AM BEING INTERROGATED BY MY PARTNER OR FAMILY MEMBER TO GIVE THEM EVERY DETAIL OF THE SESSION?

If you feel that your partner or family member is forcing you to tell them every detail about the session and you are unable to have this private space to talk about how you feel, please let your therapist know. It is really important to be aware that controlling and coercive behaviour like this could be a sign of abuse. Have a look at this link: www.nationaldahelpline.org.uk. I really hope that you are not experiencing this, but if you are, please let someone know.

I'VE SEEN MY THERAPIST OUTSIDE THE THERAPY ROOM. WHAT SHOULD I DO?

Usually, the therapist will take the lead from the client if this hasn't been discussed and agreed in the sessions beforehand. If you smile or nod, they will too. If you look away, they will not acknowledge you, so as to maintain confidentiality. It is usual for therapist and client to have agreed in session that if they see each other outside the session unexpectedly then they will either nod or acknowledge each other with a smile or brief 'hello' and leave it at that. If you do get into a conversation, the therapist will usually aim to bring the chat to a close so as to keep that therapeutic boundary for you both.

I'VE HAD THERAPY IN THE NHS, BUT I STILL NEED HELP

In Chapter Seven we saw how the IAPT primary care mental health therapy service (primary care being something that you access as a first step either yourself or from referral by your GP), has different 'steps' to it. At the Step 2 level you will be seen either in a group or by a PWP (psychological wellbeing practitioner). PWPs are trained to deliver what is called 'low intensity' CBT. You will be given six 30-minute sessions with the PWP. At Step 3 clients will have up to 12 sessions with a CBT therapist or counsellor. Now for some people this really is all that is needed. But of course, this is not for everyone. The NHS has to budget somehow and tries to offer what it can. We need to be compassionate here towards ourselves and the services. Let's assume that everyone is doing the best that they can. The IAPT service was set up to help. It may need improvements, but its overall aim was to help offer more options to mental health services in primary care. But if you have had 6–12 sessions and they haven't touched the surface for you, what can you do?

Well, in therapy, we talk about it being a 'process'. What if these sessions started a 'process' for you? They got you thinking about what might be wrong, or helped you to notice a pattern of thoughts, feelings or behaviours. They may not have helped you to feel completely better, but they may have shifted you in some small way from the position you were in before. This can be something seemingly small like believing that you do want to get help. Change takes time and small shifts can create lasting change in the brain. Find something useful to take from the sessions if you can. Make it work for you.

WHAT TO DO IF THINGS DON'T GO AS EXPECTED

In therapy things may not always go the way that you expect. This is partly normal, although there can be other factors at play. We talked about differing expectations earlier, but there can be other reasons why things don't go how you had hoped. If you are feeling unsure in any way about your therapist or the type of therapy, unless you or the therapist obviously did something wrong, don't blame yourself or them. See it as just not the right fit for you and try someone else or a different type of therapy. If the therapist did something you are not sure about or that made you feel uncomfortable, do let them know. Hopefully you can tell them directly, but if it is more serious or you are unsure, then please do inform the body that they are registered with. If you find this hard, and it can be hard, there are mental health advocacy projects that can help you to contact these organizations.

Unfortunately, a bad experience in therapy can put people off trying again. In some cases, it can cause real harm to clients. In Chapter Eleven we will look at the evidence for the effectiveness of therapy, but also the studies that show how therapy can sometimes cause harm.

I HATE THERAPY – WHAT ARE THE OTHER OPTIONS?

Talking to one person is not the only way to feel better. There are group sessions, there is non-talking therapy, there are activities that are not therapy but can be very therapeutic, such as yoga, sound therapy and expressive writing.

In the next chapter we will take a look at some of ways that therapy has expanded recently. It's no longer the case that we only have one way of doing things. Therapy is not just about being in one room face to face with one person. It can be a walk in a forest, writing out how you feel as part of a group or feeling a sense of connection and calmness from interacting with an animal. It can also be about having technology show you what is going on inside your brain and body. We saw in Chapter Seven just how many different types of talking therapies there are, but now we have other methods that are proving to be effective. You have a large menu to choose from when it comes to finding the right mix for you.

CHAPTER TEN

Cyber Therapy, Blended Therapy and, er... Forest Bathing?! Alternatives to Standard Therapy Approaches

As I write this chapter, in September 2020, I have moved 'online therapy' out of the 'alternative' therapy section as it is now one of the main ways that therapists are continuing to operate in this post-pandemic world. Prior to March 2020 I had listed it as an alternative mode of therapy that not every therapist practised. Video-call therapies using platforms such as Zoom, Meet, Skype or Teams are now the norm in many therapy practices. Whichever video-conferencing software is used, this form of therapy has been found to be just as effective as face-to-face therapy. It doesn't suit everyone, but it can offer some benefits over and above face-to-face therapy. The client can remain in their own environment. This can be a plus or a minus for some people, but it can save on travel time and allow you to stay in an environment you feel comfortable in.

The main issue with video platforms is security and confidentiality. The therapist should aim to use a platform that is end-to-end encrypted and take steps to mediate any security breaches. They should have a policy on security and confidentiality. Check for this as it shows that they are aware of the risks and are taking steps to ensure their sessions are as secure and confidential as possible.

Telephone and text-based therapies are also becoming commonplace, particularly amongst CBT therapists. However, there has also been a swell of outdoor therapies, of which forest bathing is the most well known. In this chapter I want to list a number of these alternatives to traditional talking therapies. I hope that so far you can see that when it comes to therapy, you have many choices open to you!

ALTERNATIVE PSYCHOLOGICAL THERAPIES

Animal-Assisted Therapy – www.scas.org.uk/animal-assisted-interventions/accreditation-and-qualifications

Horses, dogs, cats, goats and even chickens are being utilized as part of outdoor therapy approaches which have nature and connection at their heart. The science of social connection and attachment supports this approach as our bonds with animals can provide us with many benefits psychologically.

Art Therapy and Art Psychotherapy – www.baat.org/About-BAAT/What-we-do

Art therapy/art psychotherapy (the terms are used interchangeably) is a state-regulated profession in the UK. Art therapists are regulated by the HCPC, so only a therapist with the appropriate training and registration can call themselves an 'Art therapist'. Art therapists are practising artists who also have training in psychotherapy – usually with a psychodynamic focus. It can be a very powerful non-verbal approach. Have a look at some of the comments from people who have experienced the approach here: www.baat.org/About-Art-Therapy/Art-Therapy-service-users-share-their-experiences.

See also Sensorimotor Arts Therapy – www.sensorimotorart-therapy.com/sensorimotor-art-therapy

Autogenic Training – www.autogenic-therapy.org.uk and www.autogenictraining.org

Autogenic training involves sets of repetitive exercises in combination with the assessment and feedback of what is happening in the body. It's aim is to promote mindful relaxation and stress reduction.

Bibliotherapy, 'the Ancient Art of Book-Healing" – www.relit.org.uk

We don't just read for pleasure. We read to understand, to learn, to be surprised, to find hope and to feel a bit less alone in the world. Reading and listening to stories can enrich our lives in so many ways. Being part of a book club helps us share stories and feel connected with others, and reading for wellbeing is also part of this movement towards harnessing the power of reading.

Here are some of the organizations and projects that are involved in bibliotherapy:

Books on prescription – reading-well.org.uk/books/
books-on-prescription/mental-health
The 'Overcoming' series – overcoming.co.uk/14/Help-for-Mental-Health
The Emergency Poet – emergencypoet.com/about/ and The Poetry
Pharmacy – www.poetrypharmacy.co.uk/
The Poetry Pharmacy – A book by William Sieghart, founder of
National Poetry Day and the Forward Prize. – www.penguin.co.uk/
authors/132348/william-sieghart.html?tab=penguin-books
Quiz – 'What is your poetry prescription?' www.penguin.co.uk/
articles/2017/poetry-pharmacy-quiz
Shared reading – www.thereader.org.uk/what-we-do

Biofeedback, Heart-rate Variability (HRV) and Neurofeedback

Psychophysiological methods are starting to be utilized by some psychotherapists. Advances in neuroscience are indicating potentially exciting avenues of integration between the brain and body, and between our relationships, environment and psychological functioning.

Blended Therapy

Blended therapy is where you have the support of a therapist or wellbeing practitioner whilst completing certain therapy modules online. You will have an assessment of what you are struggling with and the therapist will help you to set some goals for what you hope to get out of the sessions. The therapist will then help select relevant modules for you to work through and you will have review sessions to talk through how you are getting on. SilverCloud is a programme that is often used in blended CBT practice.

CBWT – Cognitive Behavioural Writing Therapy

CBWT was developed by Arnold van Emmerik as 'Interapy' and was later expanded to Internet-Based Cognitive Behavioural Writing Therapy (IB-CBWT). As a technique it is a combination of expressive writing therapy, trauma-focused therapy and cognitive behavioural therapy for trauma. In a multi-centre randomized controlled trial in 2017, it was found to be as effective as EMDR for children between the ages of 8 and 18. (Roos et al., 2017).

Cyber Therapy

This is a name that is synonymous with 'online therapy'. There are several training courses for therapists to gain skills in online working. Some use the term 'online therapist' whereas others use the term 'cyber therapist'.

Dance and Movement Therapy – admp.org.uk

Dance therapy involves helping to regulate feelings using the movements of the body. It is an integrative practice that uses the medium of the body rather than talking.

Dramatherapy – badth.org.uk

Dramatherapists are artists and clinicians and dramatherapy is the therapeutic use of theatre and dramatic arts as a psychological therapy. It makes use of a range of artistic mediums such as puppetry, mask work, story and improvisation.

Expressive Writing Therapy – See Writing and Wellbeing

Hellerwork Structural Integration – hellerwork.com/what-is-hellerwork

Hellerwork is a body-based method of structural integration that aims to integrate body, mind and movement.

Holistic Therapies

This book is about psychological therapy, which is focused on the use of psychological theories to help people who are struggling with their mental health. I have not been able to include the vast array of holistic therapies that are available, although it is fair to say that many of these have psychological effects. If you are looking for a holistic practitioner, the Complementary and Natural Healthcare Council (CNHC) provides an independent register of complementary healthcare practitioners (www.cnhc.org.uk).

Journal Therapy – See Writing and Wellbeing

Music Therapy – www.bamt.org/music-therapy/what-is-music-therapy/mental-health-care.html

Through improvised music rather than talking, music therapy can be an aid to feelings and help people to communicate in alternative ways to traditional talking therapies.

Online CBT

Text-based, Synchronous Instant Messaging

The traditional face-to-face, one-on-one therapy model has been shifting since 2010 but has accelerated in the last five years. COVID-19 restrictions forced many therapists into online and phone sessions with clients; however, a substantial number of therapists were already working online. The company IESO (formerly Psychology Online) has been offering text-based, instant-messaging therapy since 2014. The client and therapist communicate by typing into an instant message chat screen.

Online Programmes – Asynchronous (work through it in your own time)

Other companies such as SilverCloud also offer online CBT modules to clients. SilverCloud offers a series of self-contained programmes that you can work through. For example, CBT for depression would take you through a series of modules all based around different CBT strategies, such as thinking patterns, core beliefs and how they affect us, and behavioural aspects of depression.

In the NHS these online CBT modules are routinely used in practice along with telephone therapy, video therapy and the newer virtual reality therapy.

The MIND website lists other programs available as alternatives to SilverCloud: www.mindcharity.co.uk/online-self-help-programmes-websites-resources.

Email and Message App Therapy (Asynchronous, not an instant reply)

There are also some therapists who offer text-based therapy via email or messaging apps such as Signal.

Outdoor Therapy

Ecotherapy – www.goodtherapy.org/learn-about-therapy/types/econature-therapy

Ecotherapy is a generic term for doing therapeutic activities outside in nature and bringing nature into the activity in some way.

Gardening, nature-based and community conservation for wellbeing projects

farmgarden.org.uk

tcv.org.uk/greengym

groundwork.org.uk

thrive.org.uk

carryongardening.org.uk

Forest Bathing – foresttherapyinstitute.com and natureandforesttherapy.org

Also known as *shinrin yoku* in Japan, where it originated, 'forest bathing' is the term we now recognize as referring to walks in nature, in woods and forests. A large body of research has been and is currently still being carried out on the exact reasons why this is beneficial to our health, but it is being shown to have significant benefits. Even a 20-minute walk in green space is enough to make a difference.

Natural Mindfulness – natureconnection.world/category/natural-mindfulness

Mindfulness guides use nature to support mindfulness practice. The website above also lists ecotherapists and forest bathing practitioners.

Outdoor sports and Wilderness therapy –
www.blackdogoutdoors.co.uk and waveproject.co.uk

Wilderness therapy projects such as 'Black Dog Outdoors' aim to use outdoor activities and sports such as climbing, paddleboarding and biking as not only forms of exercise but ways for people to connect and be supported by others.

Phone Therapy

As we saw above with email and instant messaging, therapists have been adapting the way that they work, and phone therapy is another alternative to face-to-face therapy. It is often used by Employee Assistance Programme providers of counselling services and for CBT therapy as well. It can work effectively for some people and I have experience of this proving to be beneficial to clients. The key here is finding the method that works for the person and not assuming it will work for everyone.

Running and Walking

Dynamic Running Therapy (DRT)

A blend of mindfulness, walking/running and talk therapy along with psychoeducation on anxiety and depression. Developed by William Pullen.

ParkRun – www.parkrun.org.uk

Free, weekly meetups for people to walk, run or jog and join with others. There will be an agreed distance but participants are free to either walk, jog or run.

Walking for Health – www.walkingforhealth.org.uk

Another project which aims to connect people and improve wellbeing by taking part in walks together.

Hip Hop Therapy (HHT) – www.hiphoptherapy.com

HHT utilizes hip hop as a therapeutic medium to heal.

Safe and Sound Protocol – integratedlistening.com/ssp-safe-sound-protocol/

The Safe and Sound Protocol is a headphone-based programme that is designed to reduce stress and auditory sensitivity while enhancing social engagement and resilience. It was developed by Stephen Porges, the creator of polyvagal theory.

Sound Therapy and Sound Baths – www.britishacademyofsoundtherapy.com/what-is-sound-therapy/

Sound therapy involves the use of sound from specific instruments to influence brain waves and the person's autonomic nervous system.

Tension and Trauma Release Exercises (TRE) – traumaprevention.com/what-is-tre

TRE is a set of exercises that are designed to assist the body in releasing pockets of stress, tension and trauma.

Somatic Stress Release – www.drscottlyons.com/about

These are body-based stress release techniques devised by Scott Lyons.

Virtual Reality and Augmented Reality Therapies

VR headsets and other wearables that connect via Apple Watch, for example, can provide information on internal bodily signals such as blood pressure, heart rate, heart rate variability, muscle tension and breathing rate. Virtual reality headsets are currently being used in some NHS services to help clients with phobias and psychosis. This therapy works on the principles of exposure therapy as part of CBT and helps clients to gradually feel less threatened in situations that they would usually avoid or feel overwhelmed in. Here's a link to several studies carried out by the department of psychiatry at the University of Oxford:

www.psych.ox.ac.uk/research/oxford-cognitive-
approaches-to-psychosis-o-cap/projects-1/
oxford-virtual-reality-vr-for-mental-health

Voice

The Naked Voice Foundation – www.thenakedvoice.com

Founded by Chloë Goodchild, this is a programme of exercises and techniques to help you discover your authentic voice.

Voice Dialogue – www.voicedialogueinternational.com

A psychospiritual therapy using voice to contact the many selves within us.

Voice Analysis – www.healthoptimising.co.uk/assessments/well-mind-assessment

The Voice Analysis system aims to pinpoint patterns in your speech and identify emotional issues that can be targeted and resolved.

CHAPTER TEN

Writing and Wellbeing

Writing has become an important addition to wellbeing activities. Talking is about putting experiences into language and making meaning. Writing is also about translating experiences into language, but in a slightly different way, and it can be just as beneficial as talking. We can see this in the research into expressive writing. This area is also called 'therapeutic writing' and 'journal therapy'. It also encompasses 'poetry therapy'. In the UK, Lapidus is the main membership organization for practitioners of writing and wellbeing (www.lapidus.org.uk). There are also degree courses in therapeutic writing offered by the Metanoia Institute and the University of Sussex.

Expressive writing is the use of writing about emotions and emotional experiences, as a way to offload, release or disclose rather than suppress one's feelings. It is also a method that helps to make sense of what we feel and process difficult experiences. The 'expressive writing' paradigm is said to have begun with the work of James Pennebaker in 1986. One of the standout findings was how participants' immune responses changed after writing. Pennebaker attributed it to what he termed 'disclosure'. He found that when people disclose certain experiences, they process the associated emotions and engage in meaning making about the event, which helps to reduce distress.

This is very similar to what happens in psychotherapy, in particular trauma therapy. But writing can be a helpful addition for those who find talking difficult. Handled in the correct way, the therapy should be about safe, grounded containment, learning self-regulation skills, then processing stuck emotions and negative meanings to come to a new understanding. Emotions are multisensory events too; for example, they are the actions or unfinished actions of muscles in the body, a rise in blood pressure as the body readies itself for action. The processing of emotion in psychotherapy is a physical process, not just a cognitive one. This is described in exquisite detail in Bessel Van der Kolk's book *The Body Keeps the Score* (Van der Kolk, 2014).

Yoga Therapy

Yoga is being used frequently by some trauma-therapy centres, particularly in the US, and an evidence base is beginning to grow for its effectiveness in soothing and balancing the nervous system. An example of yoga in a therapy setting is trauma-sensitive yoga: www.traumasensitiveyoganederland.com.

Self-help and Mental Health Apps

Therapy research is fairly conclusive that the key ingredient in successful therapy is very often the therapeutic relationship that is established between you and the therapist. However, if talking to someone is hard for you, or you are on a waiting list for therapy, there are other options that are proving to be effective. Text-based therapy, self-help websites, online communities and mental health apps are all real and helpful alternatives.

The use of apps in mental health is a massive area and still growing in size. There is evidence to show the benefits that smartphone apps can have, particularly with anxiety (see Firth et al., 2017). How apps help and what they can help with is not yet completely clear, but there are two things that apps do that is potentially key to how they help us. They bring our attention towards the issue at hand so that we take notice of it rather than acting on autopilot, and they offer us information and education about what is happening so that we are better informed and have increased knowledge of how our brain and body operate.

If you are going to use an app to help with your emotional health, it is important to know how to assess its quality. How do you know that it is giving you the correct information about anxiety, for example? Whose opinion is it based on? Is it based on any evidence? Does the app company store your data and is it secure? Do you know what to do if you want to delete your data from this app and company? Will they share your personal information with anyone? Is there privacy and confidentiality of your personal information? Assessing quality is a vital skill in our digital age, where there is content everywhere and also an overwhelming number of people with opinions on all of it.

Stephen Schueller of One Mind PsyberGuide in the US estimated that there are approximately 25,000 mental health apps available at the moment and that number is still growing (Schueller, 2020). His organization reviews apps based on several criteria:

Credibility
Science-backed data
Evidence-base
User experience
Bugs
Security and privacy
Regulation

On their website you can check the ratings and reviews for different apps (onemindpsyberguide.org/apps).

In the UK, the organization Orcha (appfinder.orcha.co.uk) reviews apps and has a similar list of rated and reviewed apps. You have to pay to get access to this data, but fees start at £4 per annum.

Self-help resources and apps can give you the information that you need and the ability to track what happens for you, but they are not a replacement for professional help. The evidence in counselling and psychotherapy is showing us that the quality of the interaction with another person is a vital ingredient in what makes therapy an experience that helps and heals. That doesn't rule out the role of apps and other self-help resources at all, but it does suggest that a blend of both would be the ideal for certain people

I've compiled a brief list of some self-help sites and apps and have put these into the appendix, but of course there are many more out there!

ONLINE COMMUNITIES

Online communities can be helpful on many levels. Science is showing us how our nervous system is wired to feel safe and connected to others. We have an innate need to connect with others, and this is where groups and communities are so vital to mental health. However, there can be a downside, as anyone who has used platforms such as Twitter will be aware of. In any group of people, you will have differences of opinion and exchanges that can sometimes become quite heated and, in the worst of cases, quite hateful. How these issues are managed is a challenge for group moderators. If you are part of a group and you start to feel upset by what is happening, speak to someone outside the group and take a break from it. The ups and downs of other people's emotions can take a toll on your mental health. But tell yourself that this is their emotion, not yours, label it and separate yourself from it.

In the appendix for this chapter I have put together a brief list of some of the online communities that I could find for different groups of people. This list doesn't include the vast number that are also available on Facebook, though, so it is worth looking there also.

OFFLINE COMMUNITY PROJECTS

I have added some offline community projects to the appendix section, but there are also some community wellbeing projects in the 'Alternatives to talk therapy' section.

CHAPTER ELEVEN

Does Therapy Work?

On the surface, the fact that CBT is the most widely used therapy in the NHS and has the largest database of evidence behind it should tell us the whole story about what is and what is not effective. Except, as with most things in life, there is more to the story. Yes, CBT is effective, for certain issues and for certain people at particular points in their life where they are receptive to this type of therapy. However, there are a core group of factors that have been shown to contribute to effectiveness in therapy that have little to do with the particular type of therapy being offered. These common factors are the therapist's warmth, empathy and acceptance, and the quality of the therapeutic relationship between the client and therapist (Zilcha-Mano, 2017).

The upshot from this is that if these factors are present, in combination with a therapy that is effective for that particular client's issue, then you have the magic formula needed for a successful course of therapy. Research is moving beyond only studying single types of psychotherapy approaches and their effects on clients and is starting to consider clients as agents of change in therapy (Bohart, 2000), as well as the importance of taking an integrative approach (Zarbo et al., 2016) and not considering that one type of therapy will suit every client.

In the appendix I have listed some of the trials showing effectiveness data for various types of therapy. CBT is not the only therapy that has been shown to be effective. We need to look more broadly at the factors that therapies have in common.

WHY EVIDENCE IS NOT THE ONLY MEASURE OF SUCCESS

When we hear that a therapy is 'evidence-based', what does this actually mean? In the UK, the National Institute for Clinical Excellence (NICE) is the body that produces guidelines for the effectiveness of medical and psychological interventions. It rates evidence according to the type of studies that have been carried out and the statistical significance of those findings. Randomized controlled trials (RCTs) are said to be the 'gold standard' in evidence-based medicine. However, these are not always possible to carry out. Funding is not always available to potential researchers, and for every successful RCT there are many potential clients who were not included in the study because they did not fulfil the strict diagnostic criteria. For example, some trials of trauma therapy exclude clients who use drugs or alcohol or have other psychological issues, for example OCD. Now, as a therapist I know only too well that alcohol can be a common coping mechanism for managing or blocking out thoughts. But researchers carrying out a study have to try to make the participants as equal as possible in order to be sure that what they are measuring is not being affected by other issues. This brings us into another tricky area with regards to psychotherapy research. In order to carry out an RCT you need to categorize participants into a diagnostic category. This is not always easy for some psychotherapists who do not wish to pathologize or diagnose their clients. Thus, the language of traditional quantitative (statistics-based) research has sat uneasily with certain psychotherapy bodies. There is, however, a large and growing body of qualitative (experiential, language-based) research which gives us a richer source of information, and a sense of how a client's story has changed through therapy. You cannot get this rich information from pure numbers.

So when we look at therapies that do not yet have an evidence base, it is not fair to say immediately that they are not helpful. We need to look more deeply at what is being said, and there needs to be more equity of access to research amongst the psychotherapy field.

We also need to look at another aspect of what makes a therapy helpful: the feedback from clients themselves. This is an area that needs more work. For reasons of confidentiality, it has suffered somewhat, and feedback questionnaires still tend to be biased towards numbers. In-depth reviews of therapies are also difficult to acquire, because therapists do not wish to break the confidentiality of their clients by asking for reviews either offline or online. Clients understandably feel uncomfortable when asked to give a public review of therapy, when the process is by its very nature meant to be a private and personal conversation.

IS PSYCHOTHERAPY HARMFUL?

We also need to address not only the effectiveness of psychotherapy but whether psychotherapy is harmful. A review of this area by Scott Lilienfeld in 2007 found that some interventions proved to be not only ineffective but harmful. Among those listed in his report was 'Critical Incident Stress Debriefing' (CISD) and 'Boot Camps for Conduct Disorder'.

Curran et al. (2019) have listed several issues that potentially cause harm, such as lack of cultural sensitivity, over-controlling and rigid applications of a therapy method, not addressing client's expectations and clients feeling disempowered, silenced and devalued.

Clients' true experiences of therapy are important here, and it should also not be a numbers game. We need qualitative research from different methods of therapy, so that we can assess things from the client's perspective. Researchers have also pointed out that a more systematic approach to seeking client feedback should be prioritized, and more needs to be done to assess potential harm in psychological therapies.

CONCLUSION

JUDGEMENTS ABOUT THERAPY AND EMOTIONS

In Nadiya Hussain's recent BBC documentary *Anxiety and Me*, an anxiety sufferer, Barry, said that there is still a stigma about going to see a therapist. This seems familiar and understandable, doesn't it? I wasn't surprised to hear him state what seems to be a common attitude towards therapy. There has been a viewpoint from previous generations that you shouldn't give voice to how you feel, because this in some way makes it worse, makes it last, makes you weak or gets you labelled as 'mad'. The societal norms of emotional suppression – 'keep calm and carry on', 'don't get hysterical', 'it's weak to cry' – all reinforce this fear of being or showing upset.

The consequence of this is that people have held the view that there is something wrong with them if they find it hard to cope. That they are weak if they show an emotion, or are a burden if they tell loved ones how they feel. On the other side, if someone tells us they are struggling, we do not always know how to respond to that either. Our parents, peers and those who guide us in our younger lives are our models for how to manage emotions. If we have not been given the message that it is safe to be upset, safe to express that we are upset, and normal to do this, then how are we to know what to do?

If you are used to people around you 'brushing issues under the carpet', not saying how they feel about something or saying they are not angry or upset and then giving you the silent treatment instead, then you will learn that this is how to manage if you feel upset. This strategy doesn't make feelings go away though, and can lead to more rumination and having to find some form of 'release' for what you are experiencing. If you have been told 'it's weak to cry', then of course you will not want to be seen as weak and will prevent yourself from crying. You will need to find another way to relieve the activation in your body, or find a method of suppression or avoidance that works, such as obsessive compulsive rituals.

Emotional education is vital to help us overcome the fear of our own feeling-states, and to equip us to be able to know what to do when those around us are upset. With the help of neuroscience, we now have alternatives to the dominant suppression and avoidance paradigm that we have been stuck in for generations. Let's be curious rather than fearful and try to use the knowledge that is around at the moment to help ourselves to *feel* better, rather than putting energy into avoidance and making ourselves feel worse. When we know how to tolerate and be with our own emotions, without catastrophizing them, we can also learn to be with others who are distressed without panicking too. We just need to allow the person to experience what is happening physically in their body without rushing to take the feeling away from them.

WHAT DO WE KNOW SO FAR ABOUT EMOTIONS?

Emotions are messengers. They are made up of physical sensations, such as the dropping feeling in your gut when you feel scared or criticized, or the flinching of your muscles in response to an image of something bad happening. The images you see and the thoughts that flash through your mind are part of the emotion too. When an emotion swells and rises within us, along with frightening thoughts, it can be unsettling, because of course some feelings are warning signs – for example, of threat or potential social danger. But what has happened for some of us is that we have grown to fear these feelings themselves and have ended up trying to avoid them. Why? Because of societal attitudes and judgements, and because of a lack of education about how to manage these feeling-states.

WHAT TO DO INSTEAD OF AVOIDING EMOTIONS

The next time you get a rush of anxiety or irritation or stress – in whatever way that usually manifests itself for you – try to notice and separate the thoughts going through your mind from the physical experience of that feeling in your body. The way to do this is to notice the physical sensations or movements. As you notice this activity you might get to see how this activation rises, plateaus and then tapers off. Of course, the thoughts that you have can inflame the feeling again, and this is OK: just notice. Notice how your thoughts can do that. Notice how your brain is working so hard to explain what is going on. It might be coming up with all sorts of scenarios; for example, 'This must mean I'm having a heart attack'; 'I can't deal with this'; 'I can't put up with this any more.' The emotion is a warning or a message about something, but our predicting brains can often come up with incorrect theories. Notice what your body wants to do. If there is something to deal with, then do what you need to do. If not, pause and notice the sensations in your body. Do some slow breathing now. In for four and out for six.

Emotions can be so much easier to manage when we aim to notice the sensations rather than try to fight them, avoid them or control them. A bad day could just be a bad day. Let yourself have a bad day – it's OK. Your brain will be predicting all sorts of things like 'I always feel like this. It'll always be this way. Why do I always feel bad? Why can't I just have a good day?' Just refocus on your body and notice what it is doing. It doesn't have to mean anything about your future. See where the sensations go if you notice them and let them be. You can ride the wave to the other side.

When we fight a mood and wish it would go away this can make us feel much worse. You don't need to control it. It might feel very strongly like you need to, but this just gets you stuck in a loop. If you feel anxious, another way of viewing it could be that your body and brain are activating you to deal with something threatening, to try to keep you safe and protected. But if there isn't a threat around right now, don't fight the feeling. Work with it. Notice that your body is activated and ask yourself if you need to deal with anything right now? If not, then let your nervous system 'stand down'. Sometimes when I am working with clients who have suffered childhood trauma, we talk about having a dialogue with that part of you that feels activated, and saying: 'I know you are just trying to keep me safe – that's OK – but you can stand down because I don't need to be on alert. Right now I am safe.'

DEVELOPING INTEROCEPTIVE AWARENESS

If you want to go deeper into managing emotions, then it can really help to develop your interoceptive awareness. This involves the deliberate practice of noticing and accepting the sensations and physical movements of your body. Interoceptive awareness will tell you a lot about your feeling-states if you listen to it. By noticing what is happening in your body and accepting that these are just sensations that do not have to mean anything negative, you will help yourself to gradually tolerate the felt sense of an emotion. This can be helpful when your brain is working hard to make predictions about what might be happening – and often coming up with distressing scenarios that are unnecessary. It is normal that the brain does this, but that doesn't mean it is always correct in its assumptions. This is the essence of CBT: noticing that the brain is making assumptions based on past experience but that these may not be serving you in the best way in the present.

Pause and bring your awareness back to your body. Do you need to deal with anything right now? If not, tell your nervous system this. Notice the wave, let it come, and let it go. Let the activation 'stand down'. You do not need to take action right now.

If you get the urge to cry, let your body cry. Crying brings that much sought-after feeling of relief, if only we can get used to letting it happen. Can you let it happen the next time you feel the tears coming? Or if someone close to you is upset, could you let them have the feeling, without thinking that you need to take their upset away? It is OK to be upset. Let them cry and just be with them.

THERAPY CAN HELP

It can also help to see a therapist to unpack what is upsetting you, and to uncover past patterns that are keeping you stuck. Some of us have the belief that seeing a therapist means we are weak or cannot cope. But these are sadly incorrect and also dangerous assumptions. Coping is about feeling, not avoiding feelings. Strength is about tolerating and leaning-into rather than leaning back and ignoring. There is a powerful feeling of confidence that can come from noticing, labelling and accepting your own feelings.

A therapist can help you out of the loops you might be stuck in and will know how to help you to work with the emotions you might be struggling with. If no one has ever helped you to express how you feel and to manage emotions then how can you be expected to know what to do? Why would it be wrong to go and see someone who can help you with this? We don't expect that we will know everything about how a car works. We just accept that a mechanic will have knowledge that can help us out. We accept that we don't know how to cut hair, so we go to the hairdressers. The human body is far more complex than a car, and emotions are much harder to see than hair is, so why is it OK to ask for the service of a hairdresser or mechanic but not the services of a therapist?

EMOTIONAL HEALTH NOT MENTAL HEALTH

Looking after our emotional health is vital to our whole system, and as the body and brain are both involved in our feeling-states it no longer makes sense to separate mental from physical. For this reason I believe that the term emotional health is more accurate than 'mental health'.

Science is showing us how the body and brain work together: via our nervous system, heart and gut, to continually predict what resources are needed moment to moment. This activity is what gives rise to an emotion.

Our system scans for threats to keep us safe, but also checks for safety and seeks connection to keep us engaged and motivated. This 'connection and safety system' as some researchers call it, is key to our wellbeing. It is what helps us to create and maintain relationships and be able to work together in groups. Without a sense of safety and connection, we can get caught in threat-based patterns or in dissociative or shutdown states.

Emotional health is also about the connections that we form with others. If we have had early relationships that have led to hurt, criticism, neglect or abuse, this manifests itself through our nervous system and body, as well as in our assumptions and thinking patterns. We learn to manage ourselves and our emotions in specific ways as a result. But importantly we can learn new attachment patterns, and we can learn to feel safe with people again and develop connections that feel right for us.*

KEY MESSAGES

We are wary of therapy because we do not want to experience the feeling of being upset.

Suppression is normal, but we need to balance it out with discharging and processing what we have suppressed.

We can manage emotions by learning to tolerate the physical feeling of an emotion, rather than trying to fight or suppress. This physical feeling is our interoceptive network in action. It is the bridge through which our brain and body communicate with our autonomic nervous system.

We could support and educate our children to notice and label their feelings, rather than try to make their feelings go away.

---

* There is a helpful article in the magazine *Aeon* that explains how this works in therapy: aeon.co/essays/how-attachment-theory-works-in-the-therapeutic-relationship.

There are some new emotion words that would be helpful to start bringing into our daily lives: Safety, Connection, and Relief. Our nervous system needs a balance of these three feeling-states. Safe places and people we feel safe with; people and activities and places that give us a sense of belonging and affiliation; a sense of being activated just enough to feel engaged and interested; and an ability to be able to notice and discharge emotions and activation to get to a feeling of relief. Feeling 'relief' is important for us. Crying is one way to get this feeling. We need to let ourselves do this and not be afraid of it. We can learn to 'bleed' our systems like we bleed our radiators. Offload, discharge, process. If we all did this more regularly and mindfully we would be less afraid of emotions, feel less need to suppress and struggle much less as a result.

Feeling safe *and* connected is a vital part of our emotional health.

If someone you know is upset, sit with them and let them be with the feeling. Processing an emotion with the support of another person who we feel safe and secure with is an ideal condition for healing.

Avoidance puts a distance between us and our feelings. This distance means we are less likely to be able to fine-tune how we feel and label how we feel, because we are always trying to keep the experience at arm's length. Avoidance can make us feel even more upset and out of control.

* * * * *

I hope that this book has helped in some small way to offer another way of dealing with emotions and perhaps to show that it isn't wrong to be upset. It doesn't mean you are weak and it doesn't mean you are crazy. Seeing a therapist to offload or process how you feel can be helpful in taking control of your feelings and learning to cope with them rather than fight against them. It is OK to talk, but talking is not the only method available. The chapter on alternatives to talking therapy show that there are many options out there for you. Please don't struggle alone.

RE-TEST YOURSELF

Now, let's revisit those questions you asked yourself in the Introduction.

EMOTIONS

1. I often don't understand my emotions or where they come from. ☐

2. I wish I didn't feel emotions. ☐

3. I hate the sensations of some emotions. ☐

Add these three to get your total score for your current discomfort with emotions.

Total score ☐

    Now do the same for therapy:

THERAPY

1. I feel uncomfortable about seeing a therapist ☐

2. I don't know how or where to look to find help for myself ☐

3. I don't want to try therapy ☐

Add these three to get your total score for your current thoughts about therapy.

Total score ☐

Compare the above with your score from the start of the book. Has there been any change, even of one point? These are your scores, what do you think they mean?

If you also did the online Emotion Beliefs Questionnaire, here is the link again:

www.researchgate.net/publication/340660428_Emotion_Beliefs_Questionnaire_EBQ_Copy_of_questionnaire_and_scoring_instructions

REFERENCES

Allsopp, K., Read, J., Corcoran, R., and Kinderman, P. (2019). 'Heterogeneity in psychiatric diagnostic classification'. *Psychiatry Research* 279: 15–22. doi: 10.1016/j.psychres.2019.07.005.

Andrews, B. (2014). 'Boys don't cry'. *Healthcare Counselling and Psychotherapy Journal* 14(3).

Aron, E. (1999). *The Highly Sensitive Person: How to Survive and Thrive When the World Overwhelms You.* London: Thorsons.

Australian Psychological Society (2018). *Evidence-Based Psychological Interventions for Mental Disorders: A Review of the Literature.* 4th edn. Available at www.psychology.org.au/getmedia/23c6a11b-2600-4e19-9a1d-6ff9c2f26fae/Evidence-based-psych-interventions.pdf.

BACP (2018). *Working with Suicidal Clients in the Counselling Professions* [Good Practice in Action 042: fact sheet]. Lutterworth: BACP. Available at https://www.bacp.co.uk/media/2157/bacp-working-with-suicidal-clients-fact-sheet-gpia042.pdf.

— — — (2020). 'Providing help at the point of need: insights from single-session therapy'. Available at www.bacp.co.uk/bacp-journals/university-and-college-counselling/may-2020/providing-help-at-the-point-of-need/.

Bai, Z., Luo, S., Zhang, L., Wu, S., and Chi, I. (2019). 'Acceptance and commitment therapy (ACT) to reduce depression: a systematic review and meta-analysis'. *Journal of Affective Disorders* 260(1): 728–37. doi: 10.1016/j.jad.2019.09.040.

Barrett, L. F. (2017). *How Emotions Are Made: The Secret Life of the Brain.* London: Macmillan.

— — — (2018). 'You aren't at the mercy of your emotions – your brain creates them' [video]. Available at www.ted.com/talks/lisa_feldman_barrett_you_aren_t_at_the_mercy_of_your_emotions_your_brain_creates_them.

Beck, A. T., Rush, A. J., Shaw, B. F., and Emery, G. (1979). *Cognitive Therapy of Depression.* New York: Guilford.

Bohart, A. C. (2000). 'The client is the most important common factor: clients' self-healing capacities and psychotherapy'. *Journal of Psychotherapy Integration* 10(2): 127–49. doi: 10.1023/A:1009444132104.

Boudewyns, P. A., Stwertka, S. A., Hyer, L. A., Albrecht, S. A., and Sperr, E. V. (1993). 'Eye movement desensitisation for PTSD of combat: a treatment outcome pilot study'. *The Behavior Therapist* 16(2): 30–33.

Brooks, A. W., Schroeder, J., Risen, J. L., Gino, F., Galinsky, A., Norton, M. L., and Schweitzer, M. E. (2016). 'Don't stop believing: rituals improve performance by decreasing anxiety'. *Organizational Behavior and Human Decision Processes* 137: 71–85.

Brown, B. (2019). *Dare to Lead*. London: Ebury.

Butler, E. A., Egloff, B., Wilhelm, F. H., Smith, N. C., Erickson, E. A., and Gross, J. J. (2003). 'The social consequences of expressive suppression'. *Emotion* 3(1): 48–67. doi: 10.1037/1528-3542.3.1.48.

Butler, E. A., Lee, T. L., and Gross, J. J. (2007). 'Emotion regulation and culture: are the social consequences of emotion suppression culture-specific?' *Emotion* 7(1): 30–48. doi: 10.1037/1528-3542.7.1.30.

Cameron, J. (1994). *The Artist's Way: A Spiritual Path to Higher Creativity*. New York: Souvenir.

Carvel, J. (2004). 'How the death of one black patient treated as a "lesser being" showed up race bias'. *Guardian*, 6 February 2004. Available at https://www.theguardian.com/uk/2004/feb/06/race.politics.

Chakrabarti, S. (2015). 'Usefulness of telepsychiatry: a critical evaluation of videoconferencing-based approaches'. *World Journal of Psychiatry* 5(3): 286–304. doi: 10.5498/wjp.v5.i3.286.

Clement, S., Schauman, O., Graham, T., Maggioni, F., Evans-Lacko, S., Bezborodovs, N., and Thornicroft, G. (2015). 'What is the impact of mental health-related stigma on help-seeking? A systematic review of quantitative and qualitative studies'. *Psychological Medicine* 45(1): 11–27. doi: 10.1017/S0033291714000129.

Connor, K. R. (2011). 'Reading from the heart out: Chief Bromden through indigenous eyes'. *Concentric* 37(1): 231–53.

Cristea, D. D., and Hofmann, S. G. (2018). 'Why cognitive behavioral therapy is the current gold standard of psychotherapy'. *Frontiers in Psychiatry* 9(4). doi: 10.3389/fpsyt.2018.00004.

Critchley, H. D., and Garfinkel, S. N. (2017). 'Interoception and emotion'. *Current Opinion in Psychology* 17: 7–14. doi: 10.1016/j.copsyc.2017.04.020.

Curran J., Parry, G. D., Hardy, G. E., Darling, J., Mason, A.-M., and Chambers, E. (2019). 'How does therapy harm? A model of adverse process using task analysis in the meta-synthesis of service users' experience'. *Frontiers in Psychology* 10:347. doi: 10.3389/fpsyg.2019.00347.

de Botton, A., and the School of Life. (2019). *The School of Life: An Emotional Education.* London: Hamish Hamilton.

Dermendzhiyska, E. (2019). 'Cradled by therapy: why therapy works is still up for debate. But, when it does, its methods mimic the attachment dynamics of good parenting'. *Aeon* [website], 19 December 2019. Available at https://aeon.co/essays/how-attachment-theory-works-in-the-therapeutic-relationship.

Dingfelder, S. F. (2008). 'Make the most of one session'. *Monitor on Psychology* 39(5): 40–41.

Ekman, P., and Friesen, W. V. (1974). 'Detecting deception from the body or face'. *Journal of Personality and Social Psychology* 29(3): 288–98. doi: 10.1037/h0036006.

Epstein, R. (2019). 'Distance therapy comes of age'. *Scientific American Mind* 22(2): 60–63.

Felitti, V. J., Anda, R. F., Nordenberg, D., Williamson, D. F., Spitz, A. M., Edwards, V., Koss, M. P., and Marks, J. S. (1998). 'Relationship of childhood abuse and household dysfunction to many of the leading causes of death in adults: the adverse childhood experiences (ACE) study'. *American Journal of Preventive Medicine* 14(4): 245–58. doi: 10.1016/S0749-3797(98)00017-8.

Filer, N. (2019). *The Heartland: Finding and Losing Schizophrenia.* London: Faber.

Firth, J., Torous, J., Nicholas, J., Carney, R., Rosenbaum, S., and Sarris, J. (2017). 'Can smartphone mental health interventions reduce symptoms of anxiety? A meta-analysis of randomized controlled trials'. *Journal of Affective Disorders* 218: 15–22. doi: 10.1016/j.jad.2017.04.046.

Freedenthal, S. (2017). 'A suicide therapist's secret past'. *New York Times*, 11 May 2017.

Friedl, R. (2021). *The Beat of Life: A Surgeon Reveals the Secrets of the Heart.* London: Hero.

Gardner, M. N., and Brandt, A. M. (2006). '"The doctors' choice is America's choice": the physician in US cigarette advertisements, 1930–1953'. *American Journal of Public Health* 96(2): 222–32.

doi: 10.2105/AJPH.2005.066654.

Gautam, A., Polizzi, C. P., and Mattson, R. E. (2019). 'Mindfulness, procrastination, and anxiety: assessing their interrelationships'. *Psychology of Consciousness: Theory, Research, and Practice* [advance online publication]. doi: 10.1037/cns0000209.

Gerada, C. (2018a). 'Doctors, suicide and mental illness'. *British Journal of Psychiatry Bulletin* 42(4): 165–8. doi: 10.1192/bjb.2018.11.

— — — (2018b). 'For doctors with mental illness, "help me" can be the hardest words'. *Guardian*, 6 June 2018. Available at www.theguardian.com/commentisfree/2018/jun/06/doctors-mental-health-problems-taboo.

Gilbert, P. (2010). *Compassion Focused Therapy: Distinctive Features*. London: Routledge.

Goleman, D. (1987). 'Embattled giant of psychology speaks his mind'. *New York Times*, 25 August 1987.

Gross, J. J., and Levenson, R. W. (1997). 'Hiding feelings: the acute effects of inhibiting negative and positive emotion'. *Journal of Abnormal Psychology* 106(1): 95–103. doi: 10.1037/0021-843X.106.1.95.

Guille, C., Zhao, Z., and Krystal, J. (2015). 'Web-based cognitive behavioral therapy intervention for the prevention of suicidal ideation in medical interns'. *JAMA Psychiatry* 72(12): 1192–8.

Hari, J. (2018). *Lost Connections: Uncovering the Real Causes of Depression – and the Unexpected Solutions*. New York: Bloomsbury.

Harris, R. (2008). *The Happiness Trap: How to Stop Struggling and Start Living*. Boston, MA: Trumpeter.

Jacobs Hendel, H. (2018). *It's Not Always Depression: A New Theory of Listening to Your Body, Discovering Core Emotions and Reconnecting with Your Authentic Self*. London: Penguin.

Johnstone, L., and Boyle, M., with Cromby, J., Dillon, J., Harper, D., Kinderman, P., Longden, E., Pilgrim, D., and Read, J. (2018). *The Power Threat Meaning Framework: Towards the Identification of Patterns in Emotional Distress, Unusual Experiences and Troubled or Troubling Behaviour, as an Alternative to Functional Psychiatric Diagnosis*. Leicester: British Psychological Society. Available at https://www.bps.org.uk/sites/bps.org.uk/files/Policy%20-%20Files/PTM%20Main.pdf.

Kinman, G., and Teoh, K. (2018). *What Could Make a Difference to the Mental Health of UK Doctors? A Review of the Research*

Evidence. London: Society of Occupational Medicine. Available at www.som.org.uk/sites/som.org.uk/files/What_could_make_a_difference_to_the_mental_health_of_UK_doctors_LTF_SOM.pdf.

Lauderdale, S. A. (2017). 'Evaluating the distinction between aversive indecisiveness and procrastination: relationships with anxiety, anxiety vulnerability, and personality traits' [poster presented at the 51st annual convention of the Association for Behavioral and Cognitive Therapies, November 2017, San Diego, CA].

Lawrence, L. (2009). 'Cigarettes were once "physician" tested, approved'. Available at www.healio.com/hematology-oncology/news/print/hemonc-today/%7B241d62a7-fe6e-4c5b-9fed-a33cc6e4bd7c%7D/cigarettes-were-once-physician-tested-approved.

Levenson, R. W. (1994). 'Human emotion: a functional view'. In Ekman, P., and Davidson, R. J. (eds), The Nature of Emotion: Fundamental Questions. New York: Oxford University Press (123–6).

Levin, M. E., Haeger, J. A., and Pierce, B. G. (2016). 'Web-based acceptance and commitment therapy for mental health problems in college students: a randomized controlled trial'. *Behavior Modification* 41(1): 141–62.

Levine, P. A. (2010). *In an Unspoken Voice: How the Body Releases Trauma and Restores Goodness*. Berkeley, CA: North Atlantic.

Liddon, L., Kingerlee, R., and Barry, J. A. (2018). 'Gender differences in preferences for psychological treatment, coping strategies, and triggers to help-seeking'. *British Journal of Clinical Psychology* 57(1): 42–58.

Lilienfeld, S. O. (2007). 'Psychological treatments that cause harm'. *Perspectives on Psychological Science* 2(1): 53–70. doi: 10.1093/acrefore/9780190236557.013.68.

Megías-Robles, A., Gutiérrez-Cobo, M. J., Gómez-Leal, R., Cabello, R., Gross, J. J., and Fernández-Berrocal, P (2019). 'Emotionally intelligent people reappraise rather than suppress their emotions'. *PLoS ONE* 14(8). doi: 10.1371/journal.pone.0220688.

Millings, A., and Carnelley, K. B. (2015). 'Core belief content examined in a large sample of patients using online cognitive behaviour therapy'. *Journal of Affective Disorders* 186: 275–83. doi: 10.1016/j.jad.2015.06.044.

Mind (2018). 'Mental Health Units (Use of Force Bill) becomes law'. Mind [website], 1 November 2018. Available at https://www.mind.org.uk/news-campaigns/news/

mental-health-units-use-of-force-bill-becomes-law.

Mitmansgruber, H., Beck, T., Höfer, S., and Schüßler, G. (2009). 'When you don't like what you feel: experiential avoidance, mindfulness and meta-emotion in emotion regulation'. *Personality and Individual Differences* 46(4): 448–53. doi: 10.1016/j.paid.2008.11.013.

Mogk, C., Otte, S., Reinhold-Hurley, B., and Kröner-Herwig, B. (2006). 'Health effects of expressive writing on stressful or traumatic experiences – a meta-analysis'. *GMS Psycho-Social Medicine* 3:Doc06.

Moncrieff, J. (2009). *A Straight Talking Introduction to Psychiatric Drugs*. Monmouth: PCCS.

National Institute for Clinical Excellence (2004). *Short-Term Management of Violent (Disturbed) Behaviour in Adult Psychiatric In-Patient and Accident and Emergency Settings*. London: NICE.

Nelson R. E., and Kim J. (2011). 'The impact of mental illness on the risk of employment termination'. *Journal of Mental Health Policy Economics* 14(1): 39–52.

Office for National Statistics (2020). 'Suicides in England and Wales: 2019 registrations'. Available at www.ons.gov.uk/peoplepopulationandcommunity/birthsdeathsandmarriages/deaths/bulletins/suicidesintheunitedkingdom/2019registrations.

Osmo, F., Duran, V., Wenzel, A., Reis de Oliveira, I., Nepomuceno, S., Madeira, M., and Menezes, I. (2018). 'The negative core beliefs inventory: development and psychometric properties'. *Journal of Cognitive Psychotherapy* 32(1): 67–84. doi: 10.1891/0889-8391.32.1.67.

Park, D., Ramirez, G., and Beilock, S. L. (2014). 'The role of expressive writing in math anxiety'. *Journal of Experimental Psychology: Applied* 20(2): 103–11. doi: 10.1037/xap0000013.

Pennebaker, J. W., and Smyth, J. M. (2019). *Opening Up by Writing It Down: How Expressive Writing Improves Health and Eases Emotional Pain*. New York: Guilford.

Porges, S. W. (2011). *The Polyvagal Theory: Neurophysiological Foundations of Emotions, Attachment, Communication, and Self-Regulation*. New York: Norton.

Roos, C., Oord, S., Zijlstra, B., Lucassen, S., Perrin, S., Emmelkamp, P., and Jongh, A. (2017). 'Comparison of eye-movement desensitization and reprocessing therapy, cognitive behavioral writing therapy, and wait-list in pediatric posttraumatic stress disorder following single-incident trauma: a multicenter randomized clinical trial'. *Journal of Child Psychology and Psychiatry* 58(10): 1219–28. doi: 10.1111/jcpp.12768.

Rost, F. (2019). 'Psychotherapy in the era of evidence-based practice' [Powerpoint presentation, BACP – Working with Research in Practice, Universities and Colleges Conference, 13 June 2019].

Royal College of Nursing (2005). National Collaborating Centre for Nursing and Supportive Care (UK). *Violence: The Short-Term Management of Disturbed/Violent Behaviour in In-Patient Psychiatric Settings and Emergency Departments*. London: Royal College of Nursing (UK); 2005 Feb. PMID: 21834187. https://pubmed.ncbi.nlm.nih.gov/21834187/

Schueller, S. (2020). 'How to choose effective, science-based mental health apps' [podcast]. *Speaking of Psychology* 116. Available at https://www.apa.org/research/action/speaking-of-psychology/science-based-mental-health-apps.

Sebastian, B., and Nelms, J. (2017). 'The effectiveness of emotional freedom techniques in the treatment of posttraumatic stress disorder: a meta-analysis'. *Explore* 13(1): 16–25. doi: 10.1016/j.explore.2016.10.001.

Shapiro, E. (2009). 'EMDR treatment of recent trauma'. *Journal of EMDR Practice and Research* 3(3): 141–51. doi: 10.1891/1933-3196.3.3.141.

Sherine, A. (2018). *Talk Yourself Better: A Confused Person's Guide to Therapy, Counselling and Self-Help*. London: Robinson.

Siegel, D. J. (2011). *The Neurobiology of 'We': How Relationships, the Mind, and the Brain Interact to Shape Who We Are* [audiobook]. Louisville, CO: Sounds True.

Smith, R., Alkozei, A., and Killgore, W. (2017). 'How do emotions work?' *Frontiers for Young Minds* 5(69). doi: 10.3389/frym.2017.00069.

Szasz, T. (2010). *The Myth of Mental Illness: Foundations of a Theory of Personal Conduct*. London: Harper Perennial.

Topkaya, N. (2015). 'Factors influencing psychological help seeking in adults: a qualitative study'. *Educational Sciences: Theory and Practice* 15(1): 21–31. doi: 10.12738/estp.2015.1.2094.

Torre, J. B., and Lieberman, M. D. (2018). 'Putting feelings into words: affect labeling as implicit emotion regulation'. *Emotion Review* 10(2): 116–24. doi.org/10.1177/1754073917742706.

van der Kolk, B. A. (2014). *The Body Keeps the Score: Brain, Mind, and Body in the Healing of Trauma*. New York: Viking.

Waters, S. F., Karnilowicz, H. R., West, T. V., and Mendes, W. B. (2020). 'Keep it to yourself? Parent emotion suppression influences physiological linkage and interaction behavior'. *Journal of Family Psychology* 4(7): 784–93. doi:10.1037/fam0000664.

Webb, T. L., Miles, E., and Sheeran, P. (2012). 'Dealing with feeling: a meta-analysis of the effectiveness of strategies derived from the process model of emotion regulation'. *Psychological Bulletin* 138(4): 775–808. doi: 10.1037/a0027600.

Wegner, D. M. (1997). 'When the antidote is the poison: ironic mental control processes'. *Psychological Science* 8(3): 148–50. doi.org/10.1111/j.1467-9280.1997.tb00399.x.

Young, J. E., Klosko, J. S., and Weishaar, M. E. (2003). *Schema Therapy: A Practitioner's Guide*. New York: Guilford.

Yousaf, O., Grunfeld, E. A., and Hunter, M. S. (2015). 'A systematic review of the factors associated with delays in medical and psychological help-seeking among men'. *Health Psychology Review* 9:2: 264–76. doi: 10.1080/17437199.2013.840954.

Zarbo, C., Tasca, G. A., Cattafi, F., and Compare, A. (2016). 'Integrative psychotherapy works'. *Frontiers in Psychology* 6(2021). doi: 10.3389/fpsyg.2015.02021.

Zilcha-Mano, S. (2017). 'Is the alliance really therapeutic? Revisiting this question in light of recent methodological advances'. *American Psychologist* 72(4): 311–25. doi: 10.1037/a0040435.

Zwerenz, R., Becker, J., Knickenberg, R. J., Siepmann, M., Hagen, K., and Beutel, M. E. (2017). 'Online self-help as an add-on to inpatient psychotherapy: efficacy of a new blended treatment approach'. *Psychotherapy and Psychosomatics* 86(6): 341–50. doi: 10.1159/000481177.

APPENDIX

(BY CHAPTER)

CHAPTER ONE – THE FEAR OF THERAPY

NEGATIVE CORE BELIEFS AND POSITIVE ALTERNATIVES

Core fears and beliefs tend to cluster around themes. This is a simplified list to highlight the main themes that have been recorded in cognitive-behavioural literature. These beliefs can develop at a time of high emotion and/or trauma, or from repeated conditioning at a time when we were not able to challenge them. They can become a filter for how we view situations.

- Self-defectiveness
- Responsibility
- Control and Choice
- Safety and Vulnerability

1. Self-defectiveness (there's something wrong with me)

Negative belief	Alternative/helpful belief
I'm not good enough	I'm OK, I don't have to be perfect
I'm inadequate	I am capable, I'm enough as I am
I don't deserve love	I am worthy of love
I'm unloveable	I am loveable
I'm worthless	I have value, I am worthy
I'm weak	I am not completely weak; I can be strong when I need to be
I'm damaged	I am alive and I am able to do many things, I am not completely damaged
I'm shameful, ugly	I believe I have value as a person. I am more than my appearance. If I did do something wrong, it does mean I need to hide myself for ever
I'm stupid	There may have been things I did not know at the time, and I cannot know everything. It is OK to get things wrong. I can learn. It does not mean I am stupid just because I have forgotten or did not know something
I'm different	I am OK as I am
I'm a bad person	I care about things and am not completely bad. No one is all bad or all good. We all have our flaws. Just doing some bad action does not mean I am completely bad as a person

2. Responsibility

Negative belief	Alternative/helpful belief
I did something wrong	I did the best I could knowing what I knew at the time
It's my fault	It was not 100% within my control, there were other factors. I did what I did at the time. I can learn from it
It is my responsibility to make things right	I have a part to play, but I am not responsible for everything. I have to let others take some responsibility as well sometimes

3. Control/Choice

Negative belief	Alternative/helpful belief
I am powerless	I am allowed to have a choice and a say. I can communicate what I need. I do not have to stay silent any more
I am helpless	There are things I can do to help myself

4. Safety/Vulnerability

Negative belief	Alternative/Helpful belief
I'm vulnerable, not safe	I am safe now; I need to remind myself of this
I can't trust anyone	I can choose who to trust
I can't trust myself	I can learn to trust my judgement now
Nobody will protect me	I am not in danger, but I know what to do if I am. I can look after myself
I might die	I am safe and I am alive
	I can feel and express my emotions and nothing bad will happen
Something bad will happen if I show emotions	

One of the things I'd like to point out about these core beliefs, and perhaps you have noticed this, is that the ones on the left are like absolute labels. Statements of fact and very all or nothing. This is because the brain likes to categorize, and usually these are developed in times of high emotion or when we are quite young – both of these are times when we will not be thinking in shades of grey or in abstract terms. As a result, we develop these quick ways to label ourselves, and they can be there for many years undetected and unchallenged.

Notice how the alternatives are less global labels, and more accepting of the shades of grey in a situation, and within us.

Do any of these core beliefs resonate with you at all? Did you notice a slight flinching or movement in your body, or did you look twice at one or two of them? Do you use any of these labels at all? It maybe that you have been using them without realizing the effect they can have on you. If you did identify with any of them, I want to let you know that you can re-evaluate them. This is where therapy can be helpful, in showing you how to change patterns like these, but the first step is to know what your patterns are and that it is possible to change.

The next time you find yourself rushing to negative labels that make you feel bad, such as 'I'm just not good enough to do this' or 'I can't cope', pause and try your hardest to look for some shades of grey, don't just believe the absolute label straight away.

CHAPTER TWO –
THE TROUBLE WITH EMOTIONS

EMOTION LABELS

Similar to the core beliefs in the previous section, the labels we have for emotions can often be used without us thinking too much about them. Again, the brain's need to categorize will be one of the reasons for this, as will our shared social norms.

Words such as 'angry', 'worried', 'anxious', sad and upset get used a lot in therapy, by both clients and therapists. The familiarity of these words might make it seem obvious what they mean, but they aren't as universal as we might think. In Lisa Feldman Barrett's book *How Emotions Are Made* (2017), she reports how there is evidence from several studies to show that we do not all show emotions in the same way, even though we think that we can tell what emotion someone is displaying. For example, the way that anger is displayed can be very different: one person might display anger with a red face, a puffed-out body and pounding fists, whereas another might be very still, and stare at the object of their anger with a seething rage that has very few outward signs of aggression. Barrett mentions research that indicates that people who have more words in their vocabulary to explain how they feel appear to do better both in regulating their emotions and on measures of success. There could be many reasons for this; for example, if we are able to refine what we actually feel, then this shows we are observing what we are experiencing and will be adopting strategies to manage these feelings based on what we notice. Perhaps because we will be more attuned to the subtleties of different feelings, we may notice them earlier before they swell. An example here would be noticing and managing minor irritations rather than exploding in rage. As a result, we would have better emotional regulation than someone who does not pay much attention to how they feel and has very few labels to use to apply to their experiences.

When I say 'pay attention to how you feel', what I mean by this is noticing not only what goes through your mind, but also what is going on physically in your body. If you get a gripping sensation in your gut, this is a feeling, if you feel your breath getting faster and quicker as you say something to someone, this is a feeling. The thoughts that go through your mind as you have these sensations are part of the feeling too. A feeling does not have to be an intangible concept. Feelings are thoughts going through your mind, and sensations, impulses and movements in your body. If you start to notice these, you will get to know where you tend to 'feel' certain emotions. For example, when I feel nervous, I feel this straight away in my lower gut. It's a 'wrenching' feeling.

Have a go right now. Do a quick body scan and check if you are holding any tension anywhere. Are you biting your inner lip, or clenching your toes, or holding tension anywhere else? Take a big breath and let it flop out as you release tension.

The next time you notice you feel on edge, stressed, tense, anxious or frustrated, scan your body to see what you notice. Whereabouts is this 'on-edgeness'? Is it in your gut? Your head? Are you clenching your jaw? What words would you use to describe how you feel right now?

It can be difficult to put words to a feeling. One of the reasons for this is because we are trying to use a different part of our brain to 'describe' what we are experiencing. But this can be helpful in giving us a little bit of distance and a space within which to choose what to do next. If we practise this, we can get much better at not letting emotions blindside us.

Have a look at the list of emotion words below. Instead of using the word 'anxious', could there be another word you could use? Maybe 'apprehensive', 'doubtful', 'unsure'? Add your own words to the list if you've found one that isn't on there. This is part of our emotional literacy, and I know I wasn't taught to do this when I was younger. It's important that we can describe and manage how we feel, that we know what emotions are, how to recognize them within ourselves and how to talk to others about what we feel.

So let's have a go. I'd love to ask if we could create more words for emotions together. I'm going to start a list here and would like to invite your words too. You will have had experiences that differ from mine, so I do not have the monopoly here.

Next time you notice yourself feeling something, be it sad, thoughtful, unsure, worried, angry, embarrassed, I'd like to ask you to notice where you feel this physically in your body, and then find a word on the list to describe the feeling or put your own word to it. The more that you do this the more you will be identifying the subtleties in your own feelings. This gives you more mastery over what you feel.

AFRAID

Explanation: feeling fearful and apprehensive
Alternatives: Alarmed, anxious, apprehensive, fearful, frightened, intimidated, nervous, panicky, petrified, scared, shaken, startled

ANGRY

Explanation: feeling and/or expressing fury or annoyance
Alternatives: annoyed, cross, enraged, exasperated, furious, incensed, indignant, irate, hacked off, heated, mad, outraged, provoked, raging, ranting, raving, riled, vexed

CALM

Explanation: being at peace, still and relaxed
Alternatives: at peace, relaxed, serene, settled, soothed, tranquil, untroubled

CONNECTED

Explanation: feeling part of something, feeling like you belong (an important feeling for our nervous system)

Alternatives: affiliated, associated, engaged, kindred, linked, related, tied, connected, loved, belonging

DISGUSTED

Explanation: feeling sickened or turned off
Alternatives: appalled, nauseated, repelled, repulsed, sickened, turning away from

ENTHUSIASTIC

Explanation: feeling interested and willing
Alternatives: avid, committed, desirous, devoted, eager, ebullient, excited, fervid, keen, passionate

EXCITED

Explanation: thrilled and ready for action
Alternatives: animated, aroused, enthusiastic, expectant, high, moved, roused, stirred, stimulated, wild, yearning

FLAT

Explanation: without expression, feeling in limbo
Alternatives: empty, depressed, dispirited, downhearted, drained, numb, shocked, tired, weak, weary, without energy, worn out

FRUSTRATED

Explanation: being held back, prevented from doing something or your expectations remaining unfulfilled
Alternatives: disappointed, discouraged, disheartened, irked

INSPIRE

Explanation: to fill with energy, to make something seem possible
Alternatives: encourage, energize, galvanize, influence, infuse, motivate, persuade, stimulate

IRRITATED

Explanation: not feeling able to rest, being on edge, snappy
Alternatives: agitated, crabby, disagreeable, flustered, fractious, grumpy, hassled, impatient, miffed, nettled, tetchy, peeved

LONELY

Explanation: feeling like you can't connect to others
Alternatives: abandoned, alone, companionless, estranged, forlorn, friendless, isolated, outcast, solitary

RELIEVED

Explanation: a feeling of being able to release yourself from tension
Alternatives: cheered, comforted, glad, grateful, happy, pleased, reassured, thankful

SAD

Explanation: feeling the loss or absence of something or someone
Alternatives: blue, depressed, down, empty, gloomy, glum, grieving, low, melancholy, mournful, pensive, sombre, tearful, unhappy, wistful

SAFE

Explanation: believing that you are protected from danger in that moment (very important for a healthy nervous system to notice when you feel safe)
Alternatives: impregnable, out of danger, protected, safe and sound, secure, comforted, soothed

SURPRISED

Explanation: taken aback by something unexpected
Alternatives: astonished, astounded, baffled, bewildered, confused, confused, dismayed, embarrassed, fazed, flummoxed, mystified, perplexed, puzzled, stumped, stunned

SUPPORTED

Explanation: feeling like you have the help that you need (something to do for ourselves, as well as for others)
Alternatives: advocate, aid, assist, boost, champion, defend, encourage, help, hold, promote, stand up for, stick up for

UPSET

Explanation: an unpleasant mix of feelings
Alternatives: agitated, choked, confused, disconcerted, dismayed, distressed, disturbed, distraught, distressed, gutted, hassled, hurt, overwrought, ruffled, shaken, tormented, troubled, unhappy, wrenched

WORRIED

Explanation: thinking about what might go wrong and feeling anxious as a result
Alternatives: anxious, apprehensive, avoidant, bothered, concerned, distracted, disturbed, fretful, hesitant, jittery, nervous, on-edge, perturbed, restless, shaken, suspicious, tense, troubled, twitchy, uneasy

CHAPTER THREE –
WHY AM I UPSET? PART ONE

QUESTIONNAIRES AND SELF-TESTS

RELIABILITY AND VALIDITY

Questionnaires that you complete yourself (rather than ones that a therapist/ clinician would complete) are also called self-report measures. It takes time to develop a measure to ensure that it shows two main things: reliability and validity. Reliability is when the measure is shown to be assessing the same aspect or behaviour at different points in time – in other words, how *consistent* it is. Validity is ensured when it has been found to measure that particular aspect or behaviour, and not something else. Validity is further refined by assessing whether it appears to measure what it is meant to (face validity), is measuring that particular feature and nothing else (construct validity) and shows that it can predict the feature being measured (predictive). These areas are all important in giving you a final score that you can feel is actually measuring what it is meant to measure. There are lots of fun questionnaires available on the internet, but they may not be able to claim they have this validity and reliability, so you cannot always be sure the score is a true reflection of what the questionnaire is meant to be assessing. For example, a question on a measure about depression could ask, 'Are you irritable and anxious a lot?' This question might seem to be measuring a feeling when can have when we feel low or grumpy (face validity). However, feeling irritable and anxious are aspects of generalized anxiety and also some hyper-arousal states following traumatic experiences, so it wouldn't be a question that would show construct validity for a questionnaire that only wanted to assess depression. There would need to be more work to include something like that; perhaps a part of the measure would have space for more agitated aspects of depression. But I hope you can see that when you take a test or measure, the score that you receive at the end has to be meaningful. You have to have confidence that the test is measuring what it should be.

The next time you take one of those fun tests on social media, ask yourself: is this question measuring what it thinks it is measuring, or could there be another reason for this aspect or behaviour?

With all of this in mind I have tried to include links to measures that have been researched and show reliability and validity. The way that you can tell this for yourself is by checking the questionnaire or site for information about where the measure came from and/or who developed the measure. The page on the patient.info site that offers the PHQ9 is an excellent example here. Have a look here at the credits at the end of the questionnaire: patient.info/doctor/patient-health-questionnaire-phq-9.

CAN A QUESTIONNAIRE GIVE ME A DIAGNOSIS?

It is important to note that questionnaires such as the Anxiety and Depression test on the NHS website cannot give you a diagnosis or tell you why you are feeling the way that you do. However, if you do find that you are scoring in the moderate to severe range and this either continues for more than two weeks or is a repeating pattern for you, it would be important to contact your doctor and/or arrange an appointment with a therapist to talk through what is happening for you. Two people can both score in the severe range on the PHQ9 and the GAD7 for example, but one person may be struggling with the effects of trauma whilst another may be struggling with OCD. Both can be reasons for high scores on anxiety and significant difficulties with low mood.

LIST OF SELF-REPORT MEASURES

ACES (ADVERSE CHILDHOOD EXPERIENCES) AND RESILIENCE SCORE

acestoohigh.com/got-your-ace-score
www.threerivers.gov.uk/egcl-page/adverse-childhood-experiences-aces

ANXIETY – NHS IAPT SELF-REPORT MEASURES

patient.info/doctor/generalised-anxiety-disorder-assessment-gad-7
patient.info/doctor/iapt-phobia-scale

AUTISM AND ADHD/ADD

The ADDitude website has several self-tests for ASD, ADD and ADHD as well as other tests that may be relevant. It is a great site for information and support from a friendly and informal perspective.

www.additudemag.com/download/autism-in-adults/?src=test

Note: The self-tests on this site are for screening and information rather than to confirm a diagnosis.

COMPASSION AND CRITICISM

goodmedicine.org.uk/goodknowledge/compassion-criticism
Kristin Neff's site – self-compassion.org/resources-2/#other-sites

DEPRESSION

NHS IAPT self-report measures –
patient.info/doctor/patient-health-questionnaire-phq-9

EMOTIONS

Emotional intelligence test –
globalleadershipfoundation.com/geit/eitest.html
Several different EQ tests –
positivepsychology.com/emotional-intelligence-tests/
Emotion beliefs questionnaire –
www.researchgate.net/publication/340660428_Emotion_Beliefs_
Questionnaire_EBQ_Copy_of_questionnaire_and_scoring_instructions

FINDING THE RIGHT THERAPIST FOR YOU

Esther Perel –
estherperel.com/blog/how-to-find-the-right-therapist-for-you

GENERAL SELF-ASSESSMENT TESTS FOR ANXIETY, MOOD, SLEEP

Good Thinking, a digital mental health initiative for London, supported by the NHS – www.good-thinking.uk/self-assessments

HEALTH ANXIETY

goodmedicine.org.uk/stressedtozest/2008/12/
handouts-questionnaires-health-anxiety-disorder

HIGHLY SENSITIVE PERSON SCALE (HSP)

Also called Sensory Processing Sensitivity, the HSP scale has been developed by Elaine Aron, who has worked hard to ensure this construct is researched and shows validity and reliability. On Aron's website there is a test for HSP in adults, as well as one for children, and a high-sensation-seeking test.
hsperson.com/test/highly-sensitive-test/

MIND PLAN QUIZ – YOUR MIND MATTERS

www.nhs.uk/oneyou/every-mind-matters/your-mind-plan-quiz/

NEURODIVERSITY APP AND PROFILER

The app on this website gives you a 'spiky profile' result for neurodivergent aspects such as dyslexia, dyspraxia, ADHD, ADD and ASD.
profiler.app

OCD – OBSESSIVE COMPULSIVE DISORDER

I am linking Dr James Hawkins's page here, as he has added the OCI (Obsessive Compulsive Inventory) in MS Word form with the sub-scales tagged to help you. He also includes the shortened form of this measure. The OCD scales are underneath the Panic info on this page.
goodmedicine.org.uk/goodknowledge/
panic-ocd-depersonalization-information-assessment

PANIC

goodmedicine.org.uk/goodknowledge/panic-ocd-depersonalization-information-assessment

PERSONALITY

The Big Five – bigfive-test.com
openpsychometrics.org/tests/IPIP-BFFM/

POSTNATAL DEPRESSION

patient.info/news-and-features/quiz-do-i-have-postnatal-depression

SOCIAL ANXIETY

psychology-tools.com/test/spin
goodmedicine.org.uk/goodknowledge/social-anxiety-information-assessment

TRAUMA AND PTSD

There's some detailed info on Dr James Hawkins's page that will signpost you to some really helpful information about trauma
goodmedicine.org.uk/goodknowledge/
ptsd-assessment-images-memories-information
    The two most used self-report measures in UK therapy services are the IES-R and the PCL-5.
    PCL-5: This pdf is from Lancashire's Traumatic Stress service. It includes a scoring key to help you assess whether your score is mild/moderate/severe in accordance with the criteria in the DSM5.
www.lscft.nhs.uk/media/Publications/Traumatic-Stress-Service/newPCL5.pdf
    IES-R: This questionnaire is in both Word and PDF format on the GoodMedicine website (it is towards the bottom of the page), along with a scoring key. The IES-R has sub-scales for 'avoidance', 'intrusions', and 'hyperarousal' – all key parts of PTSD.
goodmedicine.org.uk/goodknowledge/ptsd-assessment-images-memories-information

CHAPTER SIX – WHEN SHOULD I SEE A THERAPIST?

CRISIS INFORMATION

If you are in the UK and are feeling suicidal right now, call 116123, or if you are under 19 call 0800 11 11.

If you are outside the UK click on these links for global and international helplines:

Suicide.org – International Suicide Hotlines: www.suicide.org/international-suicide-hotlines.html

USA: The National Suicide Prevention Lifeline: www.suicidepreventionlifeline.org 1-800-273-TALK (8255)

WhatsApp – Global Suicide Hotline Resources: faq.whatsapp.com/general/security-and-privacy/global-suicide-hotline-resources

Your Life Counts – Global Support Resources: yourlifecounts.org/find-help/

HELPLINES AND CRISIS SUPPORT

Alcoholics Anonymous

www.alcoholics-anonymous.org.uk/contact
Call: 0800 9177 650

Alcohol Change UK (Drinkline)

alcoholchange.org.uk/help-and-support/get-help-now

Anxiety UK

www.anxietyuk.org.uk/get-help/helpline-email-text-live-chat-services
Call: 03444 775 774 or email: support@anxietyuk.org.uk

At a Loss (support for the bereaved)

www.ataloss.org

Breathing Space, Scotland

breathingspace.scot/
Call: 0800 83 85 87

Bullying UK

www.bullying.co.uk

C.A.L.L Mental health helpline for Wales

www.callhelpline.org.uk

Campaign Against Living Miserably (CALM)

www.thecalmzone.net/help/get-help/
Call: 0800 585858

Childline

www.childline.org.uk
Call: 0800 1111

CRUSE Bereavement care

www.cruse.org.uk
Call: 0808 808 1677

Domestic Abuse

Mankind – www.mankind.org.uk
Respect – mensadviceline.org.uk
Refuge – www.nationaldahelpline.org.uk
Call: 0808 2000 247

Drinkaware support services list

www.drinkaware.co.uk/advice/support-services/alcohol-support-services

Emergency Service workers – PTSD999

www.ptsd999.org.uk/about/how-to-get-help
Call: 01223 755 130, email: support@ptsd999.org.uk or text: 07778 485 528

Family Lives (Previously Parentline)

www.familylives.org.uk/how-we-can-help/confidential-helpline

Family Rights Group

www.frg.org.uk

Farming Community Network

fcn.org.uk/help-health-issues/ or call: 03000 111 999
Galop (Helpline for LGBT+ people who have experienced hate crime or
abuse) – www.galop.org.uk/how-we-can-help/
Call: 0800 999 5428 or email: help@galop.org.uk

GamCare (helpline for problem gambling)

www.gamcare.org.uk/get-support/talk-to-us-now
Call: 0808 8020 133

LGBT Foundation

lgbt.foundation/coronavirus/wellbeing
Call: 0345 3 30 30 30

LGBT Health Scotland

www.lgbthealth.org.uk
Call: 0300 123 2523

Marijuana Anonymous

www.marijuana-anonymous.org.uk
Call: 0300 124 0373

MEIC (helpline service for children and young people up to the age of 25 in Wales)

www.meiccymru.org
Call: 0808 80 23456 or text: 84001

Mental Health Matters helplines

www.mhm.org.uk/helpline-webchat

Mermaids UK (support for trans and gender-diverse children and their families)

mermaidsuk.org.uk/about-us
Call: 0808 801 0400

MIND

Crisis planning – www.mind.org.uk/information-support/
guides-to-support-and-services/crisis-services/
List of helplines – www.mind.org.uk/information-support/
guides-to-support-and-services/crisis-services/
helplines-listening-services/

Mindline Trans+

mindlinetrans.org.uk
Call: 0300 330 5468

MindOut (online support for lesbian, gay, bisexual, trans and queer people)

www.mindout.org.uk/get-support/mindout-online/

Muslim Youth Helpline

www.myh.org.uk/helpline
Call: 0808 808 2008 or live chat on website

Narcotics Anonymous

ukna.org
Call: 0300 999 1212

OCD Action

ocdaction.org.uk/i-need-support/helpline/
Call: 0845 390 6232

Papyrus (charity dedicated to preventing suicide of young people)

www.papyrus-uk.org/hopelineuk
Call: 0800 068 4141

Panic

nopanic.org.uk/the-no-panic-helpline
Call: 0300 772 9844

Rural Support (Northern Ireland)

www.ruralsupport.org.uk/how-we-can-help/helpline/
Call: 0800 138 1678

SAMARITANS

www.samaritans.org
Call: 116123 (in UK) or email: jo@samaritans.org

SANDS (helpline for anyone affected by the death of a baby)

www.sands.org.uk
Call: 0808 164 3332 or email: helpline@sands.org.uk

Saneline

www.sane.org.uk/what_we_do/support/

Self-Injury Support for women and girls

www.selfinjurysupport.org.uk
Call: 0808 800 8088 text: 07537 432444 or email: tessmail@selfinjury-support.org.uk
SHOUT – www.giveusashout.org
Text SHOUT to 85258

The Silverline (for people over 55 years old)

www.thesilverline.org.uk/helpline
Call: 0800 4 70 80 90

Support Line (a helpline and support service aimed at those who are isolated, at risk, vulnerable and victims of any form of abuse)

www.supportline.org.uk
Call: 01708 765200 or email: info@supportline.org.uk

Survivors of bereavement by suicide (SOBS)

uksobs.org

The Survivors Trust (for people who have suffered sexual abuse)

www.thesurvivorstrust.org
Call: 0808 8 010818

Switchboard LGBT

switchboard.lgbt/about-us
Call: 0300 330 0630

Winston's Wish (support for grieving children)

www.winstonswish.org
Call: 0808 8 020 021

Young Minds

youngminds.org.uk/find-help/get-urgent-help/
Text: YM to 85258 for crisis support

Your Life Counts (global support line)

yourlifecounts.org

MY SAFETY PLAN

After you have spoken with someone on the helpline, make your own safety/crisis plan to support you. There are some great templates on the following websites:

getselfhelp.co.uk/suicidal.htm
www.stayingsafe.net/home

Note to those supporting friends and family members who are feeling suicidal: you do not have to fix the problem. It is OK to let the person feel what they are feeling, even though it can be heart-breaking to see them struggling and you will want to take this feeling away from them. Let them talk. It is OK to just 'be' with them. Too often we feel so anxious about not being able to solve the problem that this makes it hard for us to be with someone when they are upset.

CHAPTER SEVEN –
FINDING A THERAPIST

HOW TO REFER YOURSELF TO NHS PSYCHOLOGICAL THERAPY SERVICES IN THE UK:

England:
www.nhs.uk/service-search/find-a-psychological-therapies-service/

Wales:
nhswales.silvercloudhealth.com/signup/
www.wales.nhs.uk/healthtopics/conditions/mentalhealth
phw.nhs.wales/topics/latest-information-on-novel-coronavirus-covid-19/
how-are-you-doing/how-are-you-feeling/how-to-access-support/

Northern Ireland:

www.nidirect.gov.uk/articles/mental-health-services

Scotland:
clearyourhead.scot/support
www.samh.org.uk/find-help

Isle of Man:
www.gov.im/categories/caring-and-support/mental-health-service/
community-wellbeing-service/self-referral-form-for-counsellingtherapies/

Jersey:
www.gov.je/Health/Mental/Pages/JerseyTalkingTherapies.aspx
patient.info/treatment-medication/self-referral/refer-yourself-
for-nhs-talking-therapy-counselling

CHARITIES AND ORGANIZATIONS OFFERING THERAPY (SOME AT LOW COST OR FREE)

Action for Aspergers –
www.actionforaspergers.org/asperger-counselling

Anxiety UK – www.anxietyuk.org.uk/get-help/access-therapy/

Arbours Association – www.arboursassociation.org/psychotherapy/

Association of Jungian Analysts –
www.jungiananalysts.org.uk/reduced-fee-scheme/

Beyond Barriers – www.beyondbarriers.uk/pricing

Breathe UK – breathe-uk.com/counselling-services/

British Psychotherapy Foundation –

www.britishpsychotherapyfoundation.org.uk/therapy/
low-fee-intensive-therapy

Centre for Freudian Analysis & Research –
cfar.org.uk/clinical-service/

CPPD UK Ltd – cppdlondon.com/low-cost-counselling/

CRUSE Bereavement care – www.cruse.org.uk/

Free Psychotherapy Network – freepsychotherapynetwork.com/

Gestalt Centre – gestaltcentre.org.uk/find-a-counsellor-or-therapist/

Guild of Psychotherapists – guildofpsychotherapists.org.uk/psychotherapy/
reduced-fee-clinic/#.X2eB2WjYpPZ

The Help Hub – www.thehelphub.co.uk/therapists/

IOPA – Institute of Psychoanalysis –
psychoanalysis.org.uk/iopa-clinics/low-fee-scheme

LGBT Foundation – lgbt.foundation/talkingtherapies

London Friend – londonfriend.org.uk/counselling/

Metanoia – www.metanoia.ac.uk/therapy/
metanoia-counselling-and-psychotherapy-service/

The MIX – www.themix.org.uk/get-support/speak-to-our-team/
the-mix-counselling-service

The Philadelphia Association –
www.philadelphia-association.com/therapy

The Psychosynthesis Trust – psychosynthesistrust.org.uk/counselling/

Re-Vision –
www.re-vision.org.uk/find-a-therapist/low-cost-counselling/

RELATE – www.relate.org.uk/find-your-nearest-relate

SAP – The Society of Analytical Psychology – www.thesap.org.uk/
about-sap/

Tavistock Institute – www.tavistockrelationships.org/relationship-help

WPF Therapy – wpf.org.uk/need-to-talk/therapy-options/

ORGANIZATIONS PROVIDING THERAPY TO SPECIFIC GROUPS

(There are a huge number of these so if you don't see one specific to you,
do search online as I was not able to include them all here.)

Abuse

Adult survivors of abuse/neglect in Scottish care settings –
future-pathways.co.uk/
Narcissistic Abuse, the Echo Society –
www.theechosociety.org.uk/counselling-service
Woman's Trust (Domestic Abuse) – womanstrust.org.uk/?fbclid=IwAR02n-
8rtBmtWEfMn0U__wd5_JISiIf0tePtzPEjyu0b1p16TzfGQt3da9o

Addiction

Get Connected – www.getconnected.org.uk/about-us/
Drugs – www.talktofrank.com/get-help/find-support-near-you

Anxiety

No Panic – nopanic.org.uk/telephone-support-services/

Autism

Action for Aspergers –
www.actionforaspergers.org/asperger-counselling/

BAME

Aashna – www.aashna.uk/
Aashna is a service that offers long-term therapy to 'individuals diverse in culture, social background religion sexuality, age, gender, disability and other diversity, who struggle to access culturally sensitive therapy'.

Black African and Asian Therapy Network –
www.baatn.org.uk/Find-a-Therapist
Black Health Initiative – www.blackhealthinitiative.org/counselling
Chinese Mental Health Association –
www.cmha.org.uk/our-services-/counselling

Bereavement

Child Bereavement UK –
www.childbereavementuk.org/booked-telephone-support
Survivors of Bereavement by Suicide (SOBS) UK –
uksobs.org/we-can-help/e-mail/

Children and Young People

Childline – www.childline.org.uk/get-support/1-2-1-counsellor-chat/
Place2Be, mental health support for children in schools – www.place2be.
org.uk/our-services/services-for-schools/mental-health-support-in-schools/
Youth Access –
www.youthaccess.org.uk/services/find-your-local-service

Depression in New Fathers

depressioninnewdads.com/book-a-consultation/

Eating Disorders

National Centre for Eating disorders booking.eating-disorders.org.uk/counsellors/search
Beat – helpfinder.beateatingdisorders.org.uk/

Farmers and Rural Communities

Counselling for farmers – www.counsellingforfarmers.com
Countryside Counselling – countrysidecounselling.org.uk
DPJ Foundation (Wales) – www.thedpjfoundation.co.uk/contact-us/
Strong Heart – www.strong-heart.co.uk

Farsi Speakers

Farsi Speakers Counselling Service (NHS Barnet) –
www.farsophone.org.uk/index.php/en/?jjj=1600632420649

Islamic Community

Institute of Islamic Counselling and Wellbeing –
islamiccounselling.info/our-counsellors/

Jewish Community

Jami – jamiuk.org/get-support/what-we-do/online-support/

Location-Specific

Turn2Me (Ireland) – turn2me.ie/page/our-story
The Maytree Centre (London) – www.maytree.org.uk
Anxious Minds (Newcastle and Tyneside) –
www.anxiousminds.co.uk/talking-therapies-newcastle/

Refugees

Refugee Therapy Centre – refugeetherapy.org.uk

Post-Natal Depression

PANDAS Foundation – pandasfoundation.org.uk

Pregnancy

Pregnancy Crisis Care – www.pregnancycrisiscare.org.uk/about-us.php

Self Injury

Self Injury Support –
www.selfinjurysupport.org.uk/our-support-services

Sexual Abuse and Rape

Male rape and sexual abuse –
www.survivorsuk.org/young-people/counselling/
Safeline – www.safeline.org.uk/what-we-do/counselling-therapy/
Rape Crisis – rapecrisis.org.uk/get-help/want-to-talk/
Rape Crisis Scotland – www.rapecrisisscotland.org.uk/
about-local-rape-crisis-centres/

Sexual Offenders and Potential Sexual Offenders

StopSO – stopso.org.uk

THERAPY REGISTRATION AND ACCREDITATION BODIES

In the UK counselling and psychotherapy are not a regulated profession. This means that there is no legal requirement to be accredited or registered with a particular organization, and unfortunately anyone can call themselves by these titles. Despite this, it is normal for therapists to become members of a professional body and work towards 'accreditation'. Accreditation and/or registration is seen as a way of demonstrating appropriate training and upholding certain standards of practice. Membership and accreditation with one of these bodies provides some security for clients, as it shows that the therapist has appropriate training and experience, but it also provides somewhere for the client to go should they have any queries about the therapist's practice.

There is a body that oversees the work of some of these organizations; it is called the Professional Standards Authority (PSA). The PSA works with therapy bodies to ensure that standards of accreditation are upheld, and they achieve a PSA quality mark as a result. Not all therapy accrediting bodies have the PSA mark or are registered with the PSA, as it is an expensive process. You can check the list of therapy accrediting bodies that do work with the PSA and have the quality mark here: www.professionalstandards.org.uk/what-we-do/accredited-registers/find-a-register/-in-category/categories/professions/counselling

Because many therapy bodies are not listed with the PSA, I have provided a list of all of the main counselling and psychotherapy bodies in the UK. These represent a very wide range of the different therapies on offer. As there are so many different types of therapy, there are many different therapy bodies representing therapists who have trained in these different therapies. For example, there are professional associations for psychoanalysts, for CBT therapists, for family therapists and so on. The list is long, but I have tried to include as many as possible. Many of them maintain a register of therapists that are accredited/registered with them, so you can find a therapist on their site.

If you find a therapist outside these sites, for example on private directories or via a Google search, it is important to check that they are a member of one of these organizations. If you do not see any information about who they are registered or accredited with, then you won't be able to contact a specific organization if you have concerns about the therapist. This is where registration and accreditation are important in protecting you, and in providing external validation of the therapist's credentials.

ACAT, Association of Cognitive Analytic Therapy – www.acat.me.uk/page/find+a+private+cat+therapist

A registered charity that provides information on the practice and training of CAT and also has a list of CAT Therapists for the public to search.

ACC, Association of Christian Counsellors – www.acc-uk.org/find-a-counsellor/search-for-a-counsellor.html

The professional body for Christian counsellors. ACC is a registered charity and is accredited by the Professional Standards Authority.

ACP, Association of Child Psychotherapists – childpsychotherapy.org.uk/resources-families/find-child-psychotherapist

Accredited by the PSA. This is the professional accrediting body for NHS-trained child psychotherapists. The training involves master's-level study combined with 4 years in-service clinical training.

ACTO, the Association for Counselling and Therapy Online – acto-org.uk/therapists/

Offers training and resources for online therapy.

ADMP, Association for Dance Movement Psychotherapy – admp.org.uk/find-a-dance-movement-psychotherapist/

The professional organization for dance movement therapists in the UK. It is an organizational member of the Humanistic Integrative Psychotherapy College (ukcphipc.co.uk), a college of the UKCP.

AFT, Association for Family Therapy and Systemic Practice – www.aft.org.uk/consider/view/how-to-find-help.html

A registered charity aiming to promote high standards of family therapy and systemic practice.

AGIP, Association for Group and Individual Psychotherapy – agip.org.uk/psychotherapy/therapist-search

A registered charity that is also a member of the UKCP. It aims to provide psychoanalytic therapy services and a training programme for therapists.

AJA, Association of Jungian Analysts – www.jungiananalysts.org.uk/find-an-analyst/

A registered charity based in London and aiming to promote analytical psychology from a contemporary and inclusive perspective.

APCCA, Association for Person Centred Creative Arts – www.apcca.org.uk/apcca-practitioners

A new association that has been set up to bring together creative arts practitioners, counsellors, psychotherapists, psychologists and coaches who are interested in bringing the creative arts into their work.

APCP, Association of Professional Counsellors and Psychotherapists in Ireland – www.apcp.ie/find-a-counsellor-psychotherapist/

A professional organization for counsellors and psychotherapists in Ireland that aims to promote high standards of practice and training.

APPI, Association for Psychoanalysis and Psychotherapy Ireland – appi.ie/find-a-clinician/

A group for psychoanalysts working in the Freudian Lacanian tradition.

AREBT, Association for Rational Emotive Behaviour Therapy – www.arebt.one

The main association for REBT Therapists in the UK. It works with the BABCP to maintain a register of accredited CBT/REBT Therapists. To find a REBT Therapist: www.cbtregisteruk.com.

ASIIP, Adlerian Society UK Institute for Individual Psychology – asiip.org/adlerian-therapist/

A UK association setup to promote the training and practice of Adlerian Psychotherapy and Individual Psychology.

ATSAC, Association for the Treatment of Sexual Addiction and Compulsivity – atsac.org.uk/directory-counsellors/

ATSAC is a not-for-profit organization that provides information and treatment options for people who struggle with sex addiction or compulsions related to this.

Ayanay – www.ayanay.co.uk/directory.html

Ayanay Psychological Membership Ltd is a company that has been setup to provide accreditation to counsellors, therapists and life coaches.

BAAT, British Association of Art Therapists – www.baat.org/About-BAAT/Find-an-Art-Therapist

The BAAT is the professional organization that represents Art therapists in the UK. Their members are HCPC Registered Art therapists.

BABCP, British Association for Behavioural and Cognitive Psychotherapies – babcp.com

The lead organization for CBT in the UK and Ireland that also provides accreditation for CBT therapists. BABCP is a registered charity. To find/ check a CBT therapist: www.cbtregisteruk.com.

BACP, British Association for Counselling and Psychotherapy – www.bacp.co.uk/search/Therapists

BACP is a registered charity and a professional association for counselling and psychotherapy in the UK. BACP is an accredited member of the Professional Standards Authority.

BADTH, British Association of Dramatherapists – badth.org.uk/therapist-search

BADTH is a not-for-profit professional organization for dramatherapists in the UK.

BAPT, British Association of Play Therapists – www.bapt.info/find-therapist

A member of the Professional Standards Authority accredited Register, the BAPT is a registered charity and a professional organization for play therapists in the UK.

BICA, British Infertility Counselling Association – www.bica.net/find-a-counsellor

A registered charity recognized by the Human Fertilisation and Embryology Authority and the British Fertility Society in the UK.

BISS, British and Irish Sandplay Society –
www.sandplay.org.uk/members-map

A professional association for Jungian sandplay therapists.

BPA, British Psychodrama Association –
www.psychodrama.org.uk/find_a_psychotherapist.php

The BPA is accredited by the UKCP and promotes the practice of psychodrama and sociodrama in the UK and Ireland.

BPC, British Psychoanalytic Council –
www.bpc.org.uk/information-support/find-a-therapist-or-clinic/

The BPC is accredited by the Professional Standards Authority and maintains an accredited public register of psychoanalytic and psychodynamic psychotherapists. BPC incorporates several member institutions. These are:

AMPP, Association of Medical Psychodynamic Psychotherapists
Anna Freud National Centre for Children and Families –
www.annafreud.org
AJA, Association of Jungian Analysts – www.jungiananalysts.org.uk
APC, Association of Psychodynamic Counsellors
APPCOS, Association for Psychodynamic Practice and Counselling in
Organizational Settings – psychodynamicthinking.info
BPA, British Psychoanalytic Association – www.psychoanalysis-bpa.org
BPF, British Psychotherapy Foundation –
www.britishpsychotherapyfoundation.org.uk
FPC, Foundation for Psychotherapy and Counselling – www.thefpc.org.uk
FPS, Forensic Psychotherapy Society
IoP, Institute of Psychoanalysis (British Psychoanalysis Society) –
psychoanalysis.org.uk

NB: there is another website that uses the name 'British Psychoanalytic Council'. It has the website address www.psychoanalytic-council.org. The BPC have confirmed that this site is **not** connected to them.

BPS, British Psychological Society –
www.bps.org.uk/public/find-psychologist

A registered charity which operates as the representative body for psychologists and the profession of psychology in the UK. It operates by Royal Charter and maintains a register of chartered psychologists.

CFAR, Centre for Freudian Analysis and Research –
cfar.org.uk/centre-analysts

Registered with the UKCP, the CFAR accredits psychoanalysts in the UK.

COSCA –Counselling and Psychotherapy in Scotland –
finder.cosca.org.uk/searchregistrant.aspx

A charity registered in Scotland, the Confederation of Scottish Counselling Agencies is the professional body for counselling and psychotherapy in Scotland.

COSRT –College of Sexual & Relationship Therapists –
www.cosrt.org.uk/factsheets/therapists-nearest-me-search-results/

COSRT is a registered charity and the UK's professional body for sexual and relationship therapists.

CP-UK, College of Psychoanalysts UK –
psychoanalysis-cpuk.org/member-directory/

Represents psychoanalytic practitioners in the UK.

CPJA, Council for Psychoanalysis and Jungian Analysis –
www.cpja.org.uk/about-the-cpja/

The CPJA is a college of the UKCP and represents psychodynamic, psychoanalytic and Jungian psychotherapists in the UK.

EMDR UK and Ireland –emdrassociation.org.uk/find-a-therapist

The professional association for EMDR therapists in the UK and Ireland.

FDAP, Federation of Drug and Alcohol Practitioners –
www.smmgp-fdap.org.uk/fdap-practitioner-directory

A charity that operates as the professional body for workers in the substance abuse field.

FETC, Foundation for Emotional Therapeutic Counselling –
www.emotionaltherapeuticcounselling.org.uk/about

A registered charity operating as a training organization for ETC.

Gestalt Centre – gestaltcentre.org.uk/find-a-counsellor-or-therapist

The Gestalt Centre is a registered charity and training organization for gestalt therapists who are accredited with either UKCP or BACP.

GPTI, Gestalt Psychotherapy and Training Institute – gpti.org.uk/find-a-therapist

The GPTI is a member organization of the UKCP. It provides training and accreditation for gestalt psychotherapists.

GOP, Guild of Psychotherapists – guildofpsychotherapists.org.uk

A registered charity and professional body for psychoanalytic psychotherapists accredited by UKCP.

HCPC, Health and Care Professions Council – www.hcpc-uk.org/check-the-register

The HCPC is the main regulator for the health profession. It also regulates psychologists, occupational therapists and art therapists.

HGI, Human Givens Institute – www.hgi.org.uk/find-therapist

Accredited by the Professional Standards Authority, the HGI is a membership body and a professional body for Human Givens therapists.

IACP, Irish Association for Counselling and Psychotherapy – iacp.ie

A registered charity representing counselling and psychotherapy in Ireland.

IATE, Institute for the Arts in Therapy and Education – www.artspsychotherapy.org

Training institute for arts psychotherapists and child psychotherapists.

ICP, Irish Council for Psychotherapy – www.psychotherapycouncil.ie/find

The ICP is the national umbrella organization for psychotherapy in Ireland.

IGA, Institute of Group Analysis – www.groupanalysis.org/PsychotherapyReferralService/PsychotherapyReferralService.aspx

A registered charity whose mission is to promote the theory and practice of group analysis in the UK.

IGAP, Independent Group of Analytical Psychologists – www.igap.co.uk/find.html

The IGAP is a registered charity that trains Jungian analysts and maintains a register of therapists who provide low-cost therapy. Its members are UKCP registered.

IOP, Institute of Psychosynthesis – www.psychosynthesis.org/practitioners/

A member of the UKCP and the professional body for psychosynthesis practitioners.

Metanoia Institute – www.metanoiatherapists.co.uk

The Metanoia Institute trains counselling psychologists. psychotherapists and counsellors and provides a directory of therapists who have graduated from their programmes, which are accredited by the BPS, BACP and UKCP.

NCHP, National College of Hypnosis and Psychotherapy – nchp.ac.uk/

A member of UKCP, the NCHP trains and accredits hypnotherapists, hypno-psychotherapists and hypno-psychotherapeutic counsellors.

NCP, National Council of Psychotherapists – www.thencp.org

A professional organization for coaches, counsellors, psychotherapists and hypnotherapists working in any therapy modality.

NCS, National Counselling Society – nationalcounsellingsociety.org

A member of the Professional Standards Authority accredited register. NCS is a not-for-profit professional accrediting body for counselling.

PTUK, Play Therapy UK – www.playtherapy.org.uk

A member of the Professional Standards Authority accredited register. PTUK is a professional association for play and creative arts therapists in the UK.

SAP, Society for Analytical Psychology – www.thesap.org.uk/find-a-pyschotherapist/#!directory/map

A professional body for Jungian analysts and psychotherapists and a registered charity.

SEA, Society for Existential Analysis – existentialanalysis.org.uk

A member of UKCP. The SEA is a registered charity and was founded by Emmy van Deurzen in 1988. It welcomes anyone interested in existential analysis, as well as providing a training and research forum for therapists.

TPCA, The Person-Centred Association – www.the-pca.org.uk/directory/therapists/find-a-practitioner.html

Previously known as BAPCA until 2018, the PCA is an organization devoted to the maintenance and development of the person-centred approach in counselling.

UKAHPP, UK Association for Humanistic Psychology Practitioners – ahpp.org.uk/find-a-therapist/

Accredited by the Professional Standards Authority, and a member of the UKCP, the UKAHPP is the main accrediting body for practitioners who use humanistic psychology in their work.

UKSFA, UK Association for Solution Focused Practice – ukasfp.org

UK Membership organization for solution-focused practitioners.

UKATA, UK Association for Transactional Analysis – www.uktransactionalanalysis.co.uk

Formerly the Institute of Transactional Analysis, UKATA represents all forms of TA theory and practice in the UK.

UKCP, UK Council for Psychotherapy – www.psychotherapy.org.uk/find-a-therapist/

The UKCP is a registered charity and accredited member of the Professional Standards Authority. Its role is to regulate the accreditation of psychotherapists and psychotherapeutic counsellors in the UK. Individual therapists that train with one of UKCP's colleges can apply for accreditation through that college.

UPCA, Universities Psychotherapy and Counselling Association – www.upca.org.uk/find-a-therapist/

UPCA is a member of the UKCP. Its aims are to promote safe and ethical counselling and psychotherapy practices in universities. It accredits its members in accordance with UKCP rules and maintains a register of accredited therapists.

LIST OF INDEPENDENT DIRECTORIES WHERE YOU CAN FIND A THERAPIST IN THE UK

The following is a list of all the current operational therapy directories that I could find where you can search for a therapist if you are in the UK. I accessed these sites online in September 2020, so the information on there may have changed or been updated since this time. Because privacy and the security of data is vital, I put together a short list of questions that I wanted to answer for each directory when I accessed their privacy policy. I wanted to know who operated the site and where they were based, and I wanted their privacy policy to take note of the 2018 Data Protection Act. This act requires a company to be registered with the ICO and to have a named person responsible for data processing. It also requires a way of contacting the company with privacy concerns. The minimum is that the company has a privacy policy on their website, of which all but one did. Transparency, accountability and open communication are important indicators of trustworthiness. There are so many directories offering to help us find a therapist, and some of these websites will be capturing our personal information, so it is vital that we know with whom and where our data is being held.

Data and security are of course not the only indicators of whether these sites are going to offer you a good user experience, so you may wish to assess each according to your own individual criteria. The website Very Well Mind has put together a useful list of how they assess online therapy. It refers to US sites but many of the questions could be easily adapted to UK sites also. Have a look at it here: www.verywellmind.com/online-therapy-review-methodology-4777996.

The Black, African and Asian Therapy Network – www.baatn.org.uk

BAATN, BAATN 11216, PO Box 6945, London, W1A 6US

BAATN is a social enterprise that runs a directory where you can search for a therapist with a BAME heritage.

BetterHelp – www.betterhelp.com

BetterHelp, 990 Villa Street, Mountain View, CA 94041, USA

This site does ask quite a lot of questions before you can search for a therapist. Although I never completed the questionnaire, and was not on their website for too long, I was subsequently presented with adverts on Facebook for BetterHelp for several days after that one visit to the website. This is called 'remarketing' and many websites do this, but I did find it a bit annoying.

CBT Pages – www.cbtpages.com

Think CBT Ltd

CBT Pages is a directory that lists accredited CBT therapists. You can search for and book a session with the therapist of your choice on the site.

Choice Therapies – www.choicetherapies.co.uk

Choice Therapies LLP, 55 Queen Square, Bristol, BS1 4LH

Choice Therapies is a new directory that offers a range of both counselling and holistic therapies.

Counselling Directory – www.counselling-directory.org.uk

Memiah Limited, Counselling Directory, Building 3, Riverside Way, Camberley, Surrey, GU15 3YL

Counselling Directory was set up in 2005 and is one of several directories operated by Memiah Limited. The site lists counsellors and psychotherapists that you can search for and then contact directly. There are also helpful articles on the site to help you with your search and support you with information to make it easier to find the therapist for you. Memiah also operates the magazine *Happiful*.

Counsellor Directory – counsellor.directory

Counsellor Directory is a website that was set up in 2008. It has a 'Social Enterprise Initiative' badge on the homepage and states that it operates on a 'pay what you can' basis for counsellors who offer low-cost therapy. I could not find the company name, address or telephone number on the website at the time of searching.

Culture Minds Therapy – culturemindstherapy.com

CultureMinds Therapy Ltd, 1 Royal Street, London SE1 7LL

Set up in October 2020, this site states it is the 'UK's leading Therapist-matching service for the Black and Asian community'.

Dr Julian – dr-julian.com

Dr Julian Medical Group, 21 Portman Close, London W1H 6BR

Dr Julian is a website platform where you can find and book a video therapy appointment with a therapist of your choice. It was set up in 2017 by Dr Julian Nesbitt, ex-hospital doctor and now GP.

Efficacy – www.efficacy.org.uk

Efficacy Limited, 54-55 Cornhill, London EC3V 3PD

Efficacy offers CBT appointments at short notice, either by video or phone. They also offer EMDR and an online CBT program using SilverCloud.

E Therapy – www.e-therapy.uk

E-Therapy Limited Telehealth solutions offers a video platform through which you can book and have a session with either a nutritional or psychological therapist. I accessed the site from the UK, and it does offer UK therapists. I could not see a contact name or address on the day I accessed the page.

Find a therapist – www.findatherapist.co.uk

Findatherapist.co.uk Ltd, SBC House, Restmor Way, Wallington SM6 7AH

Findatherapist.co.uk was formerly known as rscpp.co.uk. It is run by therapist Richard Snowdon, and computer-science postgraduate Tommy Newman. The site lists only therapists registered and accredited by the BABCP, BACP, BPC, BPS, COSRT, HCPC, NCS and UKCP. It has a helpful self-assessment tool on there, as well as a link to which therapies are recommended by NICE for which conditions. There are also reviews of the therapists, so you can see what previous clients have said.

Find a Therapist – www.findatherapist.com

US only.

Find a Therapy – www.findatherapy.org

Find a Private Tutor Ltd, Regency House, 3 Princes Street, Bath BA1 1HL

The introductory video on this site states that they are one of the UK's leading directories of complementary therapies, but they also list psychotherapists and counsellors.

Harley Therapy – harleytherapy.com

Harley Therapy Platform Ltd and Harley Therapy Limited, 1-7 Harley Street, London W1G 9QD

A site that allows you to find and book a therapy session with a UK-registered counsellor, psychotherapist or psychologist. Sessions can be either video, phone, chat or in-person. The site has vetted the therapists it lists on the platform and assures they have the appropriate insurance, qualifications and accreditation. Harley Therapy has access to the immediate availability of its therapists, so you can see who is immediately available if you want to see someone fast.

Healing Clouds – www.healingclouds.com/about-us

Healing Clouds Ltd, 71-75 Shelton Street, Covent Garden, London WC2H 9JQ

This site is listed as a site linking clients with therapists worldwide for online therapy sessions.

Hub of Hope – hubofhope.co.uk

Chasing the Stigma, 54 St James Street Liverpool L1 0AB and Suite 2a, Cunard Building, Water St, Liverpool L3 1AH

The Hub of Hope is a directory of mental health services and support that is provided by the organization Chasing the Stigma, a charity based in the UK.

Ieso Online CBT – www.iesohealth.com

Ieso Digital Health Ltd, The Jeffreys Building, Cowley Road, Cambridge CB4 0DS

Ieso (previously known as Psychology Online), provides online text-based CBT that is free for NHS patients in most of the UK. They also offer their services to private clients too.

Inquire Talk – inquiretalk.com

Inquire Talk Ltd, 20-22 Wenlock Road, London N1 7GU (same address as ISOS Health)

A directory that offers counsellors, psychotherapists and psychologists who provide online therapy. You can choose a therapist, see their availability and book your session on the website. Sessions can be either via video, text or phone, as well as face-to-face (where appropriate). The site lists therapists as 'licensed' or 'certified' rather than as 'registered' or 'accredited'. The latter terms being familiar to therapists in the UK, whereas the former are terms used for US therapists.

ISOS – isoshealth.com/about-us

Chrysalis Health Ltd, 20 – 22 Wenlock Road, London N1 7GU

ISOS Health was setup by Kim Page, a mum, carer and sufferer of Type 1 diabetes and coeliac disease who wanted to help people get easy access to dieticians, physiotherapists and psychologists. On the site you can choose to have sessions with all three different practitioners who together work as your 'power of three' team and can share information between each other.

Muslim Counsellor and Psychotherapist Network (MCAPN) – www.mcapn.co.uk/counselling-directory

A directory for clients to find support from Muslim therapists, and for therapists to list their profiles and support and network with each other.

MYNDUP – myndup.com

MYNDUP Ltd, 44 Tempest Mead, North Weald, Essex CM16 6DY

Founded by Joel Gujral following his positive experiences with an online life coach, Myndup offers a platform where you can book video sessions with a therapist or life coach.

My Online Therapy – myonlinetherapy.com

Lekta Therapy Ltd, 2 Lansdowne Row, Suite 163, London, W1J 6HL and Lekta Therapy Ltd, Second Floor, 4-5 Gough Square, London EC4A 3DE

My Online Therapy is a new site that offers online therapy with HCPC registered psychologists.

My Therapist Online – www.mytherapistonline.co.uk

My Therapist Online Limited, 38 West Street, Helpston, Peterborough PE6 7AY

My Therapist Online was set up by BABCP accredited CBT therapist Lisa Johnston and her husband Keith.

Oliva – www.oliva.house

A website that offers to match you with the right therapist after you complete a questionnaire. The site appears to cater to UK and Spain, though I could not find a company address when I looked.

Online Counselling Service (OCS) – www.onlinecounsellingservice.co.uk

The site states that it offers worldwide 24-hour online and telephone therapy. OCS was founded in 2008 by psychological therapist Faith McMoyo. OCS offers therapy by either email, instant message, telephone or Skype.

Online Therapy – www.online-therapy.com

CRN Solutions AB, Bruksgatan 36, 26339 Höganäs, Sweden

Online Therapy offers a subscription-based online CBT model. There is a free version with worksheets and an online CBT programme, or you can pay between £23.96 and £55.96 for a service that includes daily messaging with a therapist and 1–2 weekly live sessions with a therapist.

Online Therapy 247 – onlinetherapy247.com

Online Therapy 247 Ltd, 23 Horizon Building, 15 Hertsmere Road, Canary Wharf, London E14 4AW

Online Therapy 247 allows you to choose a therapist and then arrange either telephone, email or Zoom therapy instantly (therapists available 24 hours a day).

Optimind.io

Optimind, Buckingham Palace Street, London SW1E

The site has a limited number of therapists available to provide video and phone therapy. Prior to COVID-19, the service involved face-to-face therapy in two locations: London and Suffolk.

Pink Therapy – www.pinktherapy.com

Pink Therapy, BCM 5159 London WC1N 3XX

This site states it is the 'UK's largest independent therapy organization working with gender and sexual diversity clients'. You can search for a therapist on the site who has completed training and/or had experience that enables them to offer therapy in a sexuality-affirming way. Pink Therapy also offers training and accreditation to therapists interested in working with LGBTIQ clients.

Problem Shared – www.problemshared.net

Teledoctor Ltd, 2 Frederick Street, London WC1X 0ND

A new online platform set up by Dr Nick Nabarro where you can find and book a counsellor, psychotherapist or psychologist.

Psychology Today – www.psychologytoday.com/gb

Sussex Publishers, LLC, 115 E. 23rd St., 9th Floor, New York, NY 10010, USA

This is perhaps the most well known of all the directories available. It is international so you can search by country as well as by county or city. The site lists the profiles of therapists who have been verified, and you contact the therapist via the phone number or email address on their listing.

Qwell – www.qwell.io

Kooth plc, The Epworth, 25 City Road, London EC1Y 1AA

Qwell is part of Kooth plc and aims to provide you with a support community and self-help information, and connects you with therapists you can access for therapy.

The School of Life – www.theschooloflife.com/shop/psychotherapy

Campus Group LLP, 70 Marchmont Street, London, WC1N 1AB

On the School of Life website you can book a psychotherapy session with one of their therapists. Sessions have to be paid for first in advance, and you are then contacted within a week by a therapist who has availability.

Skype Therapies – www.skypetherapies.co.uk

Skype Therapies was established by a counselling psychologist and CBT therapist with the aim of connecting clients to therapists online. It has been operating since 2014 and offers UK-based therapists to clients around the globe. You can search for a therapist and then contact them via the site.

Stillpoint Spaces – www.stillpointspaces.com

Stillpoint Zürich GmbH, Privacy & Data Protection, Schanzeneggstrasse 1, 8002 Zurich, Switzerland.

Stillpoint Spaces lists therapists worldwide but also has four physical locations in London, Berlin, Paris and Zurich. You can book and have your session with your chosen therapist using the site's video platform.

Support Room – www.supportroom.com

My Therapist Online Ltd, 20–22 Wenlock Road, London N1 7GU (same address as Inquiretalk and ISOS Health)

A website where you can search worldwide for therapists who provide online therapy via video call or instant chat. Potential clients can complete an initial questionnaire and then be matched to three therapists they can then choose from to book their session with. The session is carried out within a private instant chat or video chat room.

Talkspace – www.talkspace.com

Talkspace Network LLC, 33 W 60th Street, 8th Fl, New York, NY 10023, USA

Talkspace operates a subscription model where you can choose to chat via instant message to a therapist at any time and add on video calls to the package as well. You cannot view the therapists available until you complete a matching questionnaire, so it wasn't clear if there were therapists available in the UK.

Therapion – www.therapion.com

Therapion Consulting's website offers therapists from several different countries. You can find and book a therapist on the site for either email, phone, video or instant chat therapy.

Therapycounselling.org

A site that lists counsellors and therapists in the UK. I could not find a company name or address listed on the site. In the privacy policy section, it states that the site does not hold any personal information, and the privacy policy refers to the individual counsellors only.

Therapy Route – therapyroute.com

Therapy Route PTY Ltd's site offers a portal where therapists can list their profiles for clients to choose from. There are also articles written by the therapists on the site or guest bloggers. The site is run by Enzo Sinisi, a psychotherapist based in South Africa.

Therapy Tribe – www.therapytribe.com

Web Tribes Inc. 1055 Quartz Ct, Ste. B, San Marcos, CA 92078, USA

Therapy tribe has been operating an online support community since 2006 and now offers the ability to find a therapist on their site. It was set up by husband and wife Ryan and Kristin Fitzgerald.

Therapology – www.therapology.io

Therapologies Limited, Brulimar House, Jubilee Road, Manchester M24 4LX

Therapology is a new site that had just appeared as I wrote this. Although I could not view the app, the website stated, 'Therapology is an exciting new app that enables anyone with internet to connect rapidly with therapists in the UK and book online or face-to-face appointments, typically within the hour.'

Think CBT – thinkcbt.com

Think CBT originally offered face-to-face therapy in London and Kent, but now lists accredited CBT and EMDR therapists across the UK who provide online therapy. Think CBT also runs the cbtpages.com website.

Timewith – timewith.co.uk

Timewith Limited, 12 Constance Street, London E16 2DQ

Timewith was launched in July 2017 and offers to match you with a therapist who is right for you. The site offers a helpful step-by-step guide to therapy and a care coordinator function, where you can answer some initial questions to help you get a feel for which therapist might be right for you.

The site tells you when your chosen therapist is available, and you can book directly on the site. All their therapists are registered with established registration bodies.

UKTherapyGuide – www.uktherapyguide.com

UKTG has been operating since 2012 and aims to match you to a therapist and allow you to book and pay for your session on their website. It mentions capping the number of therapists at 250, so as to make the choice more manageable for clients, and for therapists not to be lost in a crowd.

UK Therapy Hub – www.uktherapyhub.co.uk

Private Practice Hub Limited, 4th Floor, Silverstream House, 45 Fitzroy Street, London W1T 6EB

UK Therapy Hub is operated by the people behind the Private Practice Hub. It was set up by psychotherapist Geoff Simons. There is a 'Find a therapist' tab, as well as a 'Find an online therapist' tab, and I received a different list of therapists when I used the same search term in both.

UppTherapy – upptherapy.com

Upp Therapy Ltd, 109 Colne Road, Twickenham TW2 6QL

An online video therapy platform where you can find and book therapists and coaches. The service was set up by Richard Reid (from Pinnacle Wellbeing) and Mike Tapia.

Victim Focus – victimfocus.org.uk

Dr Jessica Taylor is a psychologist and advocate for non-blaming, non-shaming treatment in mental health. On her website she has a list of therapists who have signed up to her approach to mental health and pledge to be trauma-informed, woman-centred, radical feminist, anti-victim-blaming and anti-pathologizing. Contact can be made with the therapists directly, so the site is not a directory platform like the others in this list.

We are Kiku – www.wearekiku.com

Sixteen Eighty Limited, 49 Myrtle Grove, Newcastle upon Tyne NE2 3HT

Kiku is a directory of therapists that offers a one-stop shop for you to find, book and contact your therapist using the site. There is a secure messaging service, and you can see the therapist with availability matching yours.

Welldoing – welldoing.org

Welldoing Ltd, Canterbury House, 1 Royal Street, London SE1 7LL

Welldoing has been in operation since 2014 and states it is the UK's leading directory for online and in-person therapists. You can search for a therapist yourself using a postcode, or you can answer a short questionnaire to be matched with a therapist. There is also a more personalized matching service, and there is a charge for this. On the site there is also a helpful resource section with articles and mental health resources and links to approved apps.

Well Minds Online (WellMinds Online CIC) – wellmindsonline.com

Provides access to low-cost counselling via student and qualified counsellors.

LIST OF INDEPENDENT DIRECTORIES WHERE YOU CAN FIND A THERAPIST INTERNATIONALLY

Amwell – amwell.com/cm/services/online-therapy/
Betterhelp – betterhelp.com
Chinese Counseling – directory.chinesecounseling.org/en
Counselling Online – www.counsellingonline.ie
Good Therapy – goodtherapy.com
Good Therapy Australia –
www.goodtherapy.com.au/flex/online-therapy/908/1
MDLive – www.mdlive.com/counseling
Teladoc – www.teladoc.com
Psychology Today – psychologytoday.com
Stillpoint Spaces – www.stillpointspaces.com
Talkspace – www.talkspace.com
Therapyden – www.therapyden.com
Therapy Tribe – www.therapytribe.com

CHAPTER NINE – THE TROUBLE WITH THERAPY

RESOURCES AND LINKS FOR MENTAL HEALTH AT WORK

Armed Forces

Combat Stress – www.combatstress.org.uk
Forces Online – www.forcesonline.org.uk
Help for Heroes – www.helpforheroes.org.uk
SSAFA – www.ssafa.org.uk/get-help/forcesline
Contact Armed Forces –
www.contactarmedforces.co.uk/we-can-help/i-have-served

Ambulance workers

www.nhsemployers.org/retention-and-staff-experience/
ambulance-workforce/head-first

Counsellors and Psychotherapists

The Therapist Hub has details of groups for therapists:
www.partnersforcounsellingandpsychotherapy.co.uk/the-therapist-hub.

Construction Workers

www.constructionindustryhelpline.com/app.html

Doctors

Doctors Support Network – www.dsn.org.uk/support-for-doctors
Doctors – www.practitionerhealth.nhs.uk

Education workers

www.mentalhealthatwork.org.uk/toolkit/staff-mental-health-in-education

Emergency Service Workers

www.mind.org.uk/news-campaigns/campaigns/blue-light-support

Finance and Accounts Workers

www.caba.org.uk

Football

www.thefa.com/about-football-association/heads-up

Football writers

www.mentalhealthatwork.org.uk/toolkit/
mental-health-some-pointers-for-football-writers

Frontline Workers

www.mentalhealthatwork.org.uk/toolkit/ourfrontline-socialcare

Healthcare Professionals

www.aomrc.org.uk/covid-19-mentalwellbeing/#1465858640552-4ee2b70e-5fbe
Health for Health Professionals Wales – www.hhpwales.co.uk
NHS Practitioner Support – resolution.nhs.uk/services/
practitioner-performance-advice/advice/support-for-practitioners

Legal Professionals

Law Care – www.lawcare.org.uk/information-and-support
Wellbeing at the Bar – www.wellbeingatthebar.org.uk/staying-well

Police

Oscar Kilo – oscarkilo.org.uk/category/resources/looking-after-yourself/
Police Care –
www.policecare.org.uk/get-help/people/emotional/counselling
Welfare Support Line –
www.pfoa.co.uk/support/welfare-support-programme

Veterinary workers

Vet Life – www.vetlife.org.uk/how-we-help/vetlife-health-support
Vet Mind Matters – www.vetmindmatters.org
www.rcvs.org.uk/news-and-views/publications/helping-you-help-others

CHAPTER TEN – ALTERNATIVES TO STAND-ARD THERAPY APPROACHES

SELF-HELP WEBSITES

Anna Freud Centre

www.annafreud.org/on-my-mind/self-care/

A really useful and interactive page of resources geared towards young people.

CCI, Centre for Clinical Interventions

www.cci.health.wa.gov.au/Resources/Looking-After-Yourself

Another website used often by therapists to give self-help and psychoeducation information to clients.

Esther Perel

estherperel.com/blog/how-to-find-the-right-therapist-for-you

Every Mind Matters

www.nhs.uk/oneyou/every-mind-matters

Get Self-Help

www.getselfhelp.co.uk/about.htm

A favourite of many CBT therapists, this website was set up and is managed by CBT therapist Carol Vivyan.

Local Libraries

www.gov.uk/local-library-services

Local libraries have self-help books available as well as information about local groups that you can join.

MIND

www.mindcharity.co.uk/advice-information/
how-to-look-after-your-mental-health/online-resources/

Distraction Apps

www.mind.org.uk/need-urgent-help/how-can-i-distract-myself/
videos-websites-and-apps/

Mindfulness

The Free Mindfulness Project – www.freemindfulness.org

Lots of free mindfulness exercises to download for free, plus mindfulness apps and a discussion forum.

NHS

www.nhs.uk/conditions/stress-anxiety-depression/self-help-therapies
www.nhs.uk/conditions

NHS leaflets about different mental health conditions – web.ntw.nhs.uk/selfhelp

Overcoming

overcoming.co.uk/709/Overcoming-Apps

Self-assessment, self-help and apps from the respected 'Overcoming' series.

Psychology Tools

www.psychologytools.com

A very handy resource for therapists and clients for information about different issues we can have with our mental health and info sheets on how to manage.

SAMH, Scottish Association for Mental Health

www.samh.org.uk/about-mental-health/self-help-and-wellbeing

This page of self-help resources has a questionnaire you can answer to get your 'wellbeing score'.

Self-Help Services

www.selfhelpservices.org.uk/about-us

A user-led charity providing lots of self-help resources.

Students Against Depression

www.studentsagainstdepression.org/self-help

Trauma

istss.org/public-resources/trauma-basics

The International Society for Traumatic Stress Studies (ISTSS) has some helpful info on trauma and PTSD.

The Wellness Society

thewellnesssociety.org/about

Aims to bridge the gap between private therapy and waiting for NHS services by providing self-help tools and information.

MENTAL HEALTH APPS

ACT Coach – mobile.va.gov/app/act-coach

Developed by the US Department of Veterans Affairs, this app is a good introduction to the principles of the ACT approach.

Action for Happiness – www.actionforhappiness.org/app

Babylon – www.babylonhealth.com/download-app

Speak to a doctor about any health issue.

Beat Panic – www.nhs.uk/apps-library/beat-panic

Be Mindful – www.bemindfulonline.com

BiaMother – biamother.com

App for new mothers.

Buddhify – buddhify.com

A mindfulness meditation app with lots of different options for different age groups.

CALM App – www.calm.com

A longstanding mindfulness app.

CBT Thought Diary App – www.cbtthoughtdiary.com

Catch It – www.nhs.uk/apps-library/catch-it

Chill Panda – www.nhs.uk/apps-library/chill-panda

COVE – www.cove-app.com

Daylio – daylio.net

A daily journal and mood tracker app.

Fear Tools – www.feartools.com

An app based around CBT principles for reducing fear and anxiety.

Free Mindfulness Apps – www.freemindfulness.org/apps

Happify – www.happify.com

An app that gives you a 'happiness score' and lets you plot your moods and thoughts and work towards changing habits and patterns that are not working for you any more.

Headspace – www.headspace.com/

The original mindfulness and mediation app that has been around since 2010.

Insight Timer App – insighttimer.com

An app that has a large amount of different types of meditations for you to try to help with stress, sleep problems and anxiety.

MIND

List of apps for wellbeing: www.mindcharity.co.uk/ advice-information/how-to-look-after-your-mental-health/ apps-for-wellbeing-and-mental-health/

MoodFit – www.getmoodfit.com

A well-set-out all-round app.

Moodflow – www.moodflow.co

An app that tracks your mood and gives you a clear visual on what certain periods of the year have been like for you and which days were worse or better.

MoodMission – moodmission.com

An app whose founders have carried out peer-reviewed research and a randomized controlled trial into the app's effectiveness.

NHS Recommended Apps – www.nhs.uk/oneyou/apps/

Overcoming – overcoming.co.uk/709/App

The 'Overcoming' range has apps for anxiety, depression and self-esteem.

Samaritans Self-Help App – selfhelp.samaritans.org

Sleepio – onboarding.sleepio.com/sleepio/nhs/77#1/1

A respected sleep app.

Shine – www.theshineapp.com/get-started

An app for Black, Indigenous and People of Colour.

Stressheads – www.themix.org.uk/apps-and-tools/stressheads

An app for young people by The Mix.

Thrive (NHS) – www.nhs.uk/apps-library/thrive

TOMO – hellotomo.co.uk

Worry Tree – www.nhs.uk/apps-library/worrytree

WYSA – www.wysa.io

For teenagers.

COMMUNITIES - ONLINE AND OFFLINE

ONLINE

Abuse

Adults survivors of child abuse:
www.havoca.org/resources/forum
www.isurvive.org/forum
pandys.org
nexusni.org

Anxiety

Anxious Minds – www.anxiousminds.co.uk – has an online community
and Facebook group that you can join wherever you are in the UK.
DARE – dareresponse.com/community/ – set up by Barry McDonagh,
author of the book *DARE*. The website has links to his book, App, and a
Facebook community.
Triumph Over Phobia – www.topuk.org/top-uk-groups

Autism, Aspergers and Neurodiversity:

wrongplanet.net/forums/
www.autism.org.uk/what-we-do/community

Bipolar

Bipolar UK – www.bipolaruk.org/ecommunity

Body Dysmorphic Disorder

www.bddandme.co.uk

Brain Injury

Headway – www.headway.org.uk/supporting-you/online-communities

Children and Young People

Childline – www.childline.org.uk/get-support/message-boards/
Kooth – kooth.com
The Mix – www.themix.org.uk/get-support/group-chat

Depression

depressionuk.org

Divorce

Support Group – divorcesupportgroup.co.uk/divorce-support-groups

Drugs

Families Anonymous – famanon.org.uk/meetings/online-meetings/
The Withdrawal Project – withdrawal.theinnercompass.org/page/
twp-connect

Eating Disorders

support.beateatingdisorders.org.uk/app/social/home/

Family and Relationships

Families Need Fathers –
fnf.org.uk/help-and-support-2/fnf-online-forum
Family Lives – www.familylives.org.uk/how-we-can-help/
forum-community/?_ga=2.51933609.1457503942.1600701834-
163298806.1600701834

Gambling

Gamblers Anonymous – www.gamblersanonymous.org.uk/forum
GamCare – www.gamcare.org.uk/get-support/group-chatroom

General Help

7 Cups – www.7cups.com
Befrienders – www.befrienders.org

Mental Health Forum – www.mentalhealthforum.net/about-us
Mindfulness – www.freemindfulness.org/discussion-forums
Therapy Friends – sidebyside.mind.org.uk/about (formerly 'Elefriends')
and Therapyfriends.co.uk
Hearing Voices Network –
www.hearing-voices.org/hearing-voices-groups/

Hoarding

Help for Hoarders – www.helpforhoarders.co.uk/forum

Men

Mentell – www.mentell.org.uk
An online community for men 18+ to talk.

OCD

OCD Action – www.ocdaction.org.uk/support-groups
OCD UK – www.ocduk.org/support-groups/

Peer Support Online

www.safelyheldspaces.org/about

Post-Natal Depression

pandasfoundation.org.uk/how-we-can-support-you/
social-media-and-facebook-groups/

Self Harm

Self Harm UK – www.selfharm.co.uk/alumina/signup

Spiritual

Spiritual Crisis Network –
www.meetup.com/Spiritual-Crisis-Network-Community-Forum/

Transgender

Beaumont Society–
www.beaumontsociety.org.uk/online-support-groups.html

Trauma

ACES Too High Online Community – www.acesconnection.com/

OFFLINE

Mens Sheds Association – menssheds.org.uk/about/#who-we-are
MIND – Social Spaces – www.mindcharity.co.uk/social-spaces
Park Run – www.parkrun.org.uk
Walking for health – www.walkingforhealth.org.uk/get-walking/why-walk/
healthy-minds
Wave – www.waveproject.co.uk/about-us

CHAPTER ELEVEN –
DOES THERAPY WORK?

A selection of effectiveness studies for some of the main psychotherapy areas.

EVIDENCE FOR THE EFFECTIVENESS OF THERAPY

ACT Therapy

www.sciencedirect.com/science/article/abs/pii/
S0165032719313023?via%3Dihub

Howell, A. J., & Passmore, H. (2019). Acceptance and commitment therapy (ACT) to reduce depression: A systematic review and meta-analysis. *Journal of Affective Disorders*, 260(1), 728-737. DOI: 10.1016/j.jad.2019.09.040

Levin, M.E., Haeger, J.A. and Pierce, B.G. (2016). 'Web-Based Acceptance and Commitment Therapy for Mental Health Problems in College Students: A Randomized Controlled Trial', *Behavior Modification*, 41:1.

CBT Therapy

Cristea & Hofmann (2018) outline the evidence base for CBT and argue that, whilst CBT is not perfect, it is the gold standard because it is the best standard that we have at the moment. www.ncbi.nlm.nih.gov/pmc/articles/PMC5797481/?fbclid=IwAR3aaVJflkzabEn3-dd1_ZCQBjKximg3qE0SFcVab2LQCQk8qAtjW-5pTEE

Dance Movement Therapy

The studies below are a fraction of the evidence available for dance movement therapy, but they indicate how it can help with executive function, memory and mood.

academic.oup.com/cercor/article/16/8/1157/455551

www.sciencedirect.com/science/article/abs/pii/S014976341830664X?via%3Dihub

www.sciencedirect.com/science/article/abs/pii/S1744388119300970?via%3Dihub

EMDR Therapy

Boudewyns, P.A., Stwertka, S.A., Hyer, L.A., Albrecht, S.A., & Sperr, E.V. (1993, February). 'Eye movement desensitization for PTSD of combat: a treatment outcome pilot study'. *The Behavior Therapist*, 16(2), 30-33.

Shapiro, E. (2009). EMDR treatment of recent trauma. *Journal of EMDR Practice and Research*, 3(3), 141-151.

Expressive Writing Therapy

Mogk, C., Otte, S., Reinhold-Hurley, B., & Kröner-Herwig, B. (2006). 'Health effects of expressive writing on stressful or traumatic experiences – a meta-analysis'. *Psycho-social Medicine*, 3, Doc06. www.ncbi.nlm.nih.gov/pmc/articles/PMC2736499/

Park, D., Ramirez, G. and Beilock, S.L. (2014). 'The role of expressive writing in math anxiety'. *Journal of Experimental Psychology: Applied.* 2014, 20:2, 103-111.

Online Therapy

Chakrabarti S. (2015). 'Usefulness of telepsychiatry: A critical evaluation of videoconferencing-based approaches'. *World Journal of Psychiatry*, 5(3), 286–304. doi.org/10.5498/wjp.v5.i3.286

Epstein, R. (2019). 'Distance therapy comes of age'. *Scientific American.*

www.onlinetherapyinstitute.com/wp-content/uploads/2010/02/scimind1.pdf

Guille,C., Zhao, Z. and Krystal, J. (2015). 'Web-based cognitive behavioral therapy intervention for the prevention of suicidal ideation in medical interns', *JAMA Psychiatry*, 72:12, 1192-1198.

Simpson, S, Richardson, L, Pietrabissa, G, Castelnuovo, G, Reid, C. 'Videotherapy and therapeutic alliance in the age of COVID–19'. *Clinical Psychology & Psychotherapy.* 2020; 1– 13. doi.org/10.1002/cpp.2521

Luo, C., Sanger, N., Singhal, N., Pattrick, K., Shams, I., Shahid, H. (2020). 'A comparison of electronically-delivered and face to face cognitive behavioural therapies in depressive disorders: A systematic review and meta-analysis'. *EClinicalMedicine*, Vol. 24, 100442, July 1, 2020.

Zwerenz, R., Becker, J., Knickenberg, R.J., Siepmann, M., Hagen, K. and Beutel, M.E. (2017). 'Online self-help as an add-on to inpatient psychotherapy: efficacy of a new blended treatment approach'. *Psychotherapy and Psychosomatics*, 86, 341-350.

Psychoanalytic Therapy

www.bpc.org.uk/information-support/the-evidence-base

www.bpc.org.uk/download/696/Evidence-in-Support-of-Psychodynamic-Psychotherapy.pdf

Phone Therapy

psyche.co/ideas/telephone-therapy-is-convenient-and-it-works-lets-use-it-more

Critiques of Psychotherapy

digest.bps.org.uk/2017/03/20/have-we-overestimated-the-effectiveness-of-psychotherapy

www.theguardian.com/society/2017/feb/12/online-therapy-thousands-but-does-it-work

9 781800 316843